LIMERI

5¹

/lif
e

LORD
LARRY

LORD LARRY

THE SECRET LIFE OF LAURENCE OLIVIER
A PERSONAL AND INTIMATE PORTRAIT

MICHAEL MUNN

**ROBSON
BOOKS**

First published in the United Kingdom in 2007 by
Robson Books
10 Southcombe Street
London
W14 0RA

An imprint of Anova Books Company Ltd

ISBN 10: 1861059779
ISBN 13: 9781861059772

A CIP catalogue record for this book is available from the British Library.

10 9 8 7 6 5 4 3 2 1

Typeset by SX Composing DTP, Rayleigh, Essex
Printed and bound by WS Bookwell, Finland 2007

This book can be ordered direct from the publisher.
Contact the marketing department, but try your bookshop first.

www.anovabooks.com

For Debs and Jack

CONTENTS

Introduction

'I knew, somehow at sometime, that I was not to be just a *nobody*. I knew, somehow, that I was destined to be a *somebody*. And more than that, if this does not sound too much like an idle boast, Michael, I knew I would be great.'

Coming from almost anyone else, it would sound like an idle boast. But coming from Laurence Olivier in 1978, on the set of another filmed version of Bram Stoker's *Dracula*, it seemed a perfectly natural thing for him to say in response to a question I had put to him: 'You're considered to be the world's greatest actor. Do you regard yourself as such, and how would you define what greatness is?' He didn't shun the 'greatest actor' description, but gave his answer in soft-spoken modest terms, as though he was happily resigned to his reputation.

'When I was young and full of ambition and ready to conquer the world, Sir Henry Irving was the king of theatre. He was the Old Man in the spotlight and every actor worth his salt wanted to one day take his spotlight and he wouldn't give it up. But I was determined to make the public forget Irving and to take his spotlight, and now I am the one who wears an invisible crown, which I like very much.'

At that time, there were still Sir John Gielgud and Sir Ralph Richardson living and working and proving that they were the cream of the world's acting talent. They were two of a triumvirate of British – even world – theatre, and the third was Lord Laurence Olivier. People will argue who was the best actor of that triumvirate. I don't know how you judge. Being the best and being the greatest isn't necessarily the same thing.

Whether Olivier was the best or not, many consider him the greatest in his lifetime, but that is only an opinion and can't be a proven fact. Others will argue that John Gielgud was the greater actor. Their acting styles were very different, and they were, to some extent, competitors. Gielgud actually abhorred the suggestion that he was the greatest actor. Olivier embraced it when given such praise but always with the cautionary air of a man desperately trying to maintain some sense of modesty while knowing that he was, undoubtedly, at least one of the greatest actors of his time.

Some, usually people who I suspect were jealous of his enormous talent, called him a ham.

'One does love to hear complimentary words,' he told me, 'but one also needs to remember that feet belong firmly on the ground. But you really can't help but acknowledge that you have done great work and that others look to you from time to time for some kind of inspiration. I know I always did to others. John Barrymore was my inspiration to play Hamlet. So I know that I am not, in the eyes of others, as many or as few as they may be, just *another* actor. And I would hope to God that I am *more* than just another actor. Otherwise my life's work has been in vain.

'And so I find myself in the rather strange position of knowing that others expect so much of me, but not nearly as much as I expect of myself, and yet I do feel elevated by what others say and think of me and are kind enough to let me know it. I can either be incredibly humble about it, but my ego is far too great for that, or I can hoist myself to the lofty heights every day of my life from where I will undoubtedly have already fallen with an almighty great and sickening thud.

'And so I accept it with as much graciousness as I can. Because you have to be honest with yourself that you are just a mere mortal, but the gods have sometimes blown into my ear on stage, and people recognise that. I try not to disappoint those whom I meet by either being too lofty or too lowly, because then you are just a fraud. So I try to make the effort to treat people with dignity and respect and, at times, fondness when it is warranted. To do otherwise would be a sin, surely. And at my age I can't afford too many additional sins as I would rather like a place in heaven when my time comes.'

He said he didn't want to be a fraud, but Franco Zeffirelli called him 'an old fraud', and he said it with affection. Olivier was a chameleon.

He would become whoever and whatever he needed to be. This has been accepted as just being a part of his theatrical make-up, and I might have thought so too if it had not been for one discovery I made about him when we last met in 1981. He had undergone, as a boy, a traumatic experience that marked him for life and caused him to be more of 'an old fraud' than he would have ever been. Because of that experience he withdrew from his real life and his own personality as often as he could to become someone else, and not just on stage.

That trauma was also the cause of his legendary stage fright. I came to understand much about him because I had been there too. We shared our experience, that last time we met, of being sexually abused – and in both our cases the evil perpetrator was a priest. I understood Olivier better than I ever did before, because it takes one to know one.

I believe that experience drove him to become the greatest actor of his time – for that is what he sought to be – while being watched by the whole world. The dangers of reaching for greatness are considerable, especially if one fails. Olivier knew that and tried his best to balance his achievement with the admiration and even adulation heaped upon him, which he did not shun; he managed to maintain a true humility that was not an act, while accepting that he was a highly important figure. He didn't allow his own self-importance to swamp his humanity. But he didn't deny it either. Asked why he turned down the part of the Chorus in the mediocre Italian 1954 film version of *Romeo and Juliet* – the one with a very young Laurence Harvey as Romeo – he replied, 'Because I am too fucking grand.' And he was.

He was also a war hero, and that was a big secret he kept; I realised that he enjoyed keeping some things secret. Other things, such as his abuse, he kept secret because you just do when you've been through that; I understood him.

As far as his war secret was concerned, it was his friend David Niven who let the cat out of the bag. I was interviewing Niven at Shepperton Studios where, in 1978, he was making *A Man Called Intrepid*, based on the exploits of Sir William Stephenson who had established British counter-intelligence operations in the USA; Niven had worked for him and was now playing him.

The morning I went on the set of *A Man Called Intrepid* as a journalist from *Photoplay* I found Niven, who I knew from previous interviews, in a particularly dour mood. I think he was remembering dark days and he spoke to me at some length about his experiences during the war, going into greater detail than he ever wrote about.

And then he told me something that took me completely by surprise. When the British Government asked him to stay in America to make subtle efforts to enlist support for the war effort, he had put them on to Laurence Olivier, who, according to Niven, duly obliged.

David Niven suddenly looked worried as he told me this, and said, 'Look, you might need to ask Larry about all this. It isn't my place.'

So we moved on to another subject. But I was a highly curious, often impudent and audacious young man who asked questions often without thinking first, and after lunch, when Niven was more conversational, I asked him informally, with the tape recorder off, about Olivier's work. Niven told me that Olivier had worked for Special Operations Executive (SOE) and probably MI5.

Getting the details from Larry himself was not to prove so easy. But when I met him during the week he worked on *Clash of the Titans* in 1979, he sat in his Zeus make-up and costume and told me, or rather hinted at, his great secret. He was, by Zeus, a great patriot and, I think, a hero.

My first encounter with Laurence Olivier was in 1964 when, as an eleven-year-old schoolboy hooked on films and having set my sights on becoming a film director at the age of eight, I was given a special treat by a teacher eager to encourage my aspirations and also keen for me to be introduced to the works of William Shakespeare. He managed to wangle me a day on the set of *Othello*.

I watched as Olivier, Maggie Smith, Frank Finlay and the great (yes, another 'great') Derek Jacobi introduced me, not so much to Shakespeare, but to the joy of seeing great acting. I mean really wonderful, charismatic acting.

Up to that point, my only other experience of seeing Olivier in action was as Crassus, the Roman general, in the Kirk Douglas epic *Spartacus*. I loved those Roman epics (it was seeing *Ben-Hur* that made me want to be a director). They had a certain classical quality to them – the good ones, that is. And I vividly remembered Olivier from the film as much as I recalled Kirk Douglas in the title role.

After the film's re-release in 1970, I saw *Spartacus* over and over, and I became ever more aware of what a towering performance Olivier gave. It was a performance that really inspired me. I wanted to be an actor more in the mould of Laurence Olivier than Kirk Douglas.

That wonderful experience of seeing *Othello* being re-created for the screen didn't make me want to get to know the works of the Bard as I still found his language hard to follow, but I was thrilled when our whole class was taken to the West End to see that film version of *Othello* and to feel the enormous power that emanated from the screen, mostly generated by Laurence Olivier. It also thrilled me to know that what I had seen on the set had magically transposed to the screen.

It still took some years for me to become interested in Shakespeare. But I had become very interested in the intangible power of Olivier's acting.

He was, of course, *Sir* Laurence Olivier. And then he became *Lord* Olivier. Such titles added in some mystical way to the grandeur of the man. It also gave me a dilemma, when I met him properly in 1972 while he was filming *Sleuth* at Pinewood Studios.

As a young film publicist who had nothing whatsoever to do with that film, I jumped at the chance to go with a kindly older colleague to the studios where I hoped to talk to the film's director, Joseph L. Mankiewicz. But on film sets, the least available person is the director. So Mankiewicz pointed me in the direction of Olivier's dressing room, and Lord Olivier had this enthusiastic and totally starstruck nineteen-year-old presented to him at his door. I expected him to sigh heavily and either invite me in with great reluctance, or tell me to go away.

But he invited me in with tremendous courtesy and grace – that is what first struck me about him: his courtesy and grace. To my surprise, he wasn't all that tall, and with his fake moustache for the film and white hair, he looked somewhat diminished from the way I remembered him eight years before when he was blacked-up and looking virile and powerful as Othello. But there was no denying that I was in the presence of greatness.

He was delighted to learn that I had seen him working on *Othello* and encouraged me to explore Shakespeare, a subject we would return to over the years.

He was also gracious enough to accept my enthusiasm for *Spartacus* and his performance in it, and when we met he would repeatedly indulge my interest in the film and the historical details – I was, and remain, a Roman history buff – which led to discussions about the real Crassus and other aspects of Roman history.

The screen Crassus was bisexual, which was a subject Olivier would, in relation to that role, discuss at times. I didn't encourage it, but he seemed to enjoy talking about it. Sometimes it was a serious exploration of Crassus and of his performance, and sometimes he was just flirting with me.

So there I was, getting to know this great actor, which naturally makes a starstruck young man incredibly overawed, and I was quickly struck by a dilemma; I didn't know how to address him.

Everyone else called him Larry. I felt I couldn't. Calling him Mr Olivier was out of the question. I tried 'Sir Laurence', but he responded with, 'Oh, don't call me that, *please*: it sounds like I should sit around some great fucking round table.'

Lord Olivier, then?

He thought for just a few seconds, then announced, 'You may call me Lord Larry.'

I thought he was serious. Some years later he told me that he quietly chuckled to himself every time I said, 'Oh, by the way, Lord Larry . . .' In time I got to know him well enough to call him Larry. But often, for the sheer pleasure of enjoying an in-joke between us, I would call him 'Lord Larry', and we'd see the faces of the people about us look on with horror.

He loved nicknames, so he put my initials together and called me 'M and M' in such a way that it came out as Eminem, long before the rap artist Marshall Mathers thought of it.

And so to me he was always Lord Larry.

Olivier tolerated my questions about *Spartacus* and was happy to indulge me because I became familiar with the Bard's works through my interest in the Roman epics. Shakespeare, I discovered in my teens, wrote Roman epics.

In his dressing room at Pinewood Studios while filming *Clash of the Titans* in 1979, Lord Larry gave me a masterclass in delivering Antony's funeral speech – I had asked if he would teach me something about acting (I had decided I wanted to become an actor and felt it was no great shame to ask Lord Larry to teach me).

He taught me about technique, and voice control, and that an actor either has or doesn't have something that couldn't be faked – a certain power over an audience, a magnetism, a chemistry, a magic that was intangible, somewhat like a hypnotic trance.

'The audience will always want to love you if you have that,' he said. 'Without it, you can be just another very fine actor and manage to get away with a great deal. But if the audience *loves* you, then you are almost there each time. It's like making love. You can be very good at it and make your woman come and she'll have a wonderful time, but if the woman loves you, then you must still make her come, but when she does, she will be yours entirely.

'With a play, there is little time for foreplay. They must love you the moment you walk out on stage. But you can't be lulled into believing that because they loved you the last time they will always love you. Love fades. So I do what I do before I make love. I make up my mind that this will be the best fucking she will have had in her life. And for me it will be too. And I do the same before going on stage. I will stand backstage somewhere, maybe behind the curtain, and I will silently tell the audience, "Tonight I will be great, and you will love me, and this will be the best theatrical orgasm of your life."'

Olivier seduced an audience. He flirted with them first. He flirted with people he liked – and the people he wanted to like him. He couldn't help but flirt. It's what he did. He needed to be liked – to be loved. Victims of sexual abuse often need to feel *truly* loved. And it's one reason why he was such a great actor. He flirted and seduced his audience of one or many.

While at that time my Shakespearean passion was for *Julius Caesar*, Olivier's passion was for Shakespeare's sequel to it – *Antony and Cleopatra*. I'd not been aware of that play until I saw Charlton Heston's film version in 1972. Lord Larry told me, 'Heston's *Antony and Cleopatra* failed because for that play you need a *great* Cleopatra, and he didn't have a great Cleopatra.'

And so Olivier proceeded to tell me how he attempted to turn Vivien Leigh into a great Cleopatra in his Broadway production of the play. And that got him talking about Vivien. He also encouraged me to study the text closely, and the history, which I had long been doing, and he told me, 'If you *must* find yourself having to do one of the Roman plays, you *must* do *Antony and Cleopatra*.' So I did, in the year 2000.

And so Olivier was happy, over the years I knew him, to talk about the Roman plays, and the films, and the history, and from those discussions I learned so much more about Olivier than I would otherwise have – about his dedication to any part, about his acting technique, about Vivien Leigh, about his sexuality, and a whole lot more.

As well as my own experience of knowing Olivier, the opinions and anecdotes of others are a vital part of this book. Some of them, and how I came by them, may need a little explaining. I have been a messenger boy in films, a publicist, a film journalist, wrote a little for John Huston and later Lee Marvin, dabbled as an extra and actor. My life for many years was spent on film sets, in theatres and at hotels, meeting, interviewing and just talking to actors, directors and writers.

I taped my interviews and learned from the start to write everything down that I thought was of interest; having good memory retention back then, I would write down, as soon as I could, conversations that had taken place, such as the one that occurred when I sat with Sir John Gielgud and Sir Ralph Richardson at the Apollo Theatre in 1970. That illustrates the sort of quirky circumstance that often led me to be in the company of those kinds of people. I had met Gielgud on a bus, of all things, going down Oxford Street. I am sure he intended to remain anonymous as he sat right behind the driver, but I couldn't mistake him, and I excused myself for intruding and told him how much pleasure his work had given me. Before I knew it we were chatting and I was being invited to the Apollo to talk with him and Richardson.

That's what my life was like.

I learned so much about Olivier from those other two giants of the theatre. And to be with them, as I was twice (the other time would be in 1975) was an entertainment in itself.

As a journalist I got to know Charlton Heston, a friend and colleague of Olivier's, just because I always interviewed him every opportunity I got. Finally, in 1999, Heston and I were talking actor/director to actor/director – that was the last time I saw him, before Alzheimer's disease had cruelly taken its toll on him.

Back in 1972 I was asked, 'Want to come to the studio – they're making a film about Nelson?' Of course I did, and found myself at Shepperton, in the restaurant, talking to Peter Finch and Anthony Quayle. Finch talked frankly about his affair with Vivien Leigh, and that was an eye-opener.

I explain all this only to show how I come to be in the position of knowing what I know. I knew so many of Olivier's peers. And from them, and from my own relationship with Olivier, I am able to paint this personal and often intimate portrait of Lord Larry. I may not have known him as well as many others, but I think I knew him a whole lot better than some who have attempted to record his life and career.

This is my perspective, my portrait of what Olivier was like. Others might have a different perspective. One of his oldest and dearest friends was Sir Ralph Richardson. In 1970 I asked him, 'What is Laurence Olivier like?'

He replied, 'I haven't the faintest idea.'

1

Chicken

'I remember that no one could carve a chicken like Larry Olivier,' David Niven told me. We were lunching at Pinewood Studios where Niven was filming *Candleshoe* in 1976, and I had opted for the chicken. I had been given thick, generous slices of tender chicken breast, and this had provoked a memory in Niven of days during the Second World War when he would be home on leave, and he and his wife Primmie would be visited by friends who brought their own food and drink with them, including Laurence Olivier and Vivien Leigh.

'Sometimes there would be a rather large party and Larry and Vivien would always come over, and if we had a chicken Larry always did the carving. He'd been raised in a low-budget parsonage and could make a chicken do for as many as ten people.'

When I relayed Niven's anecdote to Larry in 1979, he smiled and said, 'Ahhhh, yes! That was a skill taught to me by my father. He only had to carve a chicken for five of us – my mother, my brother and sister, myself and himself, of course. But he could make those slices so thin it always looked like we had more than we did. But when you raised a slice on your fork, it wilted and dropped over the fork, like slightly coloured tissue paper. One slice barely made a mouthful. And if one complained, one was told to be grateful for the bounty we had been blessed with. I just kept eyeing the chicken that was left uncarved and wondering what became of it after we three children and my mother had finished and left the table.'

'You mean, you think your father ate it?' I asked.

'Where else did it go?' Larry replied. His memories of his father were often bitter and resentful.

His father was a priest in the High Anglican Church and earned, it seemed, not a great deal, so Larry's father always cut the chicken thin. Anything in life that cost money was rationed by him. He made the family take it in turns to have baths in the same shallow bath water. Larry was always the last because he was the youngest, and by the time he got into the bath the water was murky. This saved money, but it also made the youngest Olivier feel inferior and unimportant. It marked him for life.

I remember one day in 1979, as we sat in his dressing room at Pinewood Studios where he was playing Zeus, king of the gods in *Clash of the Titans*, he asked me, 'Do you love your father?'

'Of course,' I told him.

'I loved mine,' he said, 'but I didn't like him much. Does your father like you?' He was so eager to know.

'I think so.'

'Mine didn't like me. At least, I thought he didn't. I think sometimes that maybe he did but couldn't show it, and that was a source of some . . . disquiet in me as a small boy.'

There was, even at the age of 73, and with much of his face hidden behind his Zeus beard, a look of regret and pain when he spoke about his father. And it was no act.

Ever since I had known Olivier, I had been playfully calling him Lord Larry, and I'd asked him if Larry was a nickname he had acquired, or if he had thought it up himself, or if it had come to him some other way.

He said, 'My parents may have given myself and my siblings good solid names, but they loved to play around with names – not even our real names. They loved the game of inventing nicknames.'

Trying to establish the actual facts of Larry's earliest years is not as easy as it might seem. In 1981, just a year after I saw him for what would be the last time (when he was filming *The Jigsaw Man*), his autobiography, *Confessions of an Actor*, was published in which he wrote in some detail about those early years. But when I had asked him about those times over the years, he had replied with good humour, 'I was only a baby, you know. Very hard to remember much at all.'

But he did recall something about how and why his family had nicknames. He was first called Larry, he thought, when he was three years old. His father preferred to call him Paddy because, as a baby, he cried a great deal. 'My father thought I was always in a paddy, so I became Paddy. Before that I was simply Baby, which was the name my mother and even my nanny gave to me, which I hate to admit was not a very original nickname for a baby.

'My mother didn't much care for calling me Paddy, and when I was three I had stopped my infamous paddies, and so mother decided to call me Larry – a simple bastardisation of Laurence which Fahv hated.'

'Fahv' was the name Larry, his sister Sybille and brother Gerard gave their father.

'Mother loved the name Larry. Fahv hated it. He would upset Mother by adding a certain emphasis to my name to show he disapproved of it.'

Larry was also, at times, called Kim. But Larry was the nickname that stuck.

His siblings had nicknames too. Sybille, born in 1901, was known as Baba, which became shortened to Bar. Gerard, born in 1904, named after his father and given the middle name Dacres, became Bobo. 'They sounded like a double act – Baba and Bobo,' Larry said. Bobo later became Dickie for reasons that now seem to be lost in obscurity.

Larry decided I ought to have a nickname in 1972. People mostly called me Mike at work, although I was Mick to my friends. He didn't care for Mick and he said he didn't think Mike was 'a handsome name'. He asked me my initial. I told him – MM. 'No middle name?' he enquired. No middle name, I told him. So he put my initials together and I became Eminem sometimes, although mostly he stilled called me Michael.

Larry was born Laurence Kerr Olivier on 22 May 1907 at 26 Wathen Road in Dorking in England. He was delighted when I told him that my mother's maiden name was Kerr. 'Ah, that would be *Cairhh*,' he said when I mentioned that in my mother's case the name originated from Scotland. This was a happy coincidence that seemed to endear me to Larry.

'I have always felt that I had Scottish roots myself because the name Kerr would strongly suggest it,' he said, 'but for the most part the Olivier name comes from France.'

The Olivier family tree can be firmly established back to an eighteenth-century diamond merchant called Daniel Josias Olivier, who married Susannah, a daughter of Louis XV's court painter Jean-Baptise Masse.

Susannah gave birth to a son, Daniel Stephen Olivier, who grew to become Rector of Clifton in Bedfordshire, and his son Henry Stephens Olivier married the daughter of Vice Admiral Sir Richard Dacres (from where Dickie got his middle name) and became a lieutenant in the army and then the High Sheriff of Wiltshire.

Laurence Olivier's grandfather, Henry Arnold Olivier, was the oldest of the sheriff's three sons, all of whom became clergymen, had money and high standing. Henry married the daughter of the Deputy Lieutenant of Berkshire, and was comfortably off with homes in Wiltshire and Surrey, while his wife spent winters in Southern France.

Henry Arnold fathered ten children, four of whom were sons, the youngest being Gerard Kerr Olivier, Larry's father. 'Fahv was the last and least of the four sons,' Larry told me, when we talked more of his family in 1976 when he was recording the television production *Cat on a Hot Tin Roof*. Larry's uncle, Henry Dacres, was mentioned in dispatches for his service in the Royal Engineers and became a lieutenant colonel. Uncle Sydney became Lord Olivier and was a Governor of Jamaica and Secretary of State for India. Uncle Herbert became a famous artist and friend of the Duke of Connaught, whose mother was Queen Victoria.

'Poor Fahv just didn't have it in him to be as great as his brothers,' mused Larry. 'But despite that, I felt I had it in me to rise to greater heights, as my uncles did. It was in my blood, and if some of it had turned a little sour in my father's veins, there was no reason for me to suppose – if one might be allowed to suppose such a thing – that I may have inherited greater genes from my grandfather.'

Larry did not have much regard for Fahv. 'He didn't achieve much in life – unlike his brothers.' All four brothers had attended public schools. Gerard went to Merton College in Oxford when he was nineteen, but failed to gain a degree. But he managed to rush through a residency at Durham University with a BA in Classical and General Literature, although not with any great distinction. As late as 1898, ten years after he started at Merton, he finally took his Master's degree. He was already way behind his three older brothers in their accomplishments.

Before graduating from Durham, Gerard Olivier taught at a school near Guildford where he met Agnes Crookenden, the headmaster's sister-in-law. She had a French aristocratic great-grandmother who had escaped the French Revolution and came to England. She had traces of Dutch ancestry too, but it was the additional French blood in the family that Larry was always most proud of.

'One can't help but feel the nature of the nobility that is in the blood,' he told me once.

Gerard and Agnes married on 30 April 1898. After that, Gerard ran his own school in Dorking and, with financial aid from Agnes's family, he was able to run a large house complete with servants. There was also a nanny for baby Baba. Gerard, it seemed, was determined at least to look like he was a man of substance.

'Fahv couldn't run a school successfully so he quit teaching and became a priest.' When Larry told me this, he said it with a sigh of disappointment.

There seems to be no cohesive explanation as to why Gerard chose this vocation in particular, but he took holy orders and was ordained a priest in the High Anglican Church in 1904. As an assistant priest at St Martin's in Dorking, Gerard was unable to afford servants but could afford a nanny when Laurence Kerr Olivier was born.

'Fahv took total disinterest in me from the moment I was born,' Larry said to me in 1976. 'I think to make sure I was put in my place within the family as far as he was concerned, my father always took delight in telling me how I arrived into the world just as he was frying some sausages, and this proved most inconvenient for him. The doctor who delivered me brought me to him. I was still smeared with blood and mucus. When my father related this story, as he often did, he always said it with a sense of some disgust – like I was something impure. Quickly, he handed me back to the doctor and went on with frying his sausages.'

Olivier told this story in his autobiography. His official biographer Terry Coleman doubts that the anecdote is true, explaining that Olivier, by the nature of being an actor, was also something of an inventor of stories, citing Olivier's own question from his auto-biography, 'What is acting but lying?' As an actor I understand exactly what Larry meant. The same is true of a novelist, but that does not mean that all novelists – or indeed, all actors – lie. What they invariably do is enhance their stories to make them far more entertaining. David Niven was one of the leading exponents of this form of entertainment. So too was Peter Ustinov.

Larry complicates things all the more by confessing that as a child he had 'a compulsion to invent a story and tell it so convincingly that it was believed at first without doubt of suspicion'.

He told me, 'I told so many lies as a child. But when you act, you pretend, and that is lying, because you must convince your audience you are telling them the truth. I know I am *not* Hamlet, but I must make an audience believe I *am* Hamlet or they have wasted their cost of admission. The problem I have is that I just can't always be sure of when I am acting and when I am not, and maybe that might be considered a form of lying. I could be acting now, just for you. Because, you see, I want to show off. That's all I am. A natural and somewhat addicted show-off.'

I have no doubt that Larry's story about the day he was born is true – or at least, that it is true that his father told him this story. Whether his father was making up the story, I can't say, but Larry either believed it or at least felt it was a good story that explained his father's indifference towards him. Larry's love was reserved for his mother. He thought the world of her, and those feelings lasted all his life, or certainly up to the time I last saw him in 1981.

Larry had mixed feelings about Fahv. He was a man who, as a schoolmaster, had dealt out very severe corporal punishment to misbehaving pupils. But he never took it upon himself to punish his children; that was left to Agnes to do. Larry never questioned the need for such punishments – they were a part of life in the early twentieth century. And Larry felt he deserved the spankings because, as he said in his autobiography, he was invariably spanked for lying, which he was unable to resist doing.

One might think that Larry should have considered his father a more kindly person for not carrying out these punishments on him, but Larry believed that making Agnes the one who carried out the spankings betrayed his cruel streak. She detested doing so, and cried as she inflicted the painful punishment upon her son.

In the authorised biography, Terry Coleman pointed out that Larry's sister Sybille never remembered Larry being frequently punished, casting some doubt on Larry's version. But siblings do not always share the same memories. And the fact that Sybille did not write about the punishments in the unpublished biography she wrote of Larry does not indicate that he invented all this. When Larry told me about his memories, I could see they were bitter, sad ones. I came to understand quite a bit about his hidden sadness.

He wondered why his father couldn't bring himself to be the one to carry out the spankings. 'He was a strict disciplinarian,' he said, 'and had no trouble thrashing badly behaved boys with a cane when he was a headmaster. But he couldn't do it to us – and certainly not to me who, I'm afraid, was beaten far more than my siblings and for reasons I deserved.'

And so Larry came to two conclusions. One was that his father had to be a cruel man by making Agnes the one to inflict pain upon the youngest of the Olivier children, and the second was that, at the age of nine, Larry had to stop his lying so that his mother would no longer need to punish him. It wasn't that he couldn't take the beatings. He simply wanted to spare Agnes any further agony as the punisher.

But what was this great need to tell lies in the first place that resulted in these thrashings? Larry said he simply wanted to 'show off'. Many children do. I related to Larry that as a child I told some whoppers of my own. I am sure every child, with some rare exceptions, does the same.

But in Larry it appears to have been a need to lie that went beyond the mere joy of showing off. He gave a clue when he told me, 'I find great joy in taking people with me to another place. On the one hand I want them to see how wonderful I am in doing this, and on the other, I want to whisk myself into another time and place and it is always more fun if you can take others with you. That's what acting is all about.' This, to me, explains Larry's question, 'What is acting but lying?'

But it didn't explain everything about his need to take people to another place with him – not in later years.

He took to the stage, or a stage of sorts, at the age of five, standing on a wooden chest in front of the window, so he could use the window curtains as tabs, performing plays which, he later believed, were probably his own versions of the plays he'd seen his brother perform at school. He idolised Dickie and said in his autobiography that he looked upon his brother as his 'own special hero throughout my entire boyhood'.

His audience for these highly improvised plays was always his mother, sometimes his sister – whom Larry recalled as being 'wonderfully kind' to both him and Dickie and who always helped their mother with household chores – and on occasions relatives, whose visits inspired him to tread the boards so he could show off. Very infrequently did Fahv take an interest, except to look in for a brief moment on rare occasions.

Larry never did quite get over the harsh attitude his father displayed towards him during his earliest years. 'I was like an unwelcome burden on his time and finances,' he said. 'I always felt like the child who was a mistake. He seemed far fonder of my sister and certainly of my brother.'

In his autobiography, Olivier recalled how his father would complain that the enormous amounts of porridge young Larry consumed at breakfast put him in a bad temper for the rest of the day.

'What I didn't appreciate was that he must have loved me and hid it for reasons best known to himself,' Larry told me in 1976. 'If only he had made known how he really felt, I most certainly wouldn't have had such unkind thoughts about him for much of my life.'

He regretted his own dislike of his father, and the torment he suffered through his father's seeming indifference was indelibly etched upon his psyche.

He was, however, Agnes's clear favourite of her children. He had a sweet singing soprano voice that his mother nurtured by accompanying him on piano. For some years Agnes tried to get Larry into the All Saints choir school near Oxford Circus in London.

The last of three preparatory schools he attended was Francis Holland School in Chelsea, which was a Church of England school for girls that took in young boys also.

In 1916 Agnes eventually succeeded in getting Larry, then aged nine, into All Saints, which was High Church of England. Having had a High Anglican background myself, and having also been a choirboy (which again gave us something in common that appealed to Larry), I, like him, remembered the Mass and the smell of incense. 'Funny, isn't it,' Larry told me, 'how the smell of incense never leaves your nostrils. I loved it, and I felt very close to God. I believed in God wholeheartedly.'

He had a good education, as well as training in the choir. He was taught English, Latin, French, mathematics, history, and the Bible. During his years there he improved considerably academically; it was a fine school.

He was spellbound each Sunday as the congregation were regularly admonished by Father Geoffrey Heald. He was officially the Reverend Heald, but this being a High Anglican church – closer in many ways to the Catholic Church than to the general Church of England – the priest preferred to be known as Father Heald.

'He was my first real acting teacher,' said Larry, 'because he could deliver such highly dramatic outbursts that had the congregation quaking in their seats, but he also added some brilliantly witty touches, and his flair to hold us all – his audience – not only fascinated me but taught me what I am sure were my first lessons in acting. He loved plays and acting. So he cast me in *Julius Caesar*. It was the Christmas play at All Saints. Not the usual Nativity play. Father Heald preferred to do *Julius Caesar*. But not the whole play – just the first half, concluding with Antony's funeral speech.'

It was 1917 when Larry made his debut in *Julius Caesar*; his second Christmas at All Saints. He was cast as the Second Citizen. 'That's when I discovered that Shakespeare could write great humour. I was very pleased with myself because I was very funny in the role and during rehearsals I enjoyed making the rest of the cast and our vicar, who was directing it, laugh.'

He so impressed Father Heald, in fact, that when the boy playing Cassius proved to be either unable or unwilling to continue in the part, he was replaced by the boy playing Brutus and Larry was recast as Brutus. The original Cassius was relegated to Second Citizen.

Among the audience was Gerard Olivier's friend Canon A J Thorndike, father of Sybil Thorndike, who was already an established actress, and he brought with him Ellen Terry, the great actress (and aunt of John Gielgud) who said in her diary, published in 1933, that Larry was 'already a great actor'.

In doing *Julius Caesar* Larry discovered a joy in acting that had not quite been there before. 'It was my introduction to Shakespeare,' he told me in 1972.

'It was mine too,' I said.

He frowned. 'But you said it was *Othello*.'

Almost apologetically, I explained, 'But *Julius Caesar* is all about Romans, you see.'

Larry laughed. I explained to him that I discovered *Julius Caesar*, not from reading the text or from seeing a play, but first of all from reading a comic book, complete with well-drawn pictures of Romans and battles, that was adapted from the play. Although much abridged, the text was Shakespeare's. It made understanding the Bard relatively easy.

I showed this comic book to Larry when I went to see him at the National in 1974 (he was directing *Eden End*) and he was not entirely unimpressed.

'They should make all of Shakespeare available to children in this manner, and then they should be forbidden from reading them after the age of twelve,' he said. 'Then every child should be taken to see the plays – even the films, yes – so they can see all the good and the bad that actors have done to his works, and judge for themselves.'

This seemingly draconian decree from his Lordship was all delivered with a twinkle in the eye. But he no doubt meant what he said, and with a teasing smile he remarked, 'If it can work for you, lad, it can work for all.'

It seemed that Olivier found some kind of mutual bond in the simple fact that we both found Shakespeare through *Julius Caesar*, which had, certainly for some years, been my favourite of all plays, regardless of the author. And it was certainly my favourite of Shakespeare's plays for a while. It wasn't just due to the comic book but to hearing over and over again the hour-long soundtrack album of dialogue highlights from the MGM film version. I listened to it so many times that I knew this abridged version, if not the whole text, by heart, and I loved more than anything Antony's funeral speech. At that time I had not seen the film so I had only the LP soundtrack to enjoy.

This interest in a diluted Shakespeare was enough to make Larry feel that I wasn't entirely a philistine. There was hope for me yet, obviously.

And it turned out I was more familiar with the text of that play than he was by 1979 when he made me recite Antony's funeral speech for him in his dressing room at Pinewood Studios (and that is saying something where Laurence Olivier and Shakespeare are concerned). But that's because it was a play Larry never really enjoyed.

'There is not enough of a great role there for me to ever want to do it,' he said. 'Julius Caesar himself gets killed halfway through, and no actor wants to die too soon before the curtain comes down. Antony arrives late in the play and has the best speech of the play but having then peaked he never makes an impact after it. Brutus and Cassius are the only two parts that are there from beginning to end. Brutus is too dull to want to play. Cassius is the best part. But I have never had enough passion for the part or the play.

'It is also a very unsatisfactory play. It reaches its zenith with Antony's funeral speech and after that it really loses its way as a great piece of drama.'

Larry taught me that the better play was *Antony and Cleopatra* – and he was right.

And so Larry made his stage debut, albeit in a Christmas production, abridged but still gaining him recognition from Ellen Terry as a 'great actor'. Maybe it was too soon to describe him as such, but he had the talent and the confidence to believe that he could become at least a very good actor – and at some point he realised he could actually be a truly great actor.

*

In 1918 Gerard Olivier became rector in Old Letchworth, thirty miles outside of London. He was given a handsome house and a decent salary of £400 a year. The distance from Letchworth to the centre of London was too great and so Larry boarded at All Saints. For much of his time now, Larry was out of reach of his parents, except at weekends. His greatest mentor was Father Heald. At Christmas 1918 *Julius Caesar* was revived because of its great success the previous year.

The 1919 Christmas show was more of a mix of songs and little sketches, but the following year Father Heald produced what was basically a series of scenes from *Twelfth Night*. Larry played Maria. Ellen Terry again came to watch and again was impressed.

In 1920, when Larry was 12, his beloved mother Agnes died at the age of 48 of a brain tumour. It wasn't from his father that Larry received the terrible news but from Father Heald. Larry was due to sing a solo Benedictus, and Father Heald asked him if he would prefer to forgo his solo. Larry had cried his heart out at the news but insisted he still sing his solo; he sang his heart out.

Larry also sang at his mother's funeral which, at his father's insistence, took place at Church Crookham in Hampshire, far from the family home in Letchworth but where Gerard and Agnes had taken communion together some twenty years earlier.

Gerard sold his old rectory and moved to a newer house in Letchworth Garden City. His new church had a bigger congregation, and Gerard seemed to throw himself into his work to overcome his grief. Sybille, aged nineteen, took over as the woman of the household. She also chose to become an actress and began studying at the Central School of Dramatic Art.

Something was about to happen to Larry that marked him for ever. If ever he had needed his mother, it was probably then. But his mother was gone.

2:

Is God Watching?

I hesitated to include what follows. I chose only to do so while deep into writing this book. I felt it said something more about Larry's life that has been unspoken. It also served to strengthen the bond between the two of us at the very end.

No one was closer to Larry than Father Heald. The priest saw something in Larry's Maria from *Twelfth Night* that convinced him Larry could carry off the part of another female, this time Kate in *The Taming of the Shrew*; this was again not the full play but highlights, concentrating on the quarrel scenes. Father Heald took the role of Petruchio.

Larry was explaining this to me in 1979. Over the next year I considered what he had been saying, and I began wondering about something that I thought I would never to get the chance to explore with Larry again. But I did, in 1981, when we met for the last time.

Larry had told me that girls were available for the plays; the previous year Sir Toby in *Twelfth Night* had been played by the daughter of the churchwarden – she was Ethel McGlinchy, later known as Fabia Drake, one of the great Shakespearean actresses. The casting of Larry as Kate opposite Father Heald as Petruchio brought questions to my mind. I knew, from first-hand experience, that celibate priests were not always as chaste as their frocks suggested.

In 1981, we talked about God and the church and all it stood for. There were things he said about Father Heald that had been bothering me for over a year. Larry was just thirteen but he was playing love scenes as a female with an adult male who was a priest and the closest friend Larry had. And that really bothered me.

In fact, he picked up on the fact that something was bothering me, and insisted I tell him what. And so I told him how I had been the victim of a paedophile High Anglican priest. I gave him an account in painful and explicit detail. I saw that it hurt him. Finally, I asked him if anything untoward had taken place between him and Father Heald.

His eyes burned briefly with what I think was anger – possibly aimed at me, possibly at the priest – while he remained silent. Then he sighed, took both my hands in his, despite the sore fingers he then had, and said, 'You look up to a priest and hold him in high regard, and expect him to know that God is watching. After all, He is, isn't He? God, I mean. And I believed in God with all my heart. Father Heald was a good man, and a likeable man. I trusted him.' And then his eyes filled with tears.

I asked him, 'Did he tell you that you would both pray and God would forgive you?'

He sat silent again for a while, then said, 'We prayed. But I never felt forgiven.'

In his autobiography, he wrote that Father Heald's 'direction was brilliant, and he injected into my consciousness that I was, in fact, being a woman'.

Larry had told me at another time, 'I was too convincing as a girl and other boys took a more than casual interest in me because of that.' And at another time he said, 'I had, as a boy, a rather feminine quality about me that the other boys at school found attractive.'

This is not to suggest that Larry was gay or even promiscuous as a boy. In fact, I am sure he rejected advances from other boys his own age. 'Sex was a terrible sin, especially between males,' he said. 'I knew that God would be rather unforgiving.'

While discussing the homosexual nature of the Roman general Crassus in *Spartacus*, Larry said, 'If, like me, you believed that sex between two males was a terrible sin against God, you fought it hard. But if, like Crassus, you saw it merely as a matter of taste and not morals, you were free of sin.'

Larry would, as an adult, battle with his own morals. As a boy at All Saints, he was convinced that a sin could be committed by a priest and then forgiven by that same priest, even if he knew different years later. That was what such a priest told me, and when I related this to

Larry – a terribly difficult thing for me to do at that time as I had only ever told one friend who had suffered the same thing – he just stared at me with sadness in his ageing eyes; he knew what I was talking about, and I sensed that he felt tremendous guilt that he never unburdened himself of.

There was one incident he would recall in his autobiography and which he made mention of to me, that happened just before he started at All Saints. He was visiting there one Sunday and wearing his traditional Sunday outfit, a kilt bearing the Kerr tartan. A large and older choirboy offered to show him the stage where the school plays were performed.

'I was thrown to the floor by him, and he threw himself on top of me, and I knew what he wanted, and I did not want any part of it.'

The older boy demanded that Larry repeat over and over, 'No, no, let me go, I don't want it.'

Larry told me, 'He treated me like a girl who was resisting. And I *was* resisting. My resistance merely acted to make him more amorous as he attempted to kiss me. There was a noise and he feared someone was coming up the stairs, so he got off me and disappeared, while I threw myself down the stairs into the arms of my mother.'

The young Olivier escaped from this boy but not from the priest he trusted, and when you have been sexually abused so young, especially by a priest, it stays with you for the rest of your life. And if I hadn't told Larry of my experience when we met in 1981, he would never have told me.

In the writing of this book, I saw a pattern in Larry's life that is symptomatic of someone who has been sexually abused. It has helped me to understand a lot more about Laurence Olivier. He told me, 'I went into a shell and never wanted to come out again.' I knew that feeling. I dealt with it by imagining I was some of the great heroes of the screen, such as John Wayne as Davy Crockett or Charlton Heston as El Cid, and later Clint Eastwood as the enigmatic Man With No Name. I did all that purely for my own sense of security. Larry dealt with it by doing what he did so well already – by becoming someone else and taking people to another place with him. He was able to make a living out of doing that, but he also did it much of the time in his life. This is illustrated in an interview I did with Franco Zeffirelli (in London in 1977 to direct Joan Plowright in *Filumena*). In 1972, Larry and Joan had gone to stay with Zeffirelli at his home in Italy. He recalled:

We had a terrible scare one night because Larry had drunk perhaps a little too much, and back at my house he announced he was going to bed. It was like a grand exit. He stood in the doorway with one last glass in his hand and flamboyantly bid us all good night, and then turned and disappeared into the darkness. Then we heard a terrible crash and glass breaking, and my assistant went to see what had happened and came back in a state of shock and told us, 'He's dying. He has fallen over and he's dying.'

But Joan, who knew his tricks of playacting, said, 'Nonsense, he is just playing the part.'

And true enough we found him being very overdramatic about his fall, although he did have a small cut on his head. That is Larry. He can't stop acting.

I went to stay with them at their home in Brighton before we had agreed on a play. I knew that he loved truffles, so I brought some with me as a gift for him. I gave them to him and without thinking I just referred to them by the Italian word *tartufi*, and in an instant Larry had made the connection with Molière's *Tartuffe*, and he launched into his own one-man production in which all the parts were taken from Italian cooking with a story about a maiden called Tagliatella and her maid Pastatina, and others called Risotto and Spaghetto. Oh, it was wonderful the way he gave them all different voices, and the story became ever more complicated with a priest called Don Ravlilo and a Neapolitan doctor called Maccherone. It was a wonderful commedia dell'arte.

That night I went to my room and feel asleep, and later I felt as though I was dreaming because there was the nurse from *Romeo and Juliet* and she was saying, 'Mistress, why, lamb! Why, lady! Fie, you slug-abed.' I thought for a minute that I had fallen asleep in the theatre, but then I remembered I was in the home of Laurence Olivier. And I was waking up to find that the nurse was Larry in my room, in his pyjamas and his dressing gown, with a towel over his head. He was waking me out of sleep by giving me a show. He couldn't just say, 'Wake up, Franco,' he had to put on a show. Yes, Larry is always acting.

He acted, or pretended, far more than other actors would in their real lives. Victims of sexual abuse often go into a shell and never come out. Some of us come out, but in disguise. Larry was the master of disguise.

There was another aspect to Larry I began to understand. He developed a need to always have control over his life. He had lost control of it as a boy; he wanted to find a way to regain it and keep it, and that need lasted all through his life.

In 1921 Gerard rented a houseboat on the Ouse at St Neots in Cambridgeshire. There Larry fell in love probably for the first time, at the age of fourteen. He also engaged in what was his first sexual activity with a girl.

'We had a houseboat called *White Wings* and next to us was the *Water Lily* where Bertha was holidaying with her family,' he told me in 1976. 'It was from Bertha that I realised my ambition to learn more about the opposite sex. I was, by that age, fighting the demons of a rush of hormones and the fear of damnation. But I was in love with Bertha who allowed me to feel her tits, which to me who had never felt such exquisiteness before was temptation that I couldn't resist. I learned how to kiss, and we had great fun telling each other secretly, so Fahv would never hear, how much we loved each other. And then the holiday was over and my heart was broken.'

Larry completed his final term at All Saints by singing 'Trinity and Unity' during his last Sunday service. Many years later Larry was to suffer terrible stage fright when he would forget his lines. But his first experience of this terrible trauma occurred during his rendition of this famous song.

'I can become overconfident,' he told me about his stage fright (in 1979). 'You always need a certain edge to a performance, and you need confidence, but you can't allow yourself to be overconfident or you will lose it. And that is the curse of an actor. I was first cursed with it in the choir, singing my last song solo [at All Saints]. I thought I could sing it with my arms folded and no sense of great concentration, and then I found the words failed me. I felt panic rising, couldn't breathe, had to stop altogether. The organist kept going. I grasped at some words I knew were there, felt secure that I was back in the song once again, relaxed and finished with a huge sense of relief to have survived. Classic stage fright. How I *hate* it.'

Larry moved on to his public-school life at St Edward's in 1921. People from overseas are often confused by the description 'public schools'. In Britain, public schools are actually *private* schools, and education in such schools costs money. Parents who pay to have their children educated at a public school expect their money's worth.

His friends from All Saints seemed to consider him someone very separate from them now, and he suddenly found himself somewhat bereft of friendship. 'I desire to be popular,' Larry said in 1978. 'It is an obsession with me. It was at school. It was probably worse then. I just wanted to be liked enormously. I am sure we all do. Or most of us. But I was obsessed with it, and when I went to public school my old friends did not want to know me so well, and that was a severe blow.'

Having barely arrived at the school, Larry found himself in the choir. Not only had he had enough of being in a choir, but he was also forced to take on the role of soloist. 'Being given any kind of authority or place of prominence was guaranteed to make the other boys dislike me.' That was a double blow to him.

It got worse in his second term when he was made vice-president of his form. He could have turned down this promotion, but he was beguiled by the faith his housemaster had in him, and couldn't resist accepting. Only after agreeing did he discover that this promotion simply separated him further from his peers. He said that he became known as 'that snidey little shit Olivier'.

'It probably didn't help that I was still an unabashed show-off, although my attempts were aimed at making myself popular. This didn't work at all with the boys my own age. But I found I was getting some attention from the older boys. And I didn't want what they wanted.'

He wrote that his feeling of superiority, his solo singing and his acting successes had 'lent my exterior a hint of show-off', and that the female roles he had played 'varnished it with an extra coat of girlishness'. This feminine quality and his desire to be popular resulted in him being, in his own words, 'a flirt'.

I became aware as I came to know him better that there was at times a feminine quality to him, and he admitted to me having had at least one homosexual relationship. There were times, upon reflection, when I can see that he was flirting with me. But it was not overt, and I doubt that he was even conscious of it. I suspect he flirted with everyone.

His flirting was, I think, another way for him to show off. He always wanted to be liked. He admitted that it was simply a part of his nature to perform. I gave him the chance to do this every time we met, not that he needed me to be his one-man audience. But when he had any kind of an audience, especially one that showed a deep interest in his work, he couldn't help but, as he put it, 'be on'.

I have often thought that to 'be on' made sure that nobody ever saw what lay beneath.

At school he found there were some boys who flirted back. Larry insisted he resisted their advances, which only made him the target of their rather sadistic tendencies. Senior prefects at public schools could cane younger and more inferior students. Larry came in for a succession of cruel beatings, and he admitted that he was unable to maintain a British stiff upper lip through it all. His crying only made the canings he received a popular spectator sport for the other boys.

There was some respite from all this pain, and yet a return to the girlish side of him, when, in April 1922, he found himself back with Father Heald and the All Saints choir, all heading off to Stratford-upon-Avon where they had been asked to perform *The Taming of the Shrew* at the Shakespeare Memorial Theatre as part of the celebrations for Shakespeare's birthday.

Critics from the national press came to see it. Since the cast of boys was not named, *The Times* wrote that 'one boy's performance as Katharina had a fire of its own . . . You felt that if an apple were thrown to this Katharina she would instinctively try to catch it in her lap, and if apples give her pleasure we hope with all gratitude that someone will make the experiment.'

The critic from the *Daily Telegraph* thought that the boy who played Kate made 'a fine, bold, black-eyed hussy, badly in need of taming'. This critic couldn't remember seeing 'any actress in the part who looked it better'.

These were the first reviews Larry ever had, and they were raves.

His two days at Stratford over – they performed the play only once as a matinee – he returned to St Edward's, where he remained generally unhappy, although he enjoyed history and English and did well in them. He was relieved to find that as he inevitably became one of the older boys, the canings gradually ceased.

In 1923, he was told he was to play Puck in *A Midsummer Night's Dream*, which the school was producing that Christmas. He seems to have taken no part in any other plays at St Edward's, and he dreaded playing the imp Puck before an audience of schoolboys who disliked him and regarded him as something of a sissy.

The producer, a senior master, had decided that Puck should make surprise appearances and dance among the audience with his face lit by two torch-lamps harnessed to his chest. He dreaded the whole enterprise.

He made up his mind, he wrote, to 'knock their bloody eyes out with it *somehow*'.

He told me in 1979, 'I learned a long time ago that when faced with a part that you feel bound to fail in for whatever reason, I can become so determined to make the audience love me in it that more often than not my plan works. There are times when I will stand at the back of the stage before the curtain has gone up, and I will say to the audience – but in my mind of course – "I will be fucking great and you will fucking love me." I will always lift myself a little higher to succeed. It works for me.'

And it worked for him as Puck. He also learned something about Shakespeare with that role: 'Shakespeare could look after himself and look after, too, the actor who trusts him.'

He was such a huge success that all of a sudden he found he had a seemingly unlimited number of peers who wanted to be seen walking with him. He had finally gained what he craved – popularity.

Then came sadness. In January 1924 his brother Dickie left home to work as a tea planter in India. For this sad farewell, Larry was allowed home, and he accompanied his father to see Dickie off at Waterloo Station. Larry cried at the parting – he would not see his hero for the next nine years.

Sybille was also away from home now, having become an actress. She also married in haste, to an actor and, to Gerard's horror, in a registry office. Larry had shown no obvious interest in following his sister on to the stage professionally. In fact, he didn't know what he wanted to do with his life.

3

A Kind of Mask

'Why did I choose the stage?' mused Larry in 1976, repeating the question I had just put to him in the studios of Granada Television where he was recording *Cat on a Hot Tin Roof*. 'I didn't want to be a priest like my father. I knew *that*. And I didn't want to follow Dickie to India. It was Fahv, of all people, who suggested I become an actor. I was at home having a bath. And he was asking me what I intended to do. I had no idea, and then he said, "Why not try the theatre?" He said that when I left school in the summer of 1924, I should do as my sister had done – she had gone to the Central School of Dramatic Art.'

Larry obtained permission to have a day away from St Edward's to audition at the Royal Albert Hall for Elsie Fogerty, the principal of the Central School. He performed Jacques' speech on the Seven Ages of Man from *As You Like It*. Afterwards, Miss Fogerty told him that it wasn't necessary to perform the part with exaggerated movements such as making fencing passes while saying 'sudden and quick in quarrel'. Apart from that criticism, she told Larry that she would allow him the scholarship, which paid the fees of £50 for the year.

'I learned something on the day I auditioned from Miss Fogerty that gave me what I think has been one of the keys to my success as an actor,' he said in 1974. 'She placed the tip of her finger against my hairline, which was really rather low on my forehead back then, ran it down into the hollow of my brow line and said, "There is a weakness

. . . *there.*" I didn't know what to do about it until I began to fill that area in with nose-putty.'

I asked him if that was why he had created such a bold Roman nose for his role of Crassus in *Spartacus*.

He replied, 'I'm not the leading man who must have applause on his first entrance. I am a character actor, and my joy comes from dressing my body, with clothing, and my face – with a nose or a beard if necessary – not for applause for a handsome profile. So yes, I nearly always have a false nose, and that's why I went as far as I could with it as Crassus.

'But apart from it providing me with a tool to change my face to fit the character, using nose-putty to fill that deep gap in my brow line simply strengthened my face, and I hope that you will not even notice it is there. It has become something of a shield for me as an actor, protecting me from the fear of one of the things that an actor dreads, and that is weakness in his face and in particular around the eyes. The eyes express so much that an actor has to say, so you can't afford to have any part of that area of your face let you down when you most need it.'

In 1978, at Shepperton Studios where he was making *The Thief of Baghdad*, Peter Ustinov told me:

Aldous Huxley once said that actors are by definition exhibitionists. I think Laurence Olivier is a case which proves the opposite. He always put false noses on whenever he could, and they were always noses which were very much like the nose which was the one God gave him but just a little pushed forward, which alters the face. It acted as a kind of mask. He only felt happy when he had some kind of pretence at a disguise like a false nose. He didn't feel he was himself any more and could then act.

When he made speeches as himself he wasn't nearly as effective as when he was *acting* somebody else making a speech. His own maiden speech in the House of Lords was never of the same quality it would have been had he been allowed to wear a false nose in the House of Lords.

I think it's likely that when Miss Fogerty told him about the weakness in his face, she hit on something that was for Larry both a curse and a blessing. It was a curse because he felt vulnerable; sexual abuse makes the victim more sensitive and vulnerable, and they need to hide it. It was a blessing because she gave him the clue about how to hide it – behind false noses and all manner of make-up to the point that, in some productions, he became almost unrecognisable. Most importantly to him, privately and professionally, he became somebody else. It was, at times, preferable to being who he was, or who he perceived himself to be.

Miss Fogerty also provided Larry with a bursary of another £50, without which the young Olivier could not have afforded to attend the Central School.

'I wasn't at all interested in anything but the acting,' he said. 'We had lectures and classes but I was such an idiot at first to not take an interest in them. I later discovered how important theatre history is to any actor.'

Larry never tired of talking about Shakespeare to me, and he never tired of educating me to his way of thinking. 'Shakespeare was the greatest dramatist of all time,' he said emphatically. 'A genius who remains unparalleled.'

Around this time, Sybille's marriage ended. She told Larry but not their father, and she begged Larry not to tell him. When Gerard finally found out, he blamed Larry for keeping him in the dark, and then he condemned Sybille from his own pulpit for adultery.

'I am afraid my father was a hypocrite,' said Larry. 'He couldn't see what pain he caused to us all at times, accusing us of terrible sins. And yet he was not sinless.'

Larry was referring to the fact that, against church law, Gerard remarried. His bride was Isobel Buchanan Ronaldson, whom he had met while on a church mission to Jamaica. The High Anglican Church, like the Catholic Church, forbade its priests from marrying, although it did allow Gerard's first marriage because he already had a wife when he took his vows. But it was forbidden for a priest to marry while already in holy orders. Consequently, Gerard left his position at Letchworth, was unable to find work for the next six months, and so began married life without an income, surviving only on a trust he had set up. He wasn't broke, but he and Isobel were living on a limited budget.

During the Christmas holiday Larry managed to find work at the St Christopher's School theatre in Letchworth Garden City, where he was paid £4 a week as assistant stage manager and general understudy in a children's play, *Through the Crack*, which opened on 1 January 1925. During the Easter break he was Lennox in *Macbeth*, as well as being assistant stage manager again.

'Never underestimate the experience of working in stage management,' he told me when I watched him directing at the Old Vic in 1974. 'You learn what happens and why and where, and that is something every actor should learn.'

At the end of his year at Central, he gained a gold medal that he shared with Peggy Ashcroft for their respective performances of Shylock and Portia in a scene they presented from *The Merchant of Venice*. Larry and Dame Peggy became lifelong friends. In fact, Larry fell madly in love with her, but for some reason a romantic relationship failed to materialise.

'I kept wanting to propose to Peggy,' Larry told me, 'but I just didn't have the courage. Maybe I was afraid of being rejected. I do so hate rejection.'

Dame Peggy told me, at the BBC in 1980, 'I love Larry dearly as a friend, and I would have to admit that in the early days I loved him very differently. But he was just too slow. In those days a young lady didn't make the first move. No, no! I gave up waiting for Larry to make his move.'

'What would have happened if he had made his move?' I asked her.

'Things would have been very different,' she replied. 'Or maybe not. Maybe there still would have been Vivien Leigh.'

Larry managed to land his first real professional acting work with Ruby Miller in *The Ghost Train*, appearing as a policeman. He was also with Miss Miller in a short piece to support *The Ghost Train*, called *The Unfailing Instinct*. It was a twelve-week tour, but in reality Larry only worked six of those weeks. He was paid £4 a week, but only for the six weeks he actually worked, even though he was with the tour for the full twelve.

Following a short period of unemployment, Larry found a job with the Lena Ashwell Players; Lena Ashwell was a well-known actress in both Britain and America who set up her company to perform Shakespeare. Larry played Antonio in *The Tempest* and then three minor parts, including Flavius, in *Julius Caesar*.

They played one-night stands in rather dingy venues in rather dingy areas of London, including boarded-over swimming pools and town halls, often having to use the lavatories and bath cubicles as dressing rooms. Larry christened the company The Lavatory Players. He had to pay his own fare to each venue – he was then living in Maida Vale – which took up most of his salary of two pounds and ten shillings a week.

During the opening scenes of *Julius Caesar* he had to take down some wreaths pinned to a black velvet backcloth, behind which female members of the cast were changing. Larry thought it a wonderful practical joke to tug at the wreaths in such a way as to make a tear in the backcloth and so reveal a glimpse of bare female bottoms for the benefit of the actor playing Marullus and possibly some members of the audience.

One night, the actor playing Antony failed to arrive when the play began, and Larry was hastily thrown into the role, to his great delight. He went on and gave his usual performance as Flavius ('Hence! Home, you idle creatures . . .') and also delivered the few lines Antony has in the early part of the play. He was ready to deliver the great funeral speech, but just as he was about to begin, 'Friends, Romans, countrymen, lend me your ears,' the real Antony arrived, insisting Larry stepped down. Reluctantly, Larry gave way and never got to play Antony again . . . except for a day in his Pinewood Studios dressing room in 1979 just for my benefit.

His diligence with The Lavatory Players was rewarded after a few weeks with a three-week engagement at Lena Ashwell's headquarters, the Century Theatre in Notting Hill. He opened as Flavius in *Julius Caesar*, and attempted to repeat his trick with the backcloth. But in his enthusiasm, he also managed to catch the long pants of Marullus, who was standing on a beer crate, and they slipped down around his ankles. Unable to control his hysterical laughter, Larry left the stage while Marullus was left immobile with his pants round his ankles; he was only able to get off after the stage manager closed the curtains. The next day, Larry was summoned to Lena Ashwell's office and fired.

It was time for Larry to use what connections he had, and so he went to see Lewis Casson, husband to star actress Sybil Thorndyke, the daughter of Gerard's friend, Canon Thorndike. Sybil had befriended Larry's sister, so Larry went to see Casson, who always directed Sybil's plays and was the company manager in partnership with Bronson Albery, to ask for work. He was rewarded with the job of assistant stage manager, as well as various spear and standard bearers and understudy to numerous actors, in *Henry VIII* at the Empire Theatre in Leicester Square. His salary was £4 a week. For some performances, Shelley's *The Cenci* was added to the bill in which he was given the part of an old servant.

Larry would always regard Sybil Thorndike and Lewis Casson as 'his second parents'. He remained close to them both, and worked with Dame Sybil years later when he directed her in *The Prince and the Showgirl*.

I had the extreme privilege of meeting Dame Sybil Thorndike at the premiere of the film *The Trojan Women* in 1971. Seeing me, whom she had never met before, she took my arm so I could lead her down some very precarious steps at a new cinema in Bloomsbury Square; it was literally an underground cinema.

'And how is Larry?' she asked me.

'Larry who?'

'Olivier, my dear. You're his son, aren't you?'

'No, I'm not,' I replied.

She stood still, looked at me, studied my face, smiled and said, 'Oh, but you *should* be.'

At the end of the screening, I sat with Dame Sybil and talked to her about Olivier. 'He was a wonderful young man when he first came to us. Very full of himself, of course. But I knew he had good reason to be. He had talent, enthusiasm and that special magic that only stars have we call charisma. See if you can get some for yourself, my dear.' And then she looked quizzically at me and said, 'You remind me of my young Larry. Yes, my dear, get yourself some charisma.'

When I told this tale to Larry while he was making *Sleuth*, he laughed until he literally wept, not with hysterics but with sheer emotion. 'Oh, dear boy, you were blessed by the wonderful Dame herself.'

That, I think, stood me in good stead with Laurence Olivier.

4

Jill

In 1926 Larry met Ralph Richardson. It was not a firm friendship at the start. 'The damn fellow was after my wife,' Richardson complained when I sat with him and John Gielgud in the Old Vic in 1975. Richardson's wife, Muriel Hewitt – or Kit as she was known – was appearing in *Marvellous History of St Bernard* at the Kingsway Theatre, and Larry had the small role of a minstrel.

'You did quite a number of plays, you and Larry,' Gielgud said to Richardson.

'I believe there were a few. I was a better-known actor than Larry, and I felt that he was trying too hard to get me to like him. So I tended to shun him a lot.'

'Oh, Ralph, that was rather harsh of you.'

'Serves him right for trying it on with my wife.'

Larry denied that he ever 'tried it on' with Richardson's wife, but he did say, 'Oh, but Kit was a beauty and every young actor fell for her. But she was forever faithful to Ralph who had to be somewhat irritated by all the attention the young men, including me, gave her.'

By the end of 1926, with several small stage credits to his name, Larry joined the Birmingham Repertory Company, where he appeared in fourteen productions throughout 1927. There were another five plays for the Birmingham Rep in 1928, and he also got to do a couple of Shakespeares at the Royal Court Theatre, appearing in *Macbeth* as

Malcolm and *The Taming of the Shrew* in the small part of a lord, appearing only at the beginning.

'Playing everything from major parts to spear carriers was the best thing to happen to me,' he told me in 1978. 'You learn your craft, you enjoy the heady heights of playing major roles, and you keep your feet nailed to the ground by being little more than an extra. Not that I didn't hate playing those small insignificant parts. I hated them with a vengeance. I wanted to be so grand and famous. I really wanted to be the greatest actor of all time. But you have to start as a little acorn.'

By this time he was establishing a friendship with Ralph Richardson, who played Tranio in *The Taming of the Shrew*.

'I think that was when Larry and I started to become friends,' Richardson told Gielgud and me in 1975. 'But it took a bit of time. I had to get to know that he was, after all, a likeable fellow. He could make me laugh.'

'I recall him making me laugh, but not for the right reasons,' said Gielgud.

'Oh, Johnnie, he is a very funny chap. We were doing a play [*Back to Methuselah*, 1928] and after we had finished a rehearsal I said to Larry, "Come on, let's get a drink." It was in the bar right by the stage [of the Royal Court Theatre]. I had half a pint and he asked for a "Gin and Pep". It was gin with peppermint. I'd never seen it before. "What's that, Larry?" I asked. And he said, "It's jolly good for the ovaries." And that made me laugh. I have no idea why. It was his delivery, Johnnie.'

John Gielgud didn't understand why it was at all funny, but that joke cemented the friendship between Olivier and Richardson.

In June 1928, Larry played the juvenile lead in *Bird in Hand* at the Royalty Theatre. His leading lady was Jill Esmond. Her father was H V Esmond, a successful actor/manager/writer, and her mother was the actress Eva Moore, who had appeared in many of her husband's plays.

Larry promptly fell in love with Jill and proposed marriage. I asked him why he proposed to her and not to Peggy Ashcroft. He said, 'Peggy was such a wonderful friend, and it seemed to me that to have her for a wife might somehow wreck our friendship. But Jill was someone I frankly had more lust for. Not that I didn't love her. But that was a complicated relationship. Long over. Best forgotten.' That was in 1976 when he told me this. In 1979, when he knew me better, he said, 'I simply had to have sex, dear boy, and I felt I couldn't unless I was married. So I was desperate to marry Jill. I simply felt I couldn't fuck her unless she wore my wedding ring.'

'Would you have felt so guilty about having sex outside of marriage?' I asked him.

'I wasn't without sin, you must understand. But I needed to break free of that burden and put all wrongs to right, dear boy.'

It surprised me at the time that an actor, and an obviously virile one at that, would consider sex outside of marriage a sin. It's true that he had a religious upbringing. But I feel it had to do with far more than that. To even refer to sex outside of marriage as a sin, at least in Larry's case, was more a reflection of the guilt that came, not from religious fervour, but from being sexually abused by a priest.

'It took Jill two years to respond to my proposal,' Larry said. That meant Larry would have had to avoid 'sin' for two more years.

While he was waiting for Jill's response – she would agree to marry him – he got on with the business of building his career. He wanted to audition for the title role in *Beau Geste*, which Basil Dean was due to direct at His Majesty's Theatre, and in the hope of 'frankly, showing off', he accepted a part in R C Sherriff's masterpiece about the First World War, *Journey's End*, playing Stanhope. It was a modest production performed only on Sunday afternoons, but he hoped it would attract the attention of Basil Dean.

It did, thanks to some very good reviews of *Journey's End* and good personal notices for Larry. But he had competition from his *Journey's End* co-star Maurice Evans; Dean was looking at both Evans and Olivier for the role of Beau. The other brothers had already been cast: Jack Hawkins as John, and Robin Irvine as Digby. Ultimately, Larry won the coveted part.

A little more than forty years after *Beau Geste* played at His Majesty's Theatre (from 30 January to 4 March 1929) I had the remarkable experience of sitting with Laurence Olivier and Jack Hawkins at some show-business event, probably around late 1972.

Hawkins had lost his voice box to throat cancer and had to speak through a hole in his throat and oesophagus by literally burping his words. He bravely talked, even though it seemed incredibly difficult and possibly even painful, although he assured me that it wasn't painful; just very tiring and somewhat undignified.

So here were these two great stars, reminiscing about their days when they were together in *Beau Geste*.

'Basil Dean was determined we should all be expert Legionnaires,' said Hawkins. 'Every morning we rehearsed in a rather horrid little gym near the Strand (in London) at nine o'clock.'

'Very dirty, damp place, I recall,' said Larry.

'Yes, and very smelly. We would work out in the gym because Basil wanted us to be really fit. And then we dragged ourselves to His Majesty's Theatre where there was a regimental sergeant major from one of the Guards regiments waiting for us to give us almost an hour of square-bashing.'

'Basil Dean was a stickler for authenticity.'

'Obsessive.'

'Then we would finally rehearse the play and after all that we had to spend an hour singing soldiers' songs,' said Larry.

'That was a tough play to do.'

'Very tough. Dangerous, too.'

'Do you remember, Larry, I was knocked out cold when we were rehearsing a fight scene? I got kicked in the head.'

'During the run? I don't remember.'

'During a dress rehearsal. We had to wear big studded army boots. I got one in the head and was out.'

'We wore *real* uniforms which Basil got hold of,' said Larry.

'He got them from the French Government,' said Hawkins. 'Real Foreign Legion uniforms that needed to be fumigated.'

'Yes, and often. Most unpleasant.'

'It's a wonder nobody got killed, Larry. I had to fire a machine gun and the blanks wouldn't work in it so we used wooden bullets.'

'Oh, yes. Very effective.'

'Too effective. The first time I used them I shot about three feet off the bottom of the cyclorama that went around the set. So I had to keep the gun at a low trajectory.'

'Which shot up sections of the stage,' Larry recalled.

'The audience was showered in splinters. Two women fainted on the first night.'

'Oh, yes, people dived for cover in the front rows. That was a very realistic battle scene.'

'It was a miracle nobody was hurt. Do you remember how in the final scene when you were dead –'

'We were *all* dead.'

'Except for me. I had to give you a Viking funeral.'

'And there was a fireman on duty there who thought the stage was on fire.'

Both men laughed, although Hawkins was very tired by now. His autobiography revealed the rest of the tale they were in the middle of.

Beau had always said he wanted a Viking funeral, so Hawkins, as brother John, laid Olivier, as brother Beau, on a bed, draped him with the flag, dumped the sergeant by the bed, and then poured petrol over the bodies. Hawkins actually poured the petrol over sand hidden by the corpses to give the illusion they were being drenched in petrol, and then smoke was generated at the switch of a button off stage and a sheet of silk flashed up to simulate flames.

On the first night, the duty fireman in the theatre was new to the job and hadn't seen the dress rehearsal, so when he saw the smoke he leaped into the prompt corner and released the fire curtain, which was made from iron and asbestos.

The handles to raise the fire curtain again couldn't be found. The audience, thinking it was all over and presumably bemused that there was no curtain call, left. By the time the curtain had been raised, the cast, assembled to take their bows, looked out on an empty auditorium.

Hawkins wrote, 'It was therefore no surprise to any of us involved that we were not set for a long run. *Beau Geste* folded after eight weeks.'

For his role as Beau, Larry grew a pencil moustache fashioned after Ronald Colman, who had starred in the silent film version of *Beau Geste*. 'I fashioned my look on Colman,' he admitted. 'I have stolen many things from other people to get the look of a character.'

He went to work for Dean again, in *The Circle of Chalk*, and then he performed in *The Stranger Within*, but what he really wanted to do was get to New York, where Jill Esmond was enjoying success in the play *Bird in Hand*.

He had a stroke of luck when actor Frank Vosper decided he didn't want to go to New York with a very successful play he was in, *Murder on the Second Floor*. Larry landed the role and set sail for New York in August 1929. He checked in at the Algonquin Hotel, and then turned up at the theatre where Jill was playing so they could meet as soon as the curtain came down.

I wanted to know how they managed to avoid committing sin, and asked Larry outright. 'We played our little games,' he said, as enigmatic as ever.

'What kind of games?' I persisted.

'Penetration is not mandatory,' he said. 'And then you can always torment each other with little fantasies. Jill wanted me to be her master. I think I might have liked Jill to have been mine.'

'So you didn't make love?'

'Not in the conventional sense.'

'In the naked sense?'

He almost belched a laugh and slapped his knees. 'Good God, boy, do you want diagrams? Yes, naked!'

Larry and Jill, then, tormented each other in their passionate state, trying hard not to 'sin', seeing each other naked, and the rest is up to the imagination. But in holding back, they indulged in fantasies that took them as far as they dared without resorting to the ultimate sin.

For two people with strong sexual drives, this had to be a form of gratification that, in time, harmed their relationship. They played at it, but failed to see it through, which to me says a great deal about the lasting effect being a victim of sexual abuse had on Larry.

But there was something more, something he hinted at because I persisted with highly personal questions. 'What kind of fantasies did you mean?' I asked.

'Oh, boy–girl, girl–boy stuff,' he said.

Without giving myself time to think, I asked, 'You mean, she'd be the boy and you'd be the girl, and then the other way round?' I immediately thought what a stupid question that had to be.

But I had hit the mark. He said, 'Yes. Something like that.'

This was in keeping with his feminine side, for him wanting to be a girl and for Jill pretending to be the boy. And this would make her the master, and this was something that, I am sure, was another reflection of his abusive experience. He was putting himself into that scenario but with the safety of knowing that this time he had Jill play-acting.

Some years after Jill and Larry divorced, she lived with female partners. She was, it turned out, bisexual – and so was he. It would seem that they were encouraging each other to explore their sexuality with their fantasies. His bisexuality might, of course, have been a part of him even without the intervention of Father Heald. But the experience of sexual abuse by a man upon a boy will invariably cause some sexual confusion to the victim. This confusion remained with Larry, but he fought it because, even as a young man, he still feared that eternal damnation might be a consequence of a sin that was greater than the sin of being with a woman.

This was particularly hard on Larry. He was, after all, someone who was particularly driven by his sexuality. In years to come he would explore, in his work, characters he felt were driven by sex, such as Hamlet and Iago. And when I asked him why that was, he said, 'But surely we are all driven by sex. It is human nature. Almost everything we do is determined according to our sexual responses, our sexual nature. We know within three seconds of meeting somebody if we find them sexually attractive. It just happens. And it leads us to actions that are directly or indirectly sexual in nature. A talk and a chance to flirt; a working relationship that, certainly in theatre and in film, creates electricity if it is there, and if it isn't you can only hope to pretend. But outside of acting, surely in any working relationship in any field, if you find yourself wanting to fuck some girl, you're going to make sure you spend more time with her, even if you know, through perhaps a sense of fidelity, it's never going to happen. But it drives you nonetheless.'

And so, driven by his sexual drive and his curiosity about his ambiguous sexual nature, which was either already a part of Jill's character or which surfaced through the games they played and the torment they went through, they were diving headlong into a life together which, by the standards of the day, was inevitably doomed. Each knew the other was bisexual and, apart from the more practical effects that would have upon them in their marriage, there was also the ever-present threat of one or other revealing the secret that both, surely, wanted to keep hidden. That could harm not just their marriage (particularly one so public), but more especially their careers.

Murder on the Second Floor finished its run rather prematurely at the Eltinge Theatre after only six weeks. Larry returned to England and went to live with his father and his new stepmother Isobel; Gerard had by now found a parish in Addington in Buckinghamshire. Larry became immediately fond of his stepmother. Because she had become Isobel Buchanan Olivier, Larry nicknamed her Ibo, from her new initials.

There was a family crisis when Sybille, who had given up acting, married a schoolteacher and writer called Gerard Day. She had a baby daughter, but suffered a nervous breakdown and lost all interest in the baby, and was then put into a mental hospital in north London; Larry was shaken by these events and wrote to Jill, now in Chicago, about them.

Her response was to cable that Sybille was his problem and not hers. She later wrote saying that she knew he wanted to do what he could to help his sister but urged him not to do anything in case he somehow also become mentally ill.

The Jill–Larry relationship was on shakier ground than ever.

5

Ambiguity

Larry found a good part in a good play, as a shell-shocked Royal Flying Corps officer in *The Last Enemy* by Frank Harvey, which enjoyed a good run at the Fortune Theatre from mid-December 1929 to mid-March 1930. It was, he felt, a play that brought him 'friendly and timely establishment as a leading character-juvenile'.

Professionally, he was happy. Privately he was miserable. Jill had promised in January that she was coming back to England. Instead, she went to New York for a couple of weeks, and then to Florida and the Bahamas. She arrived home just before the end of the run of *The Last Enemy*.

He then landed his first film role, in *The Temporary Widow*, based on a play called *Hokuspokus*. It was an English–German co-production, filmed in Berlin in two versions – one in English and the other in German. The star, Lilian Harvey, played a woman accused of the murder of her husband, and appeared in both versions. Larry did only the English-language version.

He was having a fine time in Germany, going to the opera, and taking a two-week holiday in Stolpchensee with co-star Felix Aylmer. But Jill, now back in England, was miserable without him.

It appears that he also become involved with a dancer in Berlin. Jill had spoken to him on the telephone, and they had argued. They had, however, agreed on a wedding date: 25 July 1930. Larry was suddenly sowing some wild oats before the marriage could take place and be consummated, regardless of whether it was sinful or not. But what drove him to cheat on Jill suddenly? He had certainly been angered by her failure to return home to England when she said she would, and he was upset about her lack of sympathy for his sister Sybille.

So why didn't Larry call off the wedding? He once told me, 'My first marriage was a disaster that should never have happened.'

'But you can't know that at the time,' I argued.

'I knew. I knew. But I couldn't stop it. I needed to have some sense of normality, and I thought marriage would give it to me and rid us both of some devils.'

Their devils, I am sure, was their bisexuality. Perhaps Larry thought marriage might be some kind of cure.

But having waited so long to avoid the 'sin' Larry had feared, why did he take up with a dancer? I didn't ask him about this directly because I didn't know about it at the time, in 1979, but he did say, 'Men are weak. You cannot hold out forever. Celibacy is an evil and it corrupts.' (Again, a reference to being sexually abused.) 'And while I tried to hold out, I gave in.'

'With Jill?' I asked.

'No. Before I married, I was a little . . . hmmm . . . wild.'

Larry, then, had 'sinned' in the fullest sense, and not with Jill, before their wedding night. But there was something fundamentally wrong with the marriage, and it was something Larry only discovered a few weeks before the wedding. Jill told him she didn't love him, that she loved another, and that she could never love Larry as completely as he would wish. Yet still he did not call off the wedding. He wrote that he was able to assure himself that he was 'a noble enough character' and that he would reach 'such divine perfection as a husband' that any 'petty difficulties could be outfaced'.

His film career was about to take off, even though, he insisted, he despised the medium and that it was only a way to make good money that was not available in the theatre.

In London, in May 1930, he made his second film, *Too Many Crooks*. It was just a short film, less than forty minutes long, and was only ever intended as a supporting film, so didn't get a great deal of notice.

Of more importance was an offer from Noël Coward to appear in *Private Lives*. The play focuses on two couples. Coward and Gertrude Lawrence would play the main characters, Elyot and Amanda, and he was looking for a younger couple to play Victor and Sybil.

Noël Coward told me, when I met him in 1972 at Claridge's in London, 'I needed an actor who was very handsome to play Victor, so I chose Larry Olivier, who was very physically attractive.'

Coward was still in bed, wearing exquisite Japanese silk pyjamas and eating his breakfast, when Larry went to meet him for the first time.

'I think he was a little overwhelmed,' Coward said, 'because I called him "Larry" just the once, and he behaved as though we were old friends and kept calling me "Noël" at every opportunity. I had to tell him that he was behaving just a little too actor-y.'

Private Lives was set to run from August through to December, with a tour that took in Edinburgh, Birmingham, Manchester and Southsea before opening in London, and then New York. Meanwhile, there was a wedding to organise. Jill's mother wanted them to wed at the Chapel Royal, Savoy, where she had married her late husband. Larry asked his father to marry him to Jill, but Gerard responded that he couldn't marry them at the Chapel Royal, because it was a place where divorced people were allowed to be married. Larry thought his father an outrageous hypocrite, but still, the wedding took place at All Saints.

For their honeymoon, they stayed in a house in Lulworth Cove that belonged to a friend of Jill's mother, a Lady Fripp, who saw fit to provide Larry and Jill with her two grown-up unmarried daughters to be their hostesses. Their presence in the house added to the disaster that was the honeymoon night.

In his autobiography, Larry put the failure of their attempt to consummate the marriage down to shyness and inexperience with each other, as well as the embarrassment of having two single women in the same house. He was unable, it seems, to satisfy Jill. He didn't explain why. But I think it is likely that when the moment finally came, despite having had some experience in Berlin, if not elsewhere at other times with other women, the sexual games they had played, the fantasies they had shared, all counted for nothing when the real thing finally happened. Sex was painful for her. Larry blamed himself, according to his autobiography.

Whether it was or wasn't his fault, what I think was behind that night's failure above all else was the guilt he still felt over being abused. He had tried to remain 'sinless' with Jill until sex could not be a sin within the bounds of marriage, but he was still plagued, as he would always be, by the guilt that stays with a victim of sexual abuse. He was, I would think, dealing with his sexual nature as best he could.

There is a very telling line in Olivier's autobiography regarding the wedding day. He had kept a daily journal for years, but for ten years from that day he kept no journal. More telling still, he chose that day to give up what he called his 'religious practices'. His religious beliefs and a priest had caused him what he saw as sexual dysfunction. Religion would cease to control his life. He wanted to be master of his own life, and that would become more evident as he became master of his career. He needed to be in control. And that, too, is very symptomatic of sexual abuse.

Soon after the honeymoon, rehearsals for *Private Lives* began. Adrianne Allen, wife of actor Raymond Massey, was cast as Sybil. Coward and Gertrude Lawrence had rehearsed all their scenes on holiday in the South of France, so Coward concentrated on Larry and Adrianne during a two-week period.

The play opened to tremendous success in Edinburgh. It was going to be a long way from there to New York, and on the way Noël Coward realised he had a problem with Larry, as he told me:

> Larry turned out to be a terrible giggler on stage. If I did anything that was at all funny in the part, Larry would be in fits of laughter instead of being cross, which he was supposed to be.
>
> It's all very well having an actor's joke, but it's not fair on the paying audience. I simply had to stop him, so I told him, 'From now on I'm going to try and make you laugh, and every time you do, I'll kill you.' Well, he got so angry with himself for falling for it that I ruined several of his performances. But it was worth it.
>
> In one scene Amanda chokes on her coffee and Victor had to slap her hard on the back. One performance she said to him, 'You great clob!' And I said, 'Clob?' 'Yes,' she replied, 'clob.' To which I added, 'The man with the clob foot!' Larry, of course, was dying to laugh and had to restrain himself, fearful of what I would do to him.

While he was performing *Private Lives* in the evenings in London, Larry was, for three weeks anyway, making his third film by day, *Her Strange Desire* (American title *Potiphar's Wife*), with Nora Swinburne.

During this period, Larry was spending time with someone other than Jill. It isn't exactly clear when this relationship began or exactly how it was conducted, but in his autobiography he wrote of 'my nearly passionate involvement with the one male with whom some sexual dalliance had not been loathsome for me to contemplate'. And the question that has bugged his biographers ever since is, who was that male?

Larry did have at least one homosexual relationship. He told me so. We were, of course, discussing the role of General Marcus Licinius Crassus in *Spartacus*.

'It was easy for me to play the general as a rather flirtatious man with a strong masculine side and a definite feminine side,' he told me in 1979. 'That came from me, from deep inside. Some actors might need to draw on their imagination or some research to find a way of playing out some attraction for another man. For me, it was something I did all the time. I am aware when I find a man attractive, and that's what I had to do with Tony [Curtis] in *Spartacus*. And then I had to seduce him. That wasn't so easy for me, as I was always reluctant to be the seducer. But I could be seduced.'

'By another man?' I asked.

'Oh, yes, indeed.'

In retrospect, he might have been talking about Father Heald, but what Olivier said next makes this clear it was not the priest he was referring to.

'Actors tend to be rather . . . ambiguous at times. And to be found attractive by an actor whom one admires is very appealing.'

He was, I realised, flirting with me, although he was talking literally of another actor, and I know this simply because I asked him who this other actor was.

'Oh, my dear boy, he was one of the great romantic actors and a beautiful Hamlet.'

One of the great romantic actors of that time and a beautiful Hamlet was Henry Ainley. He was born in Leeds on 21 August 1879. He acted in literally hundreds of productions, beginning his career as an amateur. Joining Frank Benson's company, he made his professional debut as a messenger in *Macbeth*. He played major parts in many Shakespeare plays, beginning with *Henry V* in 1900, and played Hamlet in 1930 at the Haymarket Theatre, London. He appeared in several films, but the stage was his real home, where he performed in Shakespeare plays almost annually over four decades.

In 1930 Ainley was 51, married and had a son. But, as Larry said, many actors are sexually ambiguous. Larry was now 23 and was not getting sexual fulfilment from Jill. And so he turned to Ainley who, I suspect, had worked some charm on him. In fact, Larry hinted that

Ainley was his inspiration for the scene in *Spartacus* in which Crassus attempts to seduce his slave, played by Tony Curtis.

'I had only to think of that very seductive actor, older than his willing slave, talking of what is moral and what is immoral, and whether morals are just a matter of taste.' In the bath scene in *Spartacus*, this was just what Crassus tells his slave in an attempt to seduce him. When Larry talked of 'that very seductive actor', I am sure he was talking of Ainley, and when he talked of 'his willing slave', he was referring to himself.

It was in 1981, during our final and rather emotional meeting, that he said to me, 'Don't fear the seemingly undesirable experiences that life has to offer if you want to be a serious actor. You might just dip your toe in, or dive in and get thoroughly soaked, but those experiences can be useful. At least, I have found so. You always wanted to know how I was able to play the ambiguous Roman (in *Spartacus*). I was ambiguous myself.

'But that ambiguity does not lead to true romance, unless you shake off that ambiguity and take on the complete mantle of a man who loves another (man). For me there is nothing more wonderful than true romance, and I could only find that with the women in my life. The men in my life could never give me that.'

And in that sentence, he gave away, maybe on purpose, that there had been more than just one man, more than just Henry Ainley. But whoever they may have been, and however many there were, none of them, it seemed to me, was as important to him as Ainley.

There was one American actor Larry became very close to, according to Michael Korda, who wrote in his book *Charmed Lives* that Vivien Leigh, during the time they played *Romeo and Juliet* in America in 1940, 'brooded darkly on his close friendship with a famous American actor'.

That in itself doesn't mean Larry was definitely engaged in a homosexual relationship. But it does seem to suggest it. The fact was there were a number of bisexual actors in Hollywood, including Cary Grant, Randolph Scott and Errol Flynn.

In 1940 Larry met and befriended Danny Kaye, and this was the time that, according to Korda, Vivien was worrying about him. But nothing Larry ever said to me suggested Kaye was a lover, and I won't speculate without what I would consider to be good grounds to do so.

And in the end, it doesn't matter. To me, his bisexuality is simply a part of the man's life experience and of his nature. And a major part of that experience was being sexually abused. And that is something that shaped his life and personality and character more than just about anything else that ever happened to him.

In 1981, when we talked about our respective abuse experiences, we agreed that when a priest tells you that homosexuality is a sin that can be forgiven, and you believe it, you question whether you are a homosexual yourself for even allowing it to happen. You question your own sexuality. You can easily be made to believe, at that age, that you will grow to be a homosexual. And then you discover that girls excite you more than anything else. And that happened to Laurence Olivier. But the doubts about his sexuality led him into sexual acts with men which clearly disgusted him; he wrote, 'I felt that the homosexual act would be a step darkly destructive to my soul.' It is more than likely that it was his enjoyment of those acts that really disgusted him.

He also wrote that he told the man I believe firmly was Henry Ainley, that he felt it desperately necessary 'to warn him that, dustily old-fashioned as it must seem, I had ideals which must not be trodden underfoot and destroyed, or I would not be able to answer for the consequences and neither would he'.

I do think, however, that his relationship with Ainley was an on–off affair that lasted for several years.

6

Hollywood

By the time *Private Lives* was due to hit New York, Adrianne Allen had fallen pregnant and was unable to go. Jill had become depressed, no doubt due to a bad marriage but also because she was not getting work. So Larry asked Coward if Jill could play the role of Sybil in New York. Coward reluctantly agreed; he did not like the idea of mixing domestic life with work. He was a homosexual and was rather unsympathetic to the needs of actors and actresses who were married and who desired not to be separated by work.

The play opened in New York in January 1931 and ran for 150 performances. During the last week of the run, Jill became ill with a cyst on her ovaries and, during surgery, had her appendix removed.

Larry believed this might have been the cause of her pain during sex. But there is another condition that might have been the cause of the wedding–night problem, called vaginismus, in which the vagina muscles go into spasm, making the vagina narrow and thereby causing sexual intercourse to be difficult and painful. If Jill had this condition, she might well have preferred never to have penetrative sex, and that in turn might have led her to prefer relationships with women. None of this would have been Larry's fault. But he was conditioned by his experience to feel guilt.

Meanwhile, RKO had spotted Larry and offered him two pictures at $1,000 a week with an option for two more at $1,400. Jill persuaded him to accept, and so while she finished her recovery in hospital, he went ahead to Hollywood, where he found a three-bedroom house and a car. When she was well enough, she followed.

Larry's Hollywood career began modestly, but then RKO was a very modest studio, making films on relatively low budgets compared to the big guns like Metro-Goldwyn-Mayer and Paramount. His first film for RKO was *Friends and Lovers*, with Adolph Menjou, Lily Damita and Erich von Stroheim. The film, as Larry noted, 'died the death of a dog'.

RKO loaned him out to Fox for *The Yellow Passport* in which he co-starred with Elissa Landi; they had previously worked together in a play, *After All*, which he did just before *Private Lives*. Next, RKO put him with Ann Harding in *Westward Passage*. These films made little impact, and further film offers were not coming thick and fast. Through 1931 he made just four films, a paltry number of pictures compared to many other leading actors. In 1932, unable to afford to remain in Hollywood, Larry accepted an offer from United Artists to make *No Funny Business* in England, at Ealing Studios, providing him and Jill with their only film together, although the star of the picture was Gertrude Lawrence.

Another British film followed, *Perfect Understanding*, again for United Artists, with Gloria Swanson, who also produced the film. She was, by then, well past her best. *Variety* wasn't impressed with the film, which it described as a 'dull and talky picture, done in the uninspiring British style'.

With his film career going nowhere fast, Larry knew it was time to get back to the stage, and he landed a good role in a good play in the West End of London, *The Rats of Norway*. It earned favourable notices and ran for 107 performances. His leading lady was Helen Spencer and, legend has it, they enjoyed a brief romantic interlude; whether they did or not, they remained good friends.

If Larry's relationship with Helen Spencer was platonic, his friendship with actress Annie Rooney almost certainly was not. 'Oh, Larry had a mistress here and there,' Ralph Richardson told me (this time on the set of *The Man in the Iron Mask* at Twickenham Studios, England, in 1976). 'Annie Rooney – lovely girl.'

'When was she on the scene?' I asked.

'Oh, round about the time Larry was back in London – just before Greta Garbo fired him.'

It was right after the run of *The Rats of Norway* that Larry was tempted back to Hollywood with a plum role opposite Greta Garbo in *Queen Christina* at MGM. For the first two weeks of production,

Larry, recognising he had no chemistry with Garbo, tried to make an impression on her.

He confessed to me in 1978:

I was far too scared of her. How ridiculous is that? So I made up my mind to find a way to break through the barrier she had put up. I found her one morning sitting on an old chest on the set and went right up to her and said the few sentences I had been practising. I had hoped I would sound charming, but she obviously found me boring. She didn't say a word. Then I started to say anything that came to mind. I tried some Noël Coward on her and that didn't work, not one bit. I thought I would be inventive and let loose some well-chosen swear words to show her I wasn't a prissy Englishman after all. I was dying a death. I did anything I could think of to get a response. I tried being pathetic, which was appropriate because I felt pathetic. Finally I ran out of things to say, and all ideas had fled my mind.

And then, finally, she spoke. She said, 'Oh, vell, life'sh a pain,' slid elegantly off the chest, stood up and walked away.

The next day Walter Wanger (the film's producer) called me in and said, 'We're crazy about you here at Metro and we want to put you under contract.' And I let him struggle to find a way to tell me I was fired, and when he did, I just said, 'Just so long as I'm paid,' and he said, 'Oh, yes, of course, glad to get on to money.'

So I got paid anyway, but felt that was the last I ever wanted to have to do with Hollywood.

Fortunately, there was work waiting for him, and for Jill, in New York that year of 1933, in the play *The Green Bay Tree*. It had been agreed upon back in London before they headed off to Hollywood, when director Jed Harris 'had charmed the daylights out of us', as Olivier put it. But in New York, Harris 'transformed himself into the most hurtful, arrogant, venomous little fiend that anyone could meet'. Olivier wrote that Harris was cruel and sadistic and he resolved that he would never allow that sort of situation to happen again, but would 'find the courage somehow to have things out'. He never spoke to Harris again.

'After *Queen Christina* I went through the indignity of being raped by a New York stage director,' Larry told me in 1979.

'Raped?' I asked in alarm.

'Emotionally, dear boy.'

Only looking back do I realise that his choice of words was more than a mere metaphor for being ill-treated and disrespected by Jed Harris. And it became ever clearer when Larry explained what the play was about.

'It was a very brave play about homosexuality. I was the young lover of an older man, and the young man I played realised he had fallen in love with a girl and was desperately trying to break free of the older man.'

'So what was the problem with the director?' I asked.

'He thought he understood better than I what it was like to be in that situation. There was nothing he could tell me about any of it.'

Larry understood bisexuality. His use of the word 'raped' said something else. To be sexually abused as a child by an adult is to be raped. That, I'm afraid, is the word for it. Larry felt that this particular director's methods of bullying him into portraying bisexuality in some artificial manner – or certainly in a manner Larry didn't agree with – was a form of rape. Maybe Larry was speaking subconsciously, or perhaps he knew exactly what he meant by it.

His experience at All Saints coloured his life to the end.

7

Olivier vs Gielgud

The Oliviers returned to London where Noël Coward directed Larry, with Ina Claire, in *Biography*, and then came the first of Larry's major historical plays, *Mary Queen of Scots*, directed by John Gielgud in 1934.

When I was with Ralph Richardson and John Gielgud in 1975, Gielgud said, 'Oh, Ralph, you know, it's all your fault that Larry became a classical actor.'

'Don't look to me for blame,' Richardson replied, as though they believed, with light hearts, that this had been a terrible thing for British Theatre. 'You put him in *Romeo and Juliet*.'

'No, Ralph, before that. You were supposed to play Bothwell.'

'Why, so I was.'

'In what?' I asked.

'Well, Mickey,' he said (Richardson had taken to calling me Mickey), 'Johnny was directing *Mary Queen of Scots* and I was playing Bothwell, but really, Johnny,' he turned back to Gielgud, 'you should cast your plays more carefully.'

'Oh, Ralph, you were always my first choice for the part,' said Gielgud.

'And what a bad choice you made. You needed a romantic leading man, not someone who played old men all his life.'

I finally got out of them that Richardson had dropped out a week before the play was due to open and, needing to fill the part quickly, Gielgud took a chance with Laurence Olivier.

When I mentioned all this to Larry in 1976, he said, 'They loved the drama of it all – we all do, laddie. The play is due to open, the leading actor realises he can't do the part, a replacement must be found – and fortune smiled on me. It was *exciting*. It was *daring*. It was great drama *off* the stage.'

The play ran for 106 performances at the New Theatre. Next came *Theatre Royal* in which Larry played an actor based on John Barrymore. It involved a great deal of athletics performed by Larry, including a dangerous leap from a balcony and a swashbuckling sword fight. This was the first of the plays in which he established himself as an actor willing to perform risky stunts. He told me, 'You must astound the audience with the kind of action they expect only in films, laddie. Make them hold their breath while they watch you risk your life, knowing it's you and not an anonymous stuntman. Give the people something in theatre they don't expect, and you can get away with murder.'

I took his advice and have managed to injure myself numerous times, but always to great effect.

For added thrills, he started taking flying lessons. He continued to be busy on the London stage through the rest of 1934. But in 1935 his stage career began to falter, and he knew his marriage was too. He made a film that year, a First World War melodrama, *Moscow Nights* (US title *I Stand Condemned*), produced by Alexander Korda and directed by Anthony Asquith. Korda, an independent producer, put Larry under contract.

Much of 1935 was taken up with stage plays that amounted to very little.

In the autumn of 1935, John Gielgud asked Olivier to alternate roles – Mercutio and Romeo – with him in *Romeo and Juliet*. Gielgud directed, and with Peggy Ashcroft as Juliet, Larry as Romeo and Gielgud as Mercutio, the play kicked off at the New Theatre in London.

During rehearsals there was an immediate clash between director/ star and new young upstart Olivier over the delivery of the verse.

In 1978, Larry told me:

In those days there was a way of doing things and you didn't change them. The public came to hear the verse spoken beautifully and anyone who didn't do what they wanted was an upstart, an outsider, so that's what I was – an outsider. They loved John, and rightly so. He had the most beautiful voice – he still does – but I felt that he allowed his voice to dominate his performances.

But he wasn't always like that. I thought his first Hamlet was wonderful because he didn't allow his voice to dominate his performance. He didn't sing it. But over time, as he played Hamlet five or six times, he began to sing it more and more, as though it was a complete aria, which I felt was a disappointment because I wanted him to do it the way he started it in the beginning, real and alive.

It was always my intention to do what John Barrymore inspired me to do – to make Shakespeare as modern as possible. More than Barrymore did, in fact. Modern to the ear, not to the eye. And in those early days I was criticised for it. People said, 'You can't *speak* the verse.' So when we did *Romeo and Juliet* the Establishment considered that I was against him, which I never was.

I felt Shakespeare needed a new style of delivery. John had a beautiful voice, but he sang the words. From my earliest performances at school I was always taught that you must speak verse as if it were the way you speak naturally. And I still feel that is true. Johnnie came from a different school of thought; that the verse and the poetry is everything, and so he didn't so much speak the lines as sing them, and that is very beautiful to hear; of that there is no doubt. But I wanted to find a sort of 1930s realism to bring to the part, and so I was much more physical in the part and tried to deliver the text as though it was real speech and not merely verse. On the other hand, you have to make sure that you don't entirely lose the beauty of the language, but you can do that, I believe, by *living* through it, by making it real.

When I spoke to Gielgud in Norfolk in 1979 (where he was filming an episode for the TV series *Tales of the Unexpected*) he recalled, 'Larry thought I was far too verse-conscious and an exhibitionist in the way I used the text. Of course, he is an exhibitionist also but very different from me. He is daring and flamboyant. He was iconoclastic, wanting to change everyone's perception of Shakespearean performance.'

Larry used his great physicality, as well as his new-style delivery, to add a new sense of realism. Romeo was a boy of sixteen, impetuous, madly in love, just a little clumsy in his eagerness to bed Juliet. When Larry entered as Romeo, he sprang onto the stage and continued to use his body language to convey the eager, passionate adolescence of the character. He told me in 1976, 'Romeo is a very difficult part because it falls so short of the rather glamorous partnership or companionship the title of the play suggests. Much like Antony in *Antony and Cleopatra*, in fact. Antony is never quite up to Cleopatra and also Romeo is never quite up to Juliet because he fails to possess the romantic valour that is expected. It isn't that it can't be found in the lines; it is certainly there in parts. But not as a whole. And so often Romeo is a letdown to the young women who come to see it and they go away complaining, "Well, he was no Romeo."

'Of course, I was so conceited that when I played the part I was convinced that I was the one and only Romeo. So when the critics slaughtered me I was so shocked that I sincerely offered to give up the part immediately.'

'Larry played Romeo for the first six weeks; I, Mercutio,' said Gielgud. 'The critics didn't take to his style at all and he was so terribly upset by the reviews the morning after we opened that he threatened not to go on the second night or ever again. But I had a little talk with him and he was soon over his tantrum.'

'I still remember the terrible headlines,' Larry told me in 1976. 'The good reviews are so much more quickly forgotten than the bad ones because they are stamped indelibly on you, so you remember the *Evening News* saying, "A beautiful Juliet but . . ." and you try to forget the rest.'

James Agate wrote in the *Sunday Times*, 'Mr Olivier's Romeo suffered enormously from the fact that the spoken poetry of the part eluded him. Throughout one wanted over and over again to stop the performance and tell the actor that he couldn't, just couldn't, rush this or that passage.'

And yet Agate thought 'this Romeo looked every inch a lover, and a lover fey and foredoomed. The actor's facial expression was varied and mobile and his smaller gestures were infinitely touching. Taking the performance by and large, I have no hesitation in saying that this is the most moving Romeo I have seen.'

There were comparisons between Olivier and Gielgud. W A Darlington of the *Daily Telegraph* thought, 'Mr Gielgud's Romeo is more romantic than was Mr Olivier's, has a much greater sense of the beauty of the language, and substitutes a thoughtfulness that suits the part for an impetuosity that did not.' Of Olivier's Mercutio, this critic said, 'This is a brilliant piece of work – full of zest, humour and virility.'

Without exception, all the critics praised Peggy Ashcroft for her performance as Juliet.

One of those who saw *Romeo and Juliet* was Alec Guinness, who was able to give me an idea of what the respective performances of Gielgud and Olivier were like:

Olivier and Gielgud were no better than each other – just different. Gielgud had his own style, which audiences and critics had enjoyed for some years before Olivier arrived with his Romeo. Olivier recited the verse well; it just happened to be a new style of delivery to Gielgud's.

When it came to the poetry of the play, Gielgud was the master and Olivier appeared to be outclassed. Or that's what the critics thought. Larry wasn't outclassed, he was just different, and you could believe he really was head over heels in love with Juliet while Gielgud was just in love. I must admit I preferred Olivier's Romeo.

And yet when they alternated roles and Olivier was Mercutio, he was even better. Acting should never be a competition, but the critics were the ones who really turned that production into a race between Olivier and Gielgud. The truth is, neither of them lost.

When I sat with Gielgud and Richardson in 1975, the subject of *Romeo and Juliet* came up when I asked them about their relationships with Olivier.

'Larry and I had a curious friendship,' said Gielgud. 'We like each other a lot. I used to get told by well-meaning friends that he was jealous of me but why he should have been I could never understand.'

'Because, my dear friend, he knew you were the greatest Shakespearean actor on the stage,' said Richardson. 'Of course he would have been jealous.'

'Do you really think so? But he always had a tremendous advantage because he had what I never had; strikingly good looks, a commanding vitality and a wonderful command of humour. When we alternated Romeo and Mercutio he was holding all of the cards but one; I had the other card. I was the director.'

'But Larry wasn't your first choice, was he, Johnnie?'

'Oh, indeed, no. I asked Robert Donat, but he was afraid of it or unwell or something. So I turned to Larry and he was most enthusiastic. I think his career hadn't really taken off at that time.'

'He'd had a few stage flops,' said Richardson, 'and he felt he needed to do some Shakespeare to be taken seriously. I remember he and Jill [Esmond] were planning to do their own *Romeo and Juliet*.'

'Oh, he was, Ralph, and he could have gone on to do it but he abandoned that idea, very generously, I thought, to work with me.'

'Oh, Johnnie, I love Larry dearly, but of course he would abandon his production if he had the chance to work with you. He told me the biggest break of his career was to work with you in *Romeo and Juliet.*'

'Is that really so?' Gielgud asked him.

In fact, when I was with Richardson at Twickenham in 1976, he told me, 'Johnnie knows very well that he gave Larry his greatest break, but you'll never hear Johnnie boast.'

It may have been Larry's greatest break, but it was one that caused some disagreement between him and Gielgud, and strangely enough, after all the years that had passed, Larry was still, in 1978, unable to get over both the triumph and the trials that play was for him.

'I fought my way through the first weeks,' he recalled. 'I had been hurt by the critics. Bad reviews are like arrows to an actor who believes he is doing his best. Dear Peggy Ashcroft, who was my Juliet, nursed me tenderly through those weeks with her tremendous support from which I derived the strength to carry on.'

I wish I could have managed to get Olivier and Gielgud and even Richardson all together at the same time. I asked Larry, 'Did John Gielgud give you his support also?'

'Of course. Johnnie was concerned not about who was the star player, which concerned me back then, but about the whole production. If the play was a disaster because of one bad performance then it was *his* disaster as the director. But he never told me that I had to play the part the way he played it. He gave me the freedom to play it the way I did. If he hadn't been happy with it, he would have fired me.'

Back again to 1975, and Gielgud and Richardson: 'But you weren't exactly over the moon about Larry's Romeo,' Richardson said to Gielgud, who replied, 'Well, you see, I felt it was interesting to have a different style of performance. When a director chooses an actor, you allow that actor to bring his own gifts, and then you try to spread those gifts evenly. He was a very romantic Romeo – far more romantic than I. But I felt that he was a little too physical in his bedroom scene with Juliet. Shakespeare carefully devised the balcony scenes as a prelude, and the farewell was a post-consummation scene, which was done in order to avoid embarrassment to the boy actor who played Juliet [in Shakespeare's day] and the boy playing Romeo, and also the audience. Larry never saw it that way.'

Larry admitted to me he saw the scene as 'one in which Romeo only wanted one thing – to get into her knickers. You can argue if it was love that drove Romeo. That it was lust, there is no question. You have to play Romeo as though he has a permanent erection.'

Gielgud felt Olivier was more successful as Mercutio. 'I know that I was more lyrically successful as Mercutio in the "Queen Mab" scene, but Larry's virility and sheer panache, in all the other scenes, and his skilful fencing, which I was never best at, all the way to his death, were far more than anything I could ever achieve in that part.'

Gielgud was, it seems, far more accepting of Olivier's style than Olivier was of Gielgud's. 'John was preoccupied with the beauty and poetry rather than reality,' said Larry. 'He was a jewel, the greatest Shakespearean actor of the time. I was the outsider. Really, you know, he had the audience before they came into the theatre. I had to try and win them to me before they left.'

Larry made a reference to his perception of himself that resulted from his abuse experience. He referred to himself as an 'outsider'. When an abuse victim loses himself, he becomes an outsider, and there are only two things he can do; either stay on the outside, or try and get back in to whatever society he wishes to be a part of. In New York Larry had almost been 'raped' by a cruel director, and with his first major Shakespeare, he was the 'outsider' up against the man then considered to be the master, John Gielgud. He wanted, more than anything, not to be the outsider any longer. That, I believe, is why the reviews were so painful to him.

And yet, despite all the problems, Larry was, ultimately, a triumph, mainly as Mercutio. He was gradually emerging as a new Shakespearean star.

'If it were not for John giving me that chance,' he admitted, 'I might have become lost in obscurity. But I believed when the chance came I had to grab it. And with John's support after the first terrible reviews, and also the love and strength that Peggy gave to me, I did rather well from it.'

People who worked with Gielgud and Olivier are split over how close they were as friends. There are those in the Gielgud camp, those in the Olivier camp, and those who enjoyed the company of both men.

One actor, who I think I should not name, told me in confidence, 'Olivier was so homophobic that he was quite repulsed by Gielgud and that always prevented them from being friends.'

But Anthony Quayle (on the set of *Murder by Decree* in 1978) said, 'It's simply not true that Larry has a problem with John in any way whatsoever. They have long been friends, but not the best of friends because that's how it is in life. Larry was always grateful to John for giving him his big break in Shakespeare. But that didn't mean they had to spend every weekend together. In fact, Larry's closer friend was Ralph [Richardson], who for years wasn't close to John, but in recent years John and Ralph have been the best of friends.'

The un-named actor was, like many others, confusing Olivier with Richardson who was, in fact, the one who was repulsed by Gielgud's homosexuality for many years. It was only around 1970 that they became much closer, performing in the plays *Home* and *No Man's Land* most successfully. When I asked Richardson why it had taken so long for him and Gielgud to become friends, he simply replied, 'Oh, I don't know. Sometimes it takes years to warm to someone.'

Larry confided to me in 1979 on *Clash of the Titans*, 'Poor Ralph was most awkward in John's presence for so long. Ralph said, "Can't stand bloody poofs." But he really loves John now.'

Of course, the other point to bear in mind is that Larry was never homophobic, having a bisexual side throughout his life.

There was professional rivalry between Olivier and Gielgud right from the start – or certainly from the time of *Romeo and Juliet*. 'I suppose it would be true to say that I was somewhat smug after my success up to that time,' said Gielgud, 'and I may have been inclined to patronise Larry from my position of authority as the greater – how I hate the word – *star* actor and also the director.'

The professional rivalry between Olivier and Gielgud continued. In 1937 Gielgud became the longest running Broadway *Hamlet*, breaking John Barrymore's record of 101 performances. Later that year he returned to London and went to see Olivier as *Hamlet* at the Old Vic.

Larry recalled, 'John came backstage after and offered me his congratulations, and then with a benign smile quietly said to me, "Of course, this is still *my* role."'

I asked Larry if he ever felt during those early weeks when they were rehearsing and performing *Romeo and Juliet* that he might have been wrong and Gielgud right. He said, 'I was arrogant enough – and confident – to believe I was right, and I still think that. I know that John will always think that he was. But what is really important is not whether we disagreed and whether people put themselves in his camp or in mine, but that we must have been bloody fascinating to watch.'

What was so interesting for me was that Olivier was convinced that Gielgud believed ever after that his delivery of the verse was correct and that Olivier's was not. But Gielgud conceded, 'Larry very rightly felt I was inclined to show off in my verse-speaking, which was becoming too much like singing. I didn't agree at the time, but Larry demonstrated there was a more natural way to speak the lines.'

So Gielgud did *not* still think that he was right, and I told Larry so. He shrugged. 'We have a strange and sometimes difficult relationship. He and Ralph are the best of friends. Ralph and I are the best of friends. John and I are just moderately friendly.'

One thing Gielgud never did like about Larry was his penchant for false noses. 'It just isn't always necessary,' said Gielgud. 'And when he wanted a false nose to play Romeo, I felt, at first, inclined to remonstrate. But there is no point in falling out over a nose, now, is there?'

I felt Sir John had a good point.

But at least Larry had finally removed the moustache he had sported since *Beau Geste*.

8

Vivien

Larry first set eyes on Vivien in the spring or early summer of 1935. She was starring in a successful play, *The Mask of Virtue*. Like almost every man who saw her he was struck by her unique and exquisite beauty, which he described as 'magical'. He wrote that she possessed 'beautiful poise' and that her neck 'looked almost too fragile to support her head and bore it with a sense of surprise'.

Without fail, every man I have talked to who knew Vivien Leigh spoke of her beauty in glowing terms and each, it seems, was easily capable of falling in love with her. John Mills, David Niven, Stewart Granger, all described her as a 'swan' and each said that they would have fallen for her had the opportunity arisen. No one was surprised when Larry fell madly in love with her, although that didn't happen straight away. But he was mesmerised by her beauty from the moment he saw her.

She was born Vivian Mary Hartley on 5 November 1913, in Darjeeling in India, to Ernest Hartley, an officer in the Indian Cavalry who was of English parentage, and Gertrude Robinson Yackje, who was of French and Irish descent.

When the family relocated to Bangalore, Vivian Hartley made her first stage appearance at the age of three, reciting 'Little Bo Peep' for her mother's amateur theatre group. Gertrude Hartley tried to instil in her daughter an appreciation of literature, and introduced her to the works of Hans Christian Andersen, Lewis Carroll and Rudyard Kipling, as well as stories of Greek mythology.

An only child, in 1920 Vivian was sent to the Convent of the Sacred Heart in Roehampton in England. Her closest friend at the convent was the future actress Maureen O'Sullivan, to whom she expressed her ambitions to become 'a great actress'.

She completed her later education in Europe, returning to her parents in England in 1931 and telling them of her ambitions to become an actress. Her father helped her to enroll at the Royal Academy of Dramatic Art in London. Later in 1931 she met Herbert Leigh Holman, known as Leigh, a barrister thirteen years her senior, and they were married on 20 December 1932. She immediately dropped out of RADA, and on 12 October 1933 she gave birth to a daughter, Suzanne.

Stifled by her domestic life, she managed to land a small role in the film *Things Are Looking Up*. She found an agent, John Gliddon, who felt that the name Vivian Holman was not suitable, and they settled on the new stage name Vivian Leigh. Gliddon recommended her to Alexander Korda as a possible film actress; ironically, Korda rejected her, feeling she lacked potential.

She found work in a number of plays, including *Murder in Mayfair* written by Ivor Novello, which premiered on 3 September 1934. This was followed by *The Green Sash*, playing a soldier's wife in Florence who is widowed during a plague. It opened in February 1935 at the Q Theatre, and she earned good notices.

She was making her fourth film, *Look Up and Laugh*, when she was cast as Henriette Duquesnoy, a reformed prostitute masquerading as 'a paragon of innocence' during the time of Louis XV in *The Mask of Virtue*. It opened on 15 May 1935. The play was a huge success, making Vivian a star of the London stage.

When she and a friend, John Buckmaster, the son of Gladys Cooper, saw Larry and Jill at the Savoy Grill in London, they noticed he was no longer sporting the *Beau Geste* moustache. Buckmaster said, 'What an odd little thing Larry looks without it.'

Vivian replied, 'Not in the least, Johnny.' She said she found him extremely attractive, 'with or without the moustache' (according to what John Buckmaster told Jesse Lasky Jr).

Olivier refers to this encounter in his autobiography, but is uncertain about all the details. He wrote that a short while after seeing Vivian in *The Mask of Virtue*, he and Jill 'ran across her – I'm almost sure this particular encounter was in the Savoy Grill lobby'.

Olivier's account suggests that Vivian's husband, Leigh Holman, was also there and that he and Jill invited the couple to visit them at their house for a weekend; they now lived in Burchett's Green in Kent.

Olivier also recounted that Vivian popped into his dressing room during a matinee of *Romeo and Juliet* to wish him luck; this was probably towards the end of the run in early 1936. He said that she gave him a soft kiss on the shoulder, and that appears to have sealed his, and Vivian's, fate.

Word had reached Hollywood of Olivier's success in *Romeo and Juliet*. They probably didn't care whether he was a better Romeo or a better Mercutio. They simply knew that he was a new Shakespearean star of the British stage, and they wanted him to play Orlando in what was only the third attempt by Hollywood to put Shakespeare on film, *As You Like It*. The first was *The Taming of the Shrew* with Douglas Fairbanks and Mary Pickford in 1929 ('with additional dialogue by Sam Taylor'!). The second was *Romeo and Juliet* with Leslie Howard and Norma Shearer in 1936.

Larry asked Richardson if there could be any artistic satisfaction in doing a Hollywood Shakespeare. Richardson told him there was 'the artistic satisfaction of £600 a week' – twice the amount he had been paid for his last Hollywood film.

The film came along just when Larry needed the money most. After *Romeo and Juliet* finished triumphantly in early 1936, he decided it was time to take his career into his own hands and become an actor-manager. It was important for him to feel more in control of his destiny – something that is common among victims of abuse. Or, as he put it to me so bluntly in what may have been a very telling statement, 'You don't want others fucking with you. I'll fuck up my own life, laddie.'

But he was cautious, going into partnership with Ralph Richardson who commissioned J B Priestley to write *Bees on the Boat Deck*, which Larry and Richardson produced and co-directed; Richardson also co-starred in it. But it was a flop and the actor-managers lost £2,000 each on the venture.

And so off to Hollywood went Larry to make his first Shakespeare film. 'Oh, that was such a terrible film,' Larry remembered in 1979. 'I was so eccentric in it. I had played a more natural form of Shakespeare in *Romeo and Juliet*, but didn't know how to make it natural on screen. And we had Elizabeth Bergner [as Rosalind] with her German accent, who never looked like a boy, even to a blind man. I made up my mind doing that picture that Shakespeare could never be done on film.'

Despite his reservations about the film, the critics seemed to like it and him in it. 'I have said before that Laurence Olivier seems to me to be one of the most brilliant actors in the world,' wrote Campbell Dixon in the *Daily Telegraph*. 'In *As You Like It* his triumph as Orlando is all the more striking for its contrast to his glamorous Romeo and his fiery Mercutio in John Gielgud's *Romeo and Juliet*.'

Playing an exiled duke in the film was Henry Ainley, Larry's one-time lover. But since 1932 Ainley's stage work had been sporadic due to ill health. Larry, I believe, secured the part in the film for Ainley, whose son Richard was also in the film, as Sylvius. It was Henry Ainley's last film. He died on 13 October 1945.

As if the fate of Larry and Vivian Leigh needed a helping hand, Alexander Korda decided he had been wrong in his estimation about the young actress, and put her under contract and cast her and Larry in a historical film drama, *Fire Over England*.

With the story of the Spanish Armada as the film's backdrop, Larry played the dashing naval lieutenant, Michael, who is sent to Spain under the orders of Queen Elizabeth (Flora Robson) to uncover traitors and save England. He also has time for some romance with Cynthia, who really has little to do with the basic story, but it provided a good role for Vivien Leigh and a chance for her and Larry to become a romantic screen couple. It also began their affair. Flora Robson told me (in 1977 at Shepperton Studios, on the set of *Dominique*), 'Oh, of course they were in love. I could see that.'

Flora Robson might have known about the affair, but it seems to have remained a secret from most other people, especially from Jill Esmond and Leigh Holman.

The affair was conducted in what Larry confessed was a life of lying and deceit, and he wrote that at first he felt like a 'worm-like adulterer' as their liaison continued at film studios and in theatre dressing rooms. He was not a man without a sense of guilt. He told me, 'I couldn't help myself with Vivien. No man could. I hated myself for cheating on Jill, but then I had cheated before, but this was something different. This wasn't just out of lust. This was love that I really didn't ask for but was drawn into. You, Michael, would not have resisted, I promise you.'

But what cut through his conscience more than anything was that, while *Fire Over England* was still in production, Jill gave birth to a son, Simon Tarquin. Whatever the true nature of their marital relations earlier, Larry and Jill had clearly consummated their marriage at some point, and the result was Tarquin. But Larry was, as he confessed, unable to stop himself from becoming obsessed with Vivien.

The public got their first glimpse of Larry and Vivien when *Fire Over England* proved to be a huge critical and commercial hit. Graham Greene wrote in the *Spectator*, '(Producer Eric) Pommer and [director William K] Howard have done one remarkable thing: they have caught the very spirit of an English public schoolmistress's vision of history.'

Following Tarquin's birth, the Oliviers and the Holmans saw a lot of each other. Did Jill and Holman really have no inkling what was going on? Rex Harrison, who appeared in a play with Vivien about that time, thought they must have. 'All Vivien ever talked about was Larry,' he said (in Norwich while filming an episode of *Tales of the Unexpected* in 1983). 'It was just so obvious to everyone; I don't see how Jill and Leigh Holman couldn't have suspected.'

But Larry was keeping another secret, although not as well as he might have thought. Rex Harrison knew the secret: he said, 'While he was falling in love with Vivien he was also off having a fling with Ann Todd.'

Larry had sexual needs that were not being met by Jill, and I believe that Jill had the same problem with him. So why, then, did they decide to have a child? That was something I was able to ask Larry, and in 1981 he told me, 'Oh, my dear boy, you have no idea how much I hated myself, how much guilt I carried, and how so very much I wanted to have a "normal" married life. And so Jill and I thought we would try for a child. I think, you know, that if Vivien hadn't been there, Jill and I might have made more of a success of things. Not forever, that's most certain. We would never have lasted the course. But maybe a little longer, yes.'

He was, maybe unwittingly, hastening the end of his marriage, which he had regarded as doomed from the beginning, as he spiralled with a headlong dive into a life with Vivien.

9

The Great Dane

In January 1937, Olivier took to the stage for the first time since *Romeo and Juliet* to perform *Hamlet*. This production served two major purposes. One, to take greater control of his career; control was vital to him. Two, he wanted to establish himself, once and for all, as a Shakespearean actor. 'You simply cannot be considered a serious actor unless you do the classics,' he told me in 1979. 'An actor should be judged entirely by his work in the classics. You cannot be a serious actor unless you do so, and I wanted to be taken seriously. I wanted to be a *great* actor. The Old Vic was the best, the only, place where I would be judged for my classical work.'

Hamlet, then, was a bold move. He approached Lilian Baylis, who ran the Old Vic Theatre where, since 1923, every one of Shakespeare's plays had been performed. It was *the* theatre in London to do Shakespeare. He sought the support of Tyrone (Tony) Guthrie, one of the most respected London stage directors, and so Larry and Miss Baylis were able to agree that he would do three productions that season. To start off, there was only one choice as far as he was concerned. He told me, 'I had decided at some point in my young and callow life that if I ever had the chance to lead a company I would start with the greatest play there is, *Hamlet*. And so I did.'

I asked him in 1979 if, when playing Hamlet for the first time, he was more confident of his style of delivery following the drubbing he'd had from the critics over his Romeo.

'I felt that I was really learning how to master the delivery by the time I did my first Hamlet,' he said. 'You know, Michael, Shakespeare was a people's playwright. He didn't write for the aristocracy but for all people, and the common folk came merrily to see his plays. People say that Shakespeare is difficult but that is only because we stopped listening. I think it might have been the actors who made us stop listening. They wanted to deliver arias.

'But the actor's job is not to deliver poetry but to take the audience on a journey. When you deal with tragedy, as in *Hamlet*, or in *Macbeth*, the journey is always predictable so the ending must be cathartic.'

'So it's not *where* the actors take them but *how* you take them?' I asked.

'Exactly.'

This made much more sense to me some years later when I was performing Shakespeare. But as I told Larry, just reading Shakespeare, as we did at school, did nothing for me.

'That's because Shakespeare is not to be read but to be performed. The best way to experience Shakespeare is to see it performed and feeling and understanding those wonderful lines through an actor's interpretation. You work hard on the rhythm and timing so that reactions seem completely spontaneous, and not expected, or not there at all. It has to be as though it is happening there and then for the first time; no matter how many times somebody may have seen it.

'My job lies in interpreting and projecting from the other side of the proscenium. That is the nature of the beast we call acting. You may not agree with my interpretation but it is my job to sell it to you the best way I can and with all the gifts I have at my disposal.'

Remembering Jason Robards' appalling performance of Brutus in the 1969 film version of *Julius Caesar*, I asked Larry how you could be sure that what the actor gives you is the right interpretation.

'You can't be sure. But an actor must always come to Shakespeare with hunger and with excitement, not just because it is a paying job for an actor. An actor must work to make his language work from the brain, where it starts, down to your fingertips and down to your toes. Only then can an actor fulfil his profession. Or you are just turning up on time and being paid.

'The wonder of a part like Hamlet in particular is that you can come back to it time and again and you will always find something new to discover, and that is true of any role in Shakespeare, so Jason Robards, who is a fine actor but not one who had that hunger, must either come back and play Brutus again with hunger, or leave him and all else Shakespeare has given us well alone.'

Robards did leave the Bard well alone, and probably just as well.

In 1937 Larry gave his first of several performances of Hamlet, and was even more determined than he had been with *Romeo and Juliet* to make the lines 'modern to the ear'.

He recalled, 'On the first night Tyrone Guthrie came to my dressing room and said, "Your make-up is every inch a Hamlet. But I think they'll find fault with you for the verse-speaking and, frankly, they may be right to a certain extent. But, Larry, I know you will come to your own decisions about that in your own good time."

'There I was, about to go on, and Guthrie had put some seed of doubt into my mind. I had to decide whether to please the critics, or do what I was sure was right and hope the critics would come along with me.'

'Was the bias still very much against you?' I asked.

'To the minds of every critic and everyone in the audience John Gielgud's Hamlet was very popular, with me also, and he was the very best when it came to verse-speaking. There is no doubt that Shakespeare knew what he was doing when he put the rhythms there and they were not meant to be just ignored.

'I couldn't do anything else but what I had chosen to do. I wanted not to deliver an aria but to convey Hamlet's thoughts to people who had never heard them before. So I went on and gave the performance I felt I had to give.'

'And what is the right performance?' I asked.

'Ah, well, dear boy, *Hamlet* is the greatest play ever written. You can play it again and again and still not get to the bottom of what it has to offer. It has it all – great climaxes, dark shadows, occasional moments of high comedy. When you play Hamlet, it never leaves you. You *have* to keep going back to it. It has never left me. I think about it each day. Talking to you now, I feel great sadness that I will never play him again, but, oh God, I wish I could.'

This was 1979. Larry was ageing and ill. His eyes were wet with tears. So, hoping I would divert him from his current and rather morbid train of thought, I said, 'Take me back to the first time you played Hamlet.'

His eyes brightened. 'My great aim was to make the audience believe that this man lived. That he was not just a character on a stage with beautiful dialogue. I had seen other Hamlets begin the first lines in a very strange and mystical and theatrical way. I didn't want to scare my audience to death. I wanted to keep it simple.

'But I also wanted to find something that was new, and so I went with Tony Guthrie to see Professor Ernest Jones, who was a great psychiatrist who had studied *Hamlet* and wrote a book called *What Happens in Hamlet*. He believed that Hamlet was a prime example of the Oedipus complex. Hamlet is over-devoted to his father, and Professor Jones believed that nobody is that fond of his father unless he feels guilty about his mother. It might just be a subconscious guilt. Hamlet worships his mother but it is false; it is manufacture by Hamlet to cover up his guilt.'

'But is that what Shakespeare intended?' I asked.

'I am prepared to believe that Shakespeare had so many great gifts that he could have had a truly intuitive understanding of psychology. He was, after all, the world's greatest man.'

I asked him if he felt that he was somehow able to recognise Hamlet's feelings in his own relationships with his own father and mother.

He thought before responding. 'It wasn't there because I felt no guilt about my own devotion to my mother as I never saw her as a sexual being, and I was not fond of my father. But I can understand that it could have been possible for someone, in that position, to feel a certain way to their mother and then to feign great love for their father to hide the guilt.

'I have plenty else to be guilty about in my life, but not how I felt about my mother.'

And so, I wondered, did his first *Hamlet* explore the Oedipus theory?

'I used it as a tool for my own performance. It was never overt. It was there only for me to know about. You don't have to tell the audience that part of Hamlet's reason for his predicament is because he wishes he was still at his mother's breasts. Hamlet's problem is that he wants to sleep with his mother. When I did my first *Hamlet* at the Old Vic I suggested this as much as I dared.'

Did he feel he succeeded?

'I think my first *Hamlet* was not bad. It wasn't perfection, but it was *mine*. And it has never let go of me since, nor I of it.'

Hamlet was a huge success, playing 42 performances in January and February 1937. There was never any plan to run it for longer. Larry was earning £25 a week at the Old Vic; he had been earning £500 a week in films. But he was doing the work he felt was important, and he even began to talk publicly about how unimportant films were, encouraging people to see live theatre instead. During a matinee of *Hamlet* he told the audience during his curtain speech, 'It makes me very happy that you have come here today instead, perhaps, of going to some pantomime or movie, which might seem a more amusing way of spending the afternoon.'

When the *Observer* followed up on his infamous speech, which had the film distributors rattled, especially as *Fire Over England* was opening in London, he explained that he only wanted to cheer up the kids who had been dragged to *Hamlet* by their teachers.

When asked if he would play Hamlet on screen, he replied, 'Never. I don't really like Shakespeare on the screen at all.' He added that the real trouble with a film version of *Hamlet* was 'I could never play it again in a cut version.'

He told me in 1979, 'I was always saying things that got me into trouble. I often don't think before I speak. That was my trouble always. I try to be more careful these days, but we humans are not infallible and we are designed to make mistakes so we may learn from them. I am still learning.'

He followed *Hamlet* with *Twelfth Night* as Sir Toby Belch, with Jill as Olivia. Then suddenly the names of Laurence Olivier and Vivien Leigh were being linked in the press, but only because photographs of *Fire Over England* featuring the new romantic screen team were being splashed across newspapers and fan magazines.

The film version of *As You Like It* also opened around that time, and Larry was becoming regarded as something of a movie star – and one who did Shakespeare too.

10

Cry God For Harry

In April and May he performed *Henry V*. It was another tremendous success. With the first three of his Old Vic plays he had chosen to play very different characters. He told me in 1979, 'When I did my first season at the Old Vic, I wanted to be completely different in every performance. That is what every actor *should* be about. So when I joined the Old Vic I looked for a way of showing off how versatile I was. So after deciding to start with *Hamlet*, and then Sir Toby Belch I felt it would be a tremendous contract to do *Henry V*.'

The film version he would make of *Henry V* in 1944 was a moral booster during the Second World War; I asked him if the play had any relevance for a 1937 audience.

He said, 'Actually, when it came time to do *Henry V*, I panicked. I suddenly realised it wasn't the right play to do at that time when the First Great War had become a memory and we had moved away from such plays as *Journey's End* which was such a success a decade earlier. In the 1930s we only wanted to see pleasurable stories, not heroics.

'So I asked Ralph [Richardson] what he thought about it. He said with some disgust, "Yes, Henry V. He's a scoutmaster." He fell silent for a few moments, thought about it, and then said, "But he raises scoutmastership to godlike proportions, which is just what Shakespeare always does. Of course you must play him." So that's what I did.'

But Larry was still concerned about the heroic overtones of the play.

I started rehearsals fighting against the heroism and getting underneath the lines. I was waving no banners with 'God for Harry, England and Saint George'. I was delivering it in a natural way, not letting it ring out over the footlights.

Tyrone Guthrie hadn't given me a great deal of direction in our previous plays; he always let me have my head. In fact, he didn't really help you very much with your acting. He wasn't that kind of director. What he was very good at doing was blocking. I always thought of him as someone who shoved people round you, and giving actors a lot of movement. He was never happy unless something was happening all the time. When I direct, I like to have times when there is complete stillness. But that was Tony's way and I was often glad to be allowed by him to have my own head with a part.

But at our first rehearsal he said, 'Umm . . . Larry, let's have it properly.'

I said, 'Properly? Tony, I am doing it properly.'

He said, 'No, I mean like this.' And he went into, 'This day is call'd the feast of Crispian. . .' and as he built up towards the end his voice got louder and stronger and it was clear he wanted me to give the speech the heroic touch I was avoiding. Then he looked at me and said, 'That's the way to do it.'

I said, 'But, Tony –'

And he said, 'If you don't do it like that and enjoy doing it like that, you'll lose the audience. They won't go with you.'

And he was right. How lucky I was to have Tony Guthrie direct me. Nobody could have been more heroic than I was. I didn't show off, but I played Henry as clearly and as truthfully as I could.

Among the cast of *Henry V* was Anthony Quayle, who told me, 'I first worked with Olivier in *Henry V* at the Old Vic. Tony Guthrie asked me to play the Chorus and I jumped at the chance to work with Olivier who was the young actor of the moment. I rehearsed on my own so I saw little of Larry, and then on the opening night I sat in my dressing room, very nervous, waiting to go on, and there was a knock at the door, which was Larry. He had come to wish me luck. There he stood, his hair shaved high at the sides in a pudding basin, wearing a long scarlet gown, a great heavy gold chain around his neck, and a circlet on his head. The man wishing me luck was Larry Olivier, but the man I saw was Henry Plantagenet himself. And, I suppose, it was Laurence Olivier on his way into theatrical history.'

Alec Guinness was also in the play, as was Jessica Tandy, who played Princess Katherine. I have found, during my years in the film and theatre world, that almost everywhere I turned I was meeting actors who had worked with Olivier, and they had seen theatre history being made.

11

Elsinore

Perhaps to top up his bank balance, or perhaps for more personal reasons – or both – while Larry was performing *Henry V* each evening, he was spending the days making a film with Vivien Leigh. It was called *Twenty-One Days*, a modern-day melodrama, produced by Alexander Korda and directed by Basil Dean. It offered little more than the chance for audiences to see Olivier and Leigh together on screen for the second time, and for Larry to earn some much-needed cash and be with Vivien. It was said to me, by David Niven, 'Larry and Vivien were fucking between every take.'

In an interview on set that Vivien Leigh gave to the *Evening News*, she was asked what books she had read. She replied, '*Gone with the Wind*. I've cast myself as Scarlett O'Hara.'

Nobody took her dream to become Scarlett seriously, except Larry. To him, she had become the finest actress in the world. The truth was, Vivien was a good actress but never a great one, although she was capable of giving two great film performances in her life – as Scarlett, and as Blanche in *A Streetcar Named Desire*. She was also a very engaging and endearing actress to watch. It is impossible, except for the most hard-hearted, not to well up at the fate that befalls her as the ballerina-turned-prostitute who throws herself under a bus in *Waterloo Bridge*. Sadly, I never saw her on stage, but invariably those I spoke to who did felt she was never quite as magnificent as Larry thought she was through his rose-tinted glasses.

Twenty-One Days didn't reach the screen for another two years, mainly because it wasn't very good. It was only after the affair between Larry and Vivien was made public that the distributors were encouraged to wheel it out to make some quick bucks. And, of course, there was the success in 1939 of both *Wuthering Heights* and *Gone with the Wind* which, respectively, established Larry and Vivien as major movie stars. So even a film like *Twenty-One Days* suddenly had some box-office value, and when it was released in 1939, Paul C Mooney Jr reported in the *Motion Picture Herald*, 'Reviewed in the Rivoli Theatre, New York, an afternoon audience seemed to be more interested, judging from comments in the near vicinity of this reviewer, in the two co-stars than in the story itself.'

But before film fame, Larry was still establishing himself as a great actor on stage. And his affair with Vivien was still hidden from the public, as well as from Jill and Holman. All that was about to change when, in June 1937, Larry and Tony Guthrie took the bold step of taking *Hamlet* to Denmark to perform it in Elsinore, in the open at Kronberg Castle, where the play is actually set. This time his Ophelia was to be played by Vivien Leigh. Larry was again mixing business with pleasure. It was also a way of establishing a new leading lady in Larry's life – both his real life and his stage one. Jill Esmond had, with *Twelfth Night*, performed with her husband for the last time. The final act of the union between Larry and Jill was about to play out as the drama of Larry and Vivien's moved into a new phase, beginning, as it were, act two.

By the time I knew Larry, and no doubt for many years before, he preferred to think of the Elsinore production of *Hamlet* as a great professional triumph rather than a personal one.

I think that was one of the best performances I have ever been involved with. It was hardly the easiest play to put on as it rained nonstop, which meant we couldn't perform in the open as we had planned, so it was decided we would perform it in the ballroom, which meant the whole thing had to be restaged. Tony Guthrie was busy with other things and said to me, 'You decide how to set up and rehearse the new blocking. Just fix it for me, Larry.' And fix it I did, and enjoyed myself immensely as I let my imagination run wild.

There is nothing better in life than a group of actors who are presented with a problem and having to come up with the goods in no time. The adrenalin gets everyone in a great sense of excitement, and actors will do the impossible for you, so if you say, 'There's no other way to do this but to play the whole scene hanging from the chandelier,' that actor will just go ahead and do it.

Olivier recalled in his book *On Acting* that the performance at Elsinore was 'a great night to remember, full of magic and memories. Some say it was the best thing they'd ever seen. Whether it was or not I'll never know.'

There was a question I was bursting to ask Larry about this production of *Hamlet*. Since Vivien Leigh was playing his Ophelia, and since he and Vivien were a great romantic team of the theatre, how much of the real thing spilled over into the play?

He said, 'Oh, dear boy, it was *there* – it couldn't *not* be. We didn't have to suggest it. Vivien and I were . . . well, we couldn't keep our hands off each other and, I feel ashamed to tell you, but we made love almost under Jill's nose. It was during that time that two marriages were truly ended.'

'The passion had become that intense?' I asked.

'I feel a little sick to admit it, but yes.'

'*Hamlet*, then, was more than a performance,' I suggested.

'Oh, dear boy, the play was more than the passion of our love at that time. Hamlet is someone I can't ever fully explain and that makes him so enticing, more than any sexual act. I can tell you how I got inside Richard III, and into Othello and Henry V, but I simply can't tell you how to get inside Hamlet. He just takes you and if you are lucky he will show you the stars. He captured me the way frankly no woman can, and he has never let me go.'

Anthony Quayle was also in that production, as Laertes. I asked Quayle what he had thought of Vivien.

'Vivien was enchanting as Ophelia,' he said. 'Vivien was truly lovely and as delicate as a flower, and she could utter obscenities in a way to make your hair curl up. I know Vivien was criticised for her acting, and she wasn't the greatest stage actress of all time, but as Ophelia she was good. Not great, but good.'

When everyone returned to England, Larry told Jill that their marriage was over; Jill moved out of their house and in with her mother in the country, taking Tarquin with her. Vivien told Holman what was going on and that marriage too was severed; their daughter Suzanne remained with her father.

Elsinore had changed all their lives forever.

12

The Laird and Lady of Chelsea

Larry and Vivien escaped reality for a while and headed off on a holiday during the summer of 1937 across much of Europe. When they returned home each had film work waiting for them – *A Yank at Oxford* for Vivien, and *The Divorce of Lady X* for Larry in which he played a barrister who shares his hotel suite with a young woman (Merle Oberon) and then fears his chivalry may involve him in a divorce. This was another for Alexander Korda, now a close friend of Larry's. Korda was in love with Merle Oberon, and he had Vivien under contract; he had loaned Vivien out to MGM for *A Yank at Oxford*. They were a happy bunch of friends.

Films, or rather the money he earned from them, helped Larry to live a very comfortable life, and he was able to send money regularly to his sister Sybille, now back at home and looking after her sick husband. Larry and Vivien moved into a house in Iver, in Buckinghamshire, which was near to the major British studios. They were planning to move into a house in Chelsea in London, Durham Cottage, but that wouldn't be ready until November, when Larry and Vivien would be diving into the tragedy of *Macbeth* at the Old Vic.

Durham Cottage became a regular meeting place for their friends, as Rex Harrison recalled: 'There were a number of us living in the same area of London – John and Mary Mills, Larry Olivier and Vivien Leigh, David Lean and his wife, Anthony Havelock-Allan and Valerie Hobson, and Lilli [Palmer – Harrison's wife] and myself – and we were all very young then, always having fun, and I remember we all got together to play poker on Saturday evenings. Vivien was a wonderful hostess. Larry would get tired long before she did. She complained when we would all leave. I don't know if her mental illness was taking hold of her by then.'

There has been much talked of and written about Vivien's mental state, which quickly deteriorated once her illness eventually took hold. They used to call it manic depression; today it is known as bipolar disorder. It's surprising, looking back over the things people said about her, that so little was understood back then. Vivien would find herself unable to control her actions, and would often not even remember what she had done or said. Bipolar disorder is a terrible illness, and because it is a mental illness it has a stigma attached to it. The horrors that were to come to Larry's life and his work have too often been regarded as the work of 'mad' Vivien Leigh. But from what I have been able to gather, she was not the cruel bitch sometimes portrayed. She was just very ill.

One of her greatest champions was John Gielgud, who told me, 'Vivien became very ill, and when she did, she was not the wonderful, charming and very funny person I knew. I never forgot who she really was. It was harder for Larry, of course, as he had to try and live with her when she was at her worst. But he also lived with her and loved her when she was at her best, and the Vivien who was at her best was the true Vivien.'

John Mills, speaking in 1978, preferred to remember Larry and Vivien at their best: 'When they were on form they were the funniest couple in the world. They were both great raconteurs and would have me in stitches with their stories. People think of Larry as a very serious man, but he has a great sense of humour and so did Vivien, and so they were great foils for each other and their sense of humour was highly infectious.'

Work on *Macbeth* started, with Larry as the Laird and Judith Anderson as Lady Macbeth. Their director was Michel Saint-Denis who, with Larry, agreed on a highly stylised production, which Larry came to regret. He said, 'We made some terrible mistakes on my first outing as Macbeth, and I am happy to share the blame with my director, Michel Saint-Denis, who was a fine director with a wonderful imagination. But on this occasion he let his imagination run amok, and I let him. He wanted a highly stylised production and our make-up was so heavy it was as good as wearing masks. I had a false chin, a false putty forehead with huge eyebrows, and a huge putty nose which went straight from the forehead.'

When Larry told me this, I said to him, 'But isn't it your preference to hide behind some kind of mask?'

'Not at all, dear boy. One doesn't hide behind a mask; one *uses* make-up to finish what you have created in your mind. People misunderstand me. I do not create a false nose to create a character. That character and the performance come from the head and from the heart first and foremost. The real look of a character must come from the inside and then you can dress it with make-up. I always prefer to try to find something, even if it is just a putty-nose, to dress the character, and to strengthen what I have long perceived to be a weakness in my face at the ridge of my nose. That is my own neurosis and I'm entitled to it!

'But in the case of that first *Macbeth*, I was unable to allow the man to play through me because I had everything on the outside and not enough on the inside.'

'And that was the director's fault?' I asked.

'I share the responsibility. It was his concept, and I trusted his judgement; I should have known it was a mistake, but there are times you have to put yourself in your director's hands. I try, even today, as fucking grand as I am, not to usurp a director.'

I asked Larry if the legendary *Macbeth* curse had struck that production.

He winced. 'I do not believe in the *Macbeth* curse. That production was full of incident, and some who are superstitious would credit it to the curse. But it was not all bad luck.'

It was not all good luck either. Larry said:

Our dress rehearsal was a disaster. We worked into the night and we were clearly never going to be ready for the first night, which was only two days away. The problems were technical, to do with the lighting cues. At around three in the morning, Tony Guthrie came in, saw what was going on, and told Michel Saint-Denis that it would be a disaster if he kept the actors up all night and through the next morning and still expect them to go on stage. The decision was made to cancel the first night.

This fuelled speculation of the curse at work, but it was a blessing because we were ready for the first night. But the night before we opened dear Lilian Baylis, who founded the Old Vic, passed away. I heard it said that it was the shock of the cancellation of the first night that brought it on and that was part of the curse. I disagreed. I believe that no Old Vic production had been postponed before, and Miss Baylis, who was greater than all of us who trod those boards, simply departed quietly while her theatre was engulfed in a rare silence. It could have happened with any play, but this happened to be *Macbeth*.

The critics were not pleased. James Agate of the *Sunday Times* had mixed feelings about Olivier's performance: 'His voice, which in the "Tomorrow and tomorrow" and "Sere and yellow leaf" speeches should vibrate like a cello, is of a pitch rather higher than the average. He is not a natural bass and has some difficulty getting down to baritone.' But Agate had some praise for Olivier: 'All the same, he brings off some magnificent vocal effects, and his verse-speaking has improved.'

Macbeth proved to be the most successful play the Old Vic had enjoyed up to that time. The curse of *Macbeth* did not triumph; the play did. Larry continued to rise as a Shakespearean star.

13

Protecting Puss

In February 1938 Olivier and Ralph Richardson joined forces to perform *Othello,* with Richardson as the Moor and Larry as Iago. The story of *Othello* is complex, and Larry would attempt to make it more complex than the basic story might suggest. Othello's old and hateful lieutenant, Iago, is determined to bring about the downfall of Othello's new favourite, Cassio, and destroy Othello in the process by casting aspersions on Othello's new bride. His mind poisoned by Iago, Othello murders Desdemona.

In the cast, as Cassio, was Anthony Quayle who in 1978, said to me:

Ralph Richardson played Othello, but it wasn't right for him. Or he wasn't right for the Moor. And Tony Guthrie was the wrong director for the play. His strength was in wit and satire – in acerbity. *Othello* was none of that.

But what it did have was Olivier as Iago. While Ralph was really a disaster as Othello, Larry was a triumph. He threw himself into the part with all his boundless animalism and his sheer magnetism. And I say *threw* literally because Larry had learned from the eminent Professor Ernest Jones that Iago's hatred for Othello was because Iago had a homosexual love for Othello. Larry and Tony hatched a plot to play this without telling Ralph, who would have been mortified.

It was really left, I recall, until the morning of the opening night when we did a final rehearsal, and then we got to the last scene where Iago is led away to be tortured. Larry paused as he was passing Ralph on his way to the torture – Ralph was reclining on a divan, and I could see him looking at Larry, who hadn't paused there before. Larry bent over him and was about to plant a kiss on him.

Ralph said, 'What are you doing, cock?'

And Larry said, 'Tony and I thought it would be a good idea if, as I was being taken away, I bent over you and gave you a kiss.'

'Indeed?' said Ralph. 'Then let me give you due warning; if you do, I'll get straight up and walk off the stage.'

So the kiss was abandoned.

Quayle felt that the fame and stardom Olivier was now enjoying had a mixed effect on him. On the one hand he could be incredibly generous, but he could also be brutally frank and unwittingly hurtful. Said Quayle:

One night Larry came up to me in the wings and put his arm affectionately around my shoulders. By this time he was a great star – one of the demigods of theatre. He whispered, 'You got anything lined up when this ends?'

I said, 'No, I'm really rather worried.'

He gave me a very reassuring hug and said, 'You never have to worry. You'll never be out of work for long. And I'll tell you why. It's because you are a bloody good actor – *bloody* good.' I was really quite overwhelmed by his warmth and generosity. He paused, very slightly, and then said, 'And you haven't enough personality to worry a leading man.'

And that was like a heavy punch to the heart. I felt floored by it. And I never forgot it.

He was right about not being out of work for long. And I went on to play *Henry V*, which was really his part. And as much as it hurt to hear from him that I would never be a leading man, he was right about that too. But I think I would have preferred to have found that out for myself rather than be told so frankly by Larry.

Giving praise to Larry's Iago was John Gielgud, who told me, 'There is a great fascination to Larry's Iago, and the same is true of his Richard III – you watched him as Iago and Richard delighting in his own wicked cleverness and sharing his pleasure with the audience. Larry always knows what he wants to communicate to the audience, and what comes across is not an *actor* who knows he is being clever, but the characters themselves who are letting the audience in on their evil secrets.'

Larry continued his successful run at the Old Vic, next in *The King of Nowhere*, a modern play for once, written by James Bridie, in which Larry played Vivaldi, an actor who becomes a political leader. The critics didn't like it, but audiences still came to see the now 'great' Laurence Olivier.

Then it was back to Shakespeare with *Coriolanus*, considered just a notch below the four great tragedies – *Hamlet, King Lear, Macbeth* and *Othello*. Coriolanus was a military and political leader of ancient Rome, and Shakespeare borrowed heavily, as he also did for *Antony and Cleopatra*, from the Roman historian Plutarch.

For his death scene, Larry literally threw himself down a staircase in a complete somersault which shook the stage, rolled over three times on his side and almost crashed into the footlights before expiring.

Meanwhile, Vivien had been a success as Titania in *A Midsummer Night's Dream* at the Old Vic, directed by Tyrone Guthrie. Also in that production was John Mills, as Puck; he credited Larry and Vivien with landing him what was to be a landmark role for him. He told me (in 1978, on a foggy location for the TV series *Quatermass*):

There was a time in my life (in 1938) when I was out of work and convinced I would never work again. I had been doing well in musical theatre, you see, as well as a few films, but the work had just suddenly stopped and I was getting no offers at all. I was very depressed and thinking of giving up acting. I spent many evenings with Larry and Vivien, who did their best to keep my spirits up. They were such great chums and made me feel like I wasn't such a lost cause after all.

There was one night I shall never forget. Vivien was curled up on the sofa, and she was one of the most exquisite creatures I had ever seen. Larry was mixing drinks, making fireballs. And out of the blue Tony Guthrie arrived at their house. He and Larry got to discussing Tony's upcoming season at the Old Vic. I just sat quietly, and Larry said to Tony, 'What are you starting the season off with?'

Tony said he was doing just two productions that season – *A Midsummer Night's Dream* and *She Stoops to Conquer*. He was talking about how *Dream* had been done so often that he was doing something new with it. He had asked Robert Helpmann, the great dancer, to play Oberon, and he was looking for a sort of off-beat casting for Puck and he couldn't find one anywhere.

Then Larry said, 'You can stop looking, Tony, because the actor you want is right there,' and he was pointing at me with his glass. I was speechless. There was a terribly long pause and I was convinced Tony Guthrie was going to burst into laughter, but he said, 'My God, how absolutely right. But you'd never consider it, would you?'

I said, 'Why wouldn't I?'

He said, 'Because you must be making a fortune with all those musicals and we could pay you only fifteen pounds a week to perform at the Vic, and you couldn't possibly accept that amount.'

I couldn't think what to say and then Larry piped up with, 'Oh, stop waffling, Tony, and make him an offer if you want him.'

So Tony Guthrie said, 'Johnnie, will you play Puck for me at the Vic for fifteen pounds a week?' as though I was doing *him* a favour.

I said, 'I'll play Puck at the Vic or anywhere else you want me to play it for fifteen shillings a week if you want me to.'

Larry rather winced at my overenthusiasm, but not only did Tony Guthrie give me the part of Puck in *A Midsummer Night's Dream* but he also cast me in *She Stoops to Conquer* as Young Marlowe. And those productions literally saved me.

I have always suspected that Larry arranged all that, but he insists he didn't. I'm pretty sure Larry had a hand in getting Tony Guthrie there when I was there also. So thank God for Larry Olivier.

Mills had more to be grateful for, as he explained:

The success of those two plays led to me getting the role of George in Steinbeck's *Of Mice and Men* in London. When the play moved from the tiny experimental theatre called The Gate to the Apollo, Larry and Vivien came to see it and after they came to my dressing room and raved about the play and my performance which was a tremendous boost to the ego. Vivien had found the last scene so incredibly sad that she had started crying, and she was still in tears in my dressing room.

We went to supper and I said to Larry, 'OK, let me have it. I know you meant what you said about my performance and I am thrilled about that, but we have always promised each other that we would be as honest with each other as we can, so . . . was there anything in my performance that you really didn't like?'

He said, 'Well, Johnnie, there was one thing. Just a small thing.'

I said, 'Tell me! Anything! Please just tell me.'

And he said, 'It was your exit after the murder. That lingering hand on the doorpost. Just a *shade* too much. I think that you should cut it.'

So out it went, and just because Larry Olivier said so. I trust his judgement without question.

Following *A Midsummer Night's Dream*, Vivien chose to do a small play, *Serena Blandish* at The Gate. Her leading man was a newcomer, Stewart Granger, then under contract to Basil Dean.

Granger told me (in 1981):

The first time I met Larry, and also Vivien, was in 1938. Vivien was determined to play Scarlett O'Hara, but at the time she was about to be directed by Larry in a play called *Serena Blandish* at a small theatre in London called The Gate. Vivien had the title role, naturally, and the lead male role was Lord Ivor Cream, which, I found out, was still uncast. I'd been doing some repertory work and was under contract to Basil Dean, and thought this might be my chance, so I rushed down to the Gate as soon as I heard about this play and there I met Larry, who had always been my idol. In fact, it was watching him that inspired me to become an actor, so it's all his fault. I'd rush down to the Old Vic whenever I was able to get to London to see him. He was the most exciting actor in theatre; a beautiful man in the truest physical sense, with virility and magnetism and creativity. I tried so hard to copy what he did, but I was very bad at it.

And now there I was, face to face with him, asking him if I could read for the part of Lord Ivor. He told me to run through a scene with Vivien immediately, and that's when I was introduced to Vivien, who was really a ravishing beauty. The screen never really showed her true beauty. Well, I was just so terribly nervous that I shook through the first part of the audition. I was just terrible. I'd never even read the play before. But Larry was so helpful and so generous, and he calmed me down and in the end I gave what was a fairly good audition.

Then Larry and Vivien went into a conference and I was convinced they would decide that I was far too bad an actor to be given the part, but Larry came over and told me I had the part. I couldn't believe it. He said, 'Do you understand that this only pays three pounds a week?' I said, 'Yes,' even though I was being paid a lot more by Basil Dean. And then I said, 'There is just one problem. I'm under contract to Basil Dean.' And I asked him if he could wait just two hours while I sorted that out. Larry wished me good luck and I rushed back to the theatre where I saw Dean's manager and explained everything to him and asked to be released from my contract, and he went and spoke to Dean. I expected him to come back and give me a telling-off because Dean had this and that planned for me, but he came back and said that Mr Dean thought it was a brilliant idea, and we signed some papers, and I was free to work for Olivier.

I rushed back to the Gate and told Larry and we had a drink to seal the deal. I wasn't really sure if I had done the right thing. But it was wonderful to get to know Vivien while working with her. She was not ill back then, and very hard-working and ambitious. She was passionate about Larry, and he about her. We became good friends and they came to my wedding [to Elspeth March] shortly after that.

According to Stewart Granger, Larry directed this production, but it was in fact directed by an actor called Esne Percy. Larry was clearly behind the play and not leaving Vivien's fate in the hands of anyone else. He had become very protective, or maybe even possessive.

Some think he was out to dominate her. But Larry was not the dominating kind. And Vivien was not the subjective type. She only *seemed* to need protecting. And she seemed to need him. That is exactly what Larry needed at that time of his life – someone who *needed* him. Jill had really never actually *needed* him, and he had always felt inadequate with her. He was not able to get from her the love that he required. And Larry certainly needed love. To be loved. He'd needed to feel that since he was at All Saints.

Then along came Vivien and nobody in the world loved him the way she did. That did a great deal for him. He was someone I understood. He had been through the ordeal of being abused. He felt that nobody could love him as much as he needed to be loved, in the way he needed to be loved. But then he found Vivien, and she was able to make him feel that she couldn't live without him, and that made him feel like a very special man. It meant he could be more assured about his sexuality, which was something that haunted him. When she flattered him, it was like a magic spell cast on him. That was irresistible to him. To him, she was 'Puss' and 'Vivling'. He would protect Puss with his life. And his life, back then, was protecting Puss.

He had said that if anyone was going to fuck up his career, it would be him. Nobody else was to be trusted. He felt that nobody was going to fuck up Vivien's career, either. Nobody else was to be trusted. She was the fragile swan that he would keep safe from the predators that lurked in the world of theatre and films.

They loved each other with a great passion, they made love at every opportunity, and they pledged to always work together. Larry's only failing was that he thought she was a better actress than she was.

There was a British film Larry had to make in 1938. It was called *Q Planes* in Great Britain, and *Clouds Over Europe* in the US. Produced by Alexander Korda, Olivier was teamed up with Ralph Richardson as test pilot Tony McVane and investigator Major Hammond, who together look into the mystery of why aeroplanes are disappearing.

'That was too much fun,' Richardson told me in 1976. 'The script was pretty appalling so Larry and I made most of it up, and we had trouble not giggling through every take.'

The film did well enough, but greater film success was just a continent away.

14

Hollywood Heights

David Niven and Larry were already friends when they were cast in the 1939 film version of *Wuthering Heights*.

Niven told me (in 1978, on location in London for *A Nightingale Sang in Berkeley Square*), 'I had become friends with Ann Todd when she was still an up-and-coming actress and I had not even thought of becoming an actor. But because she got me backstage on numerous productions, I became incredibly starstruck.

'When she had become a star and I was still a nobody, she introduced me to a young actor, very good-looking, just making a name for himself on the stage, and his name was Laurence Olivier. He became a lifelong friend and godfather to one of my children.'

Larry had pretty much sworn that he would not work in Hollywood again. But when he received an offer from Samuel Goldwyn for him and Vivien to be in *Wuthering Heights*, to be directed by William Wyler, he assumed that Vivien would play Cathy to his Heathcliff. But then he discovered that she was to play Isabella while Cathy would be played by Merle Oberon, now Mrs Alexander Korda. Larry was not impressed.

William Wyler came to London twice to meet with him, to try and persuade him. Wyler, speaking by telephone to me in 1976, told me, 'Olivier was very upset that Vivien was not being cast as Cathy, but I told him that the part of Isabella was a good part for an actress who was not yet established in Hollywood pictures.'

Unsure what to do, Larry called Ralph Richardson and asked him if he thought he should accept this offer from Hollywood. Richardson said, 'Yes. Bit of fame. Good.'

There was one other person he needed to consult – Vivien. 'It was Vivien who really persuaded me,' he told me in 1976. 'She could see that I liked Wyler, and that I wanted to play Heathcliff, and so she said, "You must do it." She had a cooler head than I about it all.'

And so Larry accepted, and in November 1938 he set sail for America, leaving behind a miserable Vivien, who still had *A Midsummer Night's Dream* to finish.

Larry had no idea what he was letting himself in for. William Wyler was far tougher than any director he had worked with. He was just about the toughest director in Hollywood. It wasn't that he ranted and raved at his actors. He simply made them do take after take after take, until he felt he couldn't get any more from them.

David Niven had already suffered under Wyler's direction, in the 1936 production *Dodsworth*. He had been offered the role of Edgar, the man Cathy marries, even though she and Heathcliff, cast out by her hateful brother, are in love.

Said Niven, 'Larry and I had been friends for some time and our friendship was further grounded when we both started *Wuthering Heights* sharing a deep hatred for Willie Wyler. Wyler, it seemed to me, could be very cruel and sarcastic and he assumed we were too English, too well mannered to answer him back. So David and I were like allies against the great enemy, although we both grew to like Wyler very much. But nobody could have accused Wyler of being charming on that picture.'

Niven was under contract to Samuel Goldwyn and really had no choice about doing *Wuthering Heights*, but had protested strongly nevertheless:

Samuel Goldwyn told me I was going to play Edgar, which was a part I hated and didn't want to do. And I didn't want to work for Wyler again . . . ever. So Wyler called me and said, 'David, why don't you want to play Edgar?'

I said, 'Because it is such an awful part.'

He said, 'It's not, you know,' and then he hit the ego button with, 'and you're one of the few people who can make it better than it is.'

So I said, 'But Willie, I was so bloody miserable working for you on *Dodsworth*, and I just couldn't go through it again. You're a son of a bitch to work with.'

That just made him laugh, and he said, 'I've changed. I'm not a son of a bitch any more.'

'So I reported to the studio for the costume fittings, and while I was there Larry Olivier arrived. He had just come from England, and he had the most beautiful woman on his arm – Vivien Leigh. She was like a kitten and just stunning. [Niven's memory may have been a little shaky, as Vivien had not gone to America with Larry, although she did come over later.]

Then came the first day of shooting. I had to drive up in a two-horse buggy with Merle at my side. We had a line of dialogue each. She would say, 'Come in, Edgar, and have some tea.' And I would say, 'As soon as I've put the horses away.' Not difficult stuff.

We did the first take and Wyler said, 'Cut! Just play it straight, David, this isn't a comedy.'

I had no idea I'd played it for laughs, so we did the second take, and he said, 'Cut! What's so funny, David? This is not a Marx Brothers picture. Do it again!'

And we did it forty-something times, and finally Wyler said, 'Well, if that's the best you can do, we'd better print the first take I suppose.'

I said, 'Willie, you really are a son of a bitch, aren't you?' and he said, 'Yes, and I'm going to be one for the next fourteen weeks.' And he was.

He had Larry do a long scene over and over and over, and Willie never gave any specific instructions. He just made you do it over and over, and finally Larry said, 'What do you want me to do?'

Wyler paused, thought it over, and then said, 'Just be *better*.'

Olivier's own recollection of working with Wyler was that he was 'a man who seemed impossible to please'.
Said Larry:

I didn't understand him at all. He'd tell me, 'That was lousy overacting. What are you doing, for Christ's sake? Get your arse back down here on earth and try and be better.'

So I told him, 'Willie, this little medium of yours is just too fucking anaemic for great acting.'

He just laughed and said, 'Is that what you were doing – great acting?'

I didn't see it at first, but he was toning me down. I really knew nothing about film acting; I only *thought* I did. It was Willie who taught me how to do it. He wasn't subtle about it. He said, 'Do you think you could try if our little medium can capture one of your frowns instead of a frown *and* a glare?'

I said, 'Why not a frown and a glare?'

And he said, 'On a big screen, the frown will do it. The glare just overdoes it.'

And when I finally saw the rushes, I began to realise he was right. But I was very opinionated. I thought Hollywood was lucky to have me. He knew I couldn't be told anything. He knew I would come to my senses in time. He was really very flattering because he said I was a great actor in the theatre but knew nothing about acting for the camera. I thought he was a cruel bastard. But I grew to love him.

Once Larry had become grand, he never really found a way to be anything less, even though he never meant to behave so high and mighty. But that's the way he was, and when he talked to me about his friendship with David Niven, it was almost at the expense of Niven's lesser talent as an actor. But then, Larry was always honestly frank.

David and I are very different kinds of actors and I think that is why we got on so well. He was, with all respect and love for the man, a lightweight actor and he couldn't have performed in a stage classic ever in his life, but he could easily breathe into any part he played his own great charm and humour and also sincerity, which was all very much his own. And also, when it was needed, he had tremendous pathos. So I was no threat to him as an actor and he was no threat to me, and so we got on wonderfully well. I was the heavyweight and he was the lightweight.

He carried off the part of Edgar wonderfully. In fact, I'd say he was better than Merle. He had an impossible part and he hated it, but he was perfect in it. I would watch him and think, 'He isn't even trying to act and here I am working my bloody guts out and he is going to look bad on screen.' But he was wonderful on screen. I learned a lot about screen acting from him, although I thought when we first started working on the picture that I knew more about acting than he did. And I did, when it comes to acting on stage, but he had a natural gift for screen acting which I had to work at. So when I call him a lightweight, it is not a criticism.

When I talked to Niven in 1979, he said he had heard the 'lightweight' description from Larry applied to him but was never offended by it.

'It's true what Larry said. In fact, my film career suffered later because Larry brought a new kind of style of English acting to films which the Americans liked. He was much more theatrical than I, and when he and Vivien did the two Cleopatra plays Hollywood wanted people like them and not like me, so I was struggling for a time.'

Making *Wuthering Heights* was never going to be a happy experience for Larry, even though he acknowledged that it made him into a major star. He recalled, 'It was a difficult picture in many ways, not least because Merle Oberon and I didn't get along at all on that picture, despite having worked well on *The Divorce of Lady X*, and also David and Merle had been lovers but had fallen out by then, so there was Merle who wasn't much liked by the two men in the film who were supposed to both love her.'

Despite the difficulties on set, Wyler and Olivier became good companions after the day's work. Wyler told me:

I would get Larry over to my house and I would tell him, 'You must be patient. You are wrong to despise this medium. It is the greatest medium in the world.'

He said, 'You obviously didn't see *As You Like It*.'

I told him, 'I saw it. Don't despise that picture.'

He said, 'It proves Shakespeare can't be done on film.'

I said, 'Larry, you are wrong. Shakespeare can be done if you think out how to do it right.'

He was also worried that he was playing a part with no moustache, no putty-nose, he felt he had no personality of his own to display for the camera. I told him, 'Don't worry about your personality. Just get on with acting. Think of the camera as another actor. Show it your most subtle reactions, close-up.'

He had problems with Merle, and he was anxious about Vivien, and I said, 'Oh, and one more thing. Don't bring your problems to the set.' We did just fine together.

When Vivien went over to join him, Larry made a point of introducing her to agent Myron Selznick, brother of producer David O Selznick, who was hunting high and low for his Scarlett O'Hara in *Gone with the Wind*. 'I was very keen for her to get the role of Scarlett,' Larry told me at our last meeting in 1981. 'So I told Myron that we ought to take Vivien along to meet David. So Myron drove us out to the lot where they were filming the burning of Atlanta.'

This was second-unit work in which stunt doubles played Rhett Butler and Scarlett, and the set being burned to the ground was the island set from *King Kong*. Scarlett hadn't been cast despite just about every female star name in Hollywood trying for it, but filming had to get started, and the burning of Atlanta provided a spectacular prelude to production.

'We got out of the car and I looked at Vivien and she looked spectacular with the flickering of the flames in her face – her eyes. Anyway . . .' He stopped talking, the memory of Vivien still something to haunt him in 1981. I urged him on. 'Well, George Cukor was there [directing], and David Selznick. Myron introduced Vivien to David and he said, "David, meet Scarlett O'Hara." And so Selznick arranged a screen test and she had the part. I couldn't have been happier.'

And neither could Vivien. She had the part she had wanted so badly for so long.

When I said to Wyler, 'You didn't think Vivien was a big enough star to play Cathy, but Selznick chose her to play Scarlett,' he replied, 'Then she should thank me, because if I had cast her as Cathy, she would never have been available to play Scarlett.'

He had a good point. But it is a demonstration that there is no rocket science involved in who or what makes for a great star until it is seen up there on the big screen. Larry's performance in *Wuthering Heights* established him finally as a major film star, although he didn't overwhelm all the critics of the time.

Graham Greene wrote in the *New Statesman*, 'This Heathcliff would never have married for revenge. Mr Olivier's nervous, breaking voice belongs to balconies and Verona and romantic love, and one cannot imagine the ghost of this Cathy weeping with balked passion: Miss Oberon cannot help making her a very normal girl.'

James Agate in the *Tatler* was a little more impressed: 'Mr Olivier acts best when he acts least and . . . he superbly portrays the dumb agony which the gypsy has in common with his animals.'

And Hedda Hopper wrote in her daily gossip column, 'When Laurence Olivier says, "Come here, you're mine," how gladly you'd go.'

Before heading off to America to make *Gone With the Wind*, Vivien had asked Holman to divorce her. Larry wrote to Jill, asking her to start divorce proceedings against him, which she agreed to do.

While Larry was finishing filming *Wuthering Heights*, Vivien was beginning *Gone with the Wind*. Selznick had signed Larry and Vivien to star in *Rebecca*, but until they were both ready to begin that, Larry went to New York to do a play, *No Time for Comedy*, in April 1939. The separation between Larry and Vivien was almost too much for them to bear. *Gone with the Wind* was taking forever to make, and director George Cukor had been replaced by Victor Fleming, and then other directors were brought on when Fleming had a breakdown, and the film just seemed never-ending and plagued with problems. Vivien was exhausted and becoming hysterical, so Selznick called Larry and told him to take her away for a short break.

He took time off from his final rehearsals and spent two days and nights with Vivien in Los Angeles. Then he went on to Indianapolis for the pre-New York run of *No Time for Comedy* while she went back to playing Scarlett. Following the opening night, Larry received news that his father had died from a stroke. It was physically impossible for Larry to make it home in time for the funeral.

The stress on both Larry and Vivien was growing. They spoke often on the telephone and wrote endless letters. He sometimes called her 'Mummy darling'. Sometimes their phone calls were passionate and emotional, sometimes they just argued. The magic was already beginning to wear thin.

Writer Garson Kanin, in London in 1988, told me how he saw firsthand the obvious and early signs of disintegration in the love affair before filming on *Gone with the Wind* even commenced.

I met Vivien and Larry at George Cukor's house at a Sunday lunch which was in honour of Vivien and Larry. She had been announced for the role of Scarlett O'Hara and he was going to be in *Rebecca* as Maxim de Winter. Greta Garbo was there; an exquisitely beautiful woman. I'd never met her before and couldn't take my eyes off her for three hours. And, of course, Vivien expected all male eyes to be on her.

After lunch, Garbo and Olivier went for a walk in Cukor's beautiful gardens. I stood with Vivien at my side as we watched them walk up a long flight of stone stairs, around the esplanade and then down another flight. They had such grace and poise and were deep in conversation.

We could see that he talked and she listened, and then she talked and he listened. I saw her laugh but she made no sound. They fell silent. He gesticulated and she looked surprised and asked him something, and he replied, making grand gestures to underline his response. The afternoon light was fading, I recall, and I realised that it all looked like a scene from a silent film.

Then the magic of the moment took on another dimension as I realised that Vivien, standing beside me, was seething with rage and jealousy. You see, she was accustomed to being the most beautiful creature at any gathering, and here was the great Garbo, who was spectacular in any environment, engaged in an intimate conversation with Larry.

She said to me, 'Just look at him. He's behaving like a ninny.'

I said, 'What's a ninny?'

'*Him*! Look at him, stumbling all over himself.'

I said, 'In his position, I would be stumbling too.'

'Oh, you *would*, would you?'

I said, 'You have to admit, Vivien, she's a pretty spectacular number.'

She gritted her teeth and said, 'I don't have to admit to anything of the sort. Why is he sucking up to her? I can't understand it, especially as she had him sacked.'

I said, 'Do you mean from *Queen Christina*?'

She said, 'Well, of course I mean *Queen Christina*.'

I said, 'But I understood it was Irving Thalberg or the director or –'

'It was *her*!' she said, almost stamping her foot.

Then, in a second, her face changed from taut anger to an illuminated smile and she said, 'Ah, *there* you are! *Bonne promenade*?' and I realised only then that Garbo and Olivier had returned and were approaching us.

Within five minutes I was driving Larry and Vivien home. Vivien had engineered our departure so swiftly and gracefully that I still cannot remember the details of how we came from standing with them in the garden to being in the car. I have no idea if I said goodbye and thank you to George Cukor, or if indeed Larry and Vivien had, and now there I was driving my car with Larry and Vivien sitting next to me – the most romantic couple in the world – having a terrible quarrel.

'That's the last time I ever go to lunch with *you*,' Vivien was telling Larry. 'I would rather *starve*.'

Larry was trying to calm her down. 'Now be reasonable, Puss . . .'

'Why should I be reasonable? Are *you*?'

'Of course I am.'

'*Hah*!'

'What does that mean?'

'What does what mean?'

'*Hah*! What does that mean?'

'It means that I'm fed up with that David Copperfield performance.'

Now Larry's voice was raised. 'Oh my God! Will you give it a rest?'

'Floating round the garden like some love-struck ninny.'

'All that happened was she asked me if I would like to walk a few steps. What was I to say?'

'Did you try saying *no*?'

'Of course not.'

'Why not?'

'I was being polite. It's as simple as that.'

'*Simple*, all right!'

At that point I had this idea that if I started laughing, it might be contagious and the drive back would turn into one of gaiety. So I laughed. It didn't work. They both turned on me.

'Shut up!' yelled Larry.

'What is so funny?' demanded Vivien.

And then they turned on each other again.

'And just what was so *enthralling*?' Vivien asked Larry.

'Enthralling?'

'The conversation you had with the great Garbo. What was *that* all about?'

'All right! If you insist, I shall tell you what it was about.'

'Thank you,' she said, not sounding at all thankful. 'And do not dissemble please, because you know what a rotten liar you are and I *always* know when you're lying.'

He said, 'Good God, Puss, how many battles do you expect me to fight at once?'

She said, 'Just this one, so please go on about your enthralling tête-à-tête with your latest enthusiasm, Miss Greeta Garbo.'

He said, 'One: it was *not* enthralling. Two: it was *not* a tête-à-tête. Three: she is *not* my new enthusiasm. And four: it is *not* Greeta. It's *Greta*.'

'It's *Greeta*,' Vivien insisted. 'And I don't want to hear any more of it anyway.'

'Good,' said Larry. 'Well, I'm glad *that's* all over.'

He took out a cigarette and lit it. There was calm throughout the car. And then the calm broke.

'I meant I don't want to hear any more about how her name is *pronounced*,' said Vivien. 'Who cares if it is Greeta or Greta? What I want to know is the subject of your *enthralling* little tête-à-tête.'

'Here it is, then,' Larry cried like a man who had been given the third degree, could carry on no longer and was about to confess. 'We were walking and she said, "This is a nice garden," and I said, "Yes, it *is* a nice garden."'

He was doing the greatest Garbo impression I ever heard. His imitation of her voice and accent was uncanny, and he caught the musicality of her voice to perfection. I had to keep my eyes on the road, but as Larry continued with the conversation that had taken place, it seemed to me like I now had Garbo as well as Larry and Vivien in the front seat with me.

According to Kanin, the conversation between Olivier and Garbo went like this:

GARBO: We have gardens in Sweden.

OLIVIER: Yes, you must have.

GARBO: Do you have nice gardens in England?

OLIVIER: Yes, we have many nice gardens in England.

GARBO: In some of our Swedish gardens we grow fruit. Apples.

OLIVIER: We have apples in England, too.

GARBO: And strawberries?

OLIVIER: Oh, yes. Very good strawberries.

GARBO: Do you have oranges?

OLIVIER: No. No oranges. But we do have peaches.

GARBO: We have peaches in Sweden.

OLIVIER: Oh, I am so glad that you do. Do you also have nectarines?

GARBO: No. We have no nectarines. But we have cabbages.

OLIVIER: Oh, yes, we have cabbages too. What about gooseberries?

GARBO: What are gooseberries?

OLIVIER: Gooseberries. You know. To make gooseberry jam with. Or a gooseberry pie. Or a gooseberry fool.

GARBO: A gooseberry fool? What is a gooseberry fool?

OLIVIER: Well, it's the same as a raspberry fool or a damson fool, but it's made with gooseberries.

GARBO: Oh, I see. And do you have artichokes?

OLIVIER: No, we import them but I don't think we grow them. But we do have asparagus.

GARBO: Yes, we have asparagus, too. But no Cranshaw melon.

OLIVIER: No, neither do we.

GARBO: Cranshaw melon is good.

OLIVIER: Watermelon is good.

GARBO: And cantaloupe?

OLIVIER: I'm afraid I don't much like cantaloupe.

GARBO: I like this garden. It is a nice garden.

OLIVIER: Yes, it is a very nice garden.

Kanin continued, 'And then Larry said, "And that was it until you said, 'Ah, there you are. Let's go home.'"

'And they didn't say another word until we pulled up in their driveway when Vivien said, "I don't believe a bloody word of it," and Larry said, "No, I didn't think you would."

'But, you know, I *did* believe it because I knew that Garbo didn't go in for making charming small talk and expressing opinions. To me, gardens and vegetables and fruit was *exactly* what Garbo would have talked about, and her mode of expression was an art, like music, in which her expression goes beyond words. I believed every word of Larry's story, but Vivien didn't, and he wasn't going to argue his case any longer. Whether they did when they got indoors, I have no idea. But I think it was over. I expect ice formed on the walls inside their home when they got in.

'I knew, just from that single episode, that Larry would never be able to make Vivien happy.'

15

War

Vivien finished *Gone with the Wind* although some retakes would be needed. They were both now free to film *Rebecca*, from the book by Daphne du Maurier. Selznick was producing, Alfred Hitchcock was directing, and Larry was playing Maxim de Winter, a wealthy socialite troubled by the 'accidental' death of his wife Rebecca, who died in a boating accident. Vivien was to play a shy ladies' companion whom de Winter falls in love with and marries.

But first there was the chance to return briefly to England in July 1939. Before returning to Los Angeles in the autumn, there were divorces to be arranged so that Larry and Vivien could marry as soon as possible. It was agreed that both Jill and Holman would petition for their respective divorces on grounds of adultery.

After little more than three weeks in England, Larry and Vivien sailed for New York in August. On board the *Ile de France*, they received a cable from Selznick explaining in great detail that the part in *Rebecca* was so wrong for Vivien that it threatened to damage her career which, he assured her, was about to become huge. Larry was furious that Vivien had been fired from the film.

They flew from New York to Los Angeles where Vivien did her retakes for *Gone with the Wind* and Larry prepared for *Rebecca*. On Monday, 3 September, they went sailing with Douglas Fairbanks Jr, his wife Mary Lee, Nigel Bruce, Ronald Colman and Benita Hume on a chartered yacht off Santa Catalina.

They were waiting to be joined by David Niven and fellow British actor Robert Coote when they heard over the radio that war had been declared on Germany. Vivien began to cry.

American-born pro-British Fairbanks was as devastated as his British actor friends. Olivier wrote that they 'felt blighted right through'.

Niven and Coote arrived in a small sloop; they had been told the news by an American who had come alongside them in a dinghy. 'Nobody felt like celebrating any more,' said Niven. They all retired to their respective cabins.

Fairbanks told his wife, 'I suppose I'll join up right away, if they'll have an American.'

Larry told Vivien he would try and join the RAF. Robert Coote planned to head for Canada and join the RAF. Nigel Bruce had a permanent injury to his leg which had kept him out of the First World War, and which would now keep him out of this one.

Fairbanks gathered his guests back on deck for some champagne and said, 'Well, here's to whatever it is.'

'To victory,' Larry said solemnly.

The next morning the British consul in Los Angeleshad a queue of British actors volunteering for war service. Larry was among them. The consul announced that the British Government was asking that they all remain in the US to fulfil their obligations and to do all they could to gain the friendship and sympathy of the American people. That, the consul said, would be a greater service to their country than rushing to arms, unless they were already in the reserves.

Larry could go nowhere just yet as he was still filming *Rebecca*.

The story that Larry told was that he and Vivien wanted to get married as soon as they could, but his divorce would not be absolute until August 1940, and he didn't want to return to England without first marrying her. So they decided to remain in America. They also wanted to have their children brought over to America, away from the threat of the Luftwaffe over Britain. But this wasn't to happen for another year because, according to Olivier's autobiography, George Cukor suggested to them, 'If you two kids want to make a little extra money before you go off, why don't you put on and send on the road *Romeo and Juliet*? You could make a fortune in no time at all.'

Meanwhile there was the Oscars ceremony. Vivien was nominated Best Actress for *Gone with the Wind* and Olivier Best Actor for *Wuthering Heights*. On the night, at the end of February 1940, Vivien won while Larry lost to James Stewart in *The Philadelphia Story*.

'For a time I felt, well, envious of Vivien,' Larry would tell me. 'Vanity and ego will do that. It was clear from the start that *Gone with the Wind* was going to turn Vivien into a bigger star than I could hope to be. I, naturally, pretended that this didn't bother me as I was far more interested in being an *actor* rather than a *star*. And then when Vivien won the Oscar and I didn't, I felt terribly sorry for myself. But I consoled myself by proving that I was a great actor and also a great director with *Romeo and Juliet*. They say pride comes before a fall, and, oh, how I fell.'

Larry made plans for *Romeo and Juliet* while working on his next film, *Pride and Prejudice*. Once more, they had hoped Vivien would be the leading lady and once more they were to be disappointed. Metro-Goldwyn-Mayer only ever intended to cast their reigning queen of the lot, Greer Garson, in the film. Then Larry and Vivien thought they would be together in *Waterloo Bridge*, but MGM had only Robert Taylor in mind for Vivien's leading man.

Rebecca and *Pride and Prejudice* earned good reviews for Larry, now more confident of his screen-acting technique. Of *Rebecca*, the *Monthly Film Bulletin* wrote, 'Laurence Olivier is excellent as the sardonic Maxim and makes him credible and not unsympathetic.' *Variety* thought that 'Olivier provides an impressionable portrayal as the master of Manderley.'

As for his performance in *Pride and Prejudice*, the *New Statesman* said, 'Olivier makes a fine, contemptuous, gradually unbending Darcy,' while Basil Wright of the *Spectator* wrote, 'Both Greer Garson and Laurence Olivier breathe the original zephyrs in several scenes.'

It seemed that the harder Larry and Vivien tried to work and stay together, the more they were being kept apart. *Romeo and Juliet*, then, would keep them together. But for Larry, the responsibility of directing and starring in the play took its toll, and he grew physically tired. On the opening night in San Francisco, he failed to make a dazzling leap over Juliet's wall at the end of the balcony scene, and instead barely managed to grasp the top of the wall and hang on to it, waiting only for the curtain to come down.

The San Francisco critics were lukewarm, as were the critics and the audiences in Chicago. In New York, the critics went for Larry. The *Herald Tribune* wrote that while Olivier's acting and direction of the play was bad, it was worth seeing 'for Miss Leigh's lovely Juliet'.

The play failed badly. It had cost $96,000 and was losing Larry $5,000 a week. It stumbled along for 35 performances and closed in June 1940.

Perhaps to lose himself from the disaster that had befallen him, or maybe in some vague hope that he might be able to benefit the war effort even though he was past recruitment age, he resumed his flying lessons even before *Romeo and Juliet* had ended. On 20 July he received his American pilot's licence.

Because James Stewart flew regularly, it was not surprising that he and Larry crossed paths from time to time.

'He was . . . oh . . . just a *terrible* pilot, at first,' Stewart told me. 'But he got better. A whole *lot* better.'

Olivia de Havilland, romantically involved with Jimmy Stewart in 1940, recalled, 'Wherever Jimmy and I flew, no matter what airport or field we arrived at, Larry would have been there just before us and always managed to sideswipe planes with his wing. One time we wanted to land at Monterey, but we were told on the ground that we would have to be careful because part of the field was out of commission. When we got down, we were told by someone, "Laurence Olivier has been here and caused so much damage." That's why so much of the landing strip was out of commission. But Larry was totally fearless.'

It was that fearlessness that led him to undertake what was probably the most dangerous assignment of his entire life.

The failure of *Romeo and Juliet* to please the masses, as well its failure to make money, drove Larry's desire to return to England, where he might be able to enlist.

He called Duff Cooper, Winston Churchill's Minister of Information in London; Olivier said in his autobiography that Cooper was a friend, and so he asked him if there was the possibility of finding him a job in his department.

A few days later Duff sent Olivier a cable: 'Think better where you are – stop – Korda going there.'

Olivier wrote that a day or two later, Alexander Korda phoned him and said, 'Larry, you know Lady Hamilton?'

'Not intimately,' Olivier replied. 'Wasn't she Admiral Nelson's piece?'

'Right,' said Korda. 'Arrange meetings with Vivien, Walter Reisch and R C Sherriff. I'll come at once.' Reisch and Sherriff were working on the screenplay.

Curiously, Larry wrote little more to explain how he and Vivien came to make Korda's *Lady Hamilton* (US title *That Hamilton Woman*) in which Olivier played Nelson and Vivien the title role. And more importantly, he gives no clue why Duff Cooper thought it was best for Olivier to remain in America.

Olivier's account gives the impression that Korda was on his way over to America to make *Lady Hamilton*. After all, Cooper's cable did say, 'Korda going there'.

But Korda wasn't on his way from England. Korda had been in America for some time. He had been asked to go specifically by Winston Churchill, who knew that the British film industry couldn't survive the war without a major part of it functioning in Hollywood. It was important that British films were made on a major scale, which they couldn't be in Britain, and so earn much-needed American revenue, which in turn would help pay for the import of American films that were needed to keep British spirits up. Churchill knew the value of entertainment as propaganda.

Between them, Churchill and Korda had decided that films should be made that were obviously patriotic to Britain but not blatantly propagandistic. Furthermore, such films should not be seen to have emanated from official British Government sources.

There were other reasons why Churchill sent Korda to America. MI5 and the Special Operations Executive (SOE) needed Korda as a cover for their operations. He met with officials from both secret agencies, and was told that the offices he would set up in New York and Los Angeles would be a link to a worldwide motion picture corporation which in turn would act as a perfect cover for British intelligence agents working in America.

America was still a neutral country in the war. American isolationists intended to keep it that way and had made it almost impossible for British agents to work there, so they had to go underground. Alexander Korda's film company would be the perfect cover for those agents.

Korda was also to act as a courier for these secret organisations. But it was risky. If the FBI were to become suspicious of Korda, he could be investigated and declared a foreign agent. But far more dangerous was the possibility that the Germans could discover what he was doing and have him killed.

Korda kept much of this secret throughout his life, but it was revealed in Michael Korda's book about the Korda film dynasty, *Charmed Lives*.

Before heading for America, Korda already had it in mind to find a film that met Churchill's requirements and would star Laurence Olivier and Vivien Leigh.

Why Olivier and Leigh? It would seem that they were both easily available, even though they were steeped in the misery that had become *Romeo and Juliet*.

Michael Korda, as he suggested in his book *Charmed Lives*, knew that Larry had tired of Vivien's obsessive devotion to him during *Romeo and Juliet*, which he now found suffocating. She was possessive and jealous. He wanted to have more freedom, and she was afraid of losing him. This was the time when she was brooding on his 'close friendship with a famous American actor'. Vivien began drinking heavily.

Hollywood screenwriter Jesse Lasky Jr believed that Larry was involved with an American actor around that time. He told me, 'I don't think it was something that lasted at all long. Many actors like to try the other side, so to speak. Larry had a bisexual nature at times, but not always I think. It may have taken something specific to drive him to that extreme, and if Vivien was giving him no room to breathe with her own desires and demands, he might well have opted for something that was a fast escape.'

A possible homosexual liaison, then, may have been driven purely by his need to try and escape Vivien's obsession. But there are no clues to the other actor's identity and it appears to have been something of a well-kept secret in Hollywood circles. As Lasky told me, 'Not every single private detail about anyone's life – no matter who it is – needs to be made public. Hollywood was very good at closing ranks when it wanted to.'

Alexander Korda knew of the troubles between Larry and Vivien and wanted to rescue them. He felt that a film in which they played equal roles would satisfy each of them. He also knew that Larry had wanted to show his patriotism and that he and Vivien felt guilty about remaining in America. A patriotic film would make them both feel better about having stayed in the US.

Originally Korda had thought of the story of Elizabeth and Essex. Warner Bros had made *The Private Lives of Elizabeth and Essex* a year earlier with Errol Fynn as his usual swashbuckling self as Essex and Bette Davis giving a performance of extraordinary awfulness as Queen Elizabeth.

Korda knew Larry would be a superior Essex, but he was not convinced that Vivien was right for the role of Elizabeth. It was Churchill who came up with the idea of a film about Nelson and the Battle of Trafalgar. Korda thought it was a great idea, but needed to provide Vivien with a role that equalled the part of Nelson. The answer,

Korda decided, was Lady Hamilton, Nelson's infamous mistress. He knew it would be tricky because this would be a story of adultery. But if handled right, it could emerge as a story of love and sacrifice and, above all else, patriotism. In fact, Korda, as Churchill hoped, would attempt to make a film that talked of Britain's fight for freedom.

There was not even a screenplay when Larry and Vivien arrived in Los Angeles to begin working with Korda. They moved into a house on Cedarbrook Drive and began working with Korda, Walter Reisch and Bob Sherriff on the script. Korda very cleverly titled the film *Lady Hamilton*, giving Vivien the title role, even though the film was to celebrate Admiral Nelson's victory at Trafalgar. They concocted a story whereby Lord Horatio Nelson pays a visit to Sir William Hamilton, the British ambassador to the Court of Naples, and meets Mrs Emma Hamilton. She uses her influence to recruit the soldiers he needs to fight the French, and in time she and Nelson fall in love, causing a scandal. Ultimately they plan to retire to the country, but Nelson is killed at the Battle of Trafalgar.

In Olivier's opening scene, he informs Lord Hamilton that he has received orders from Lord Admiral Hood; Larry would portray Admiral Hood 43 years later, in *The Bounty*. (Ironically, the part of Nelson, who stole Lady Hamilton from her husband, would be played in 1973 by Peter Finch – in *Bequest to a Nation* – who would steal, for a while, Vivien from her husband.)

Korda had paid a handsome advance to Larry and Vivien, allowing them to finally arrange for their children to cross the Atlantic. Jill Esmond came to Los Angeles with four-year-old Tarquin and she even managed to get some film work. Vivien's daughter Suzanne went with grandma Gertrude to stay with relatives in Vancouver, Canada.

As word got out about the subject of the film, the emphasis was not on the film's patriotic fervour but on what was perceived to be the condoning of adultery. And worse, the two adulterers were being played by two real-life adulterers. Korda did all he could to counteract this adverse publicity with a more positive spin.

The problem was solved when, in August 1940, Larry and Vivien became free to marry. They planned to wed in Santa Barbara, eighty miles north of Los Angeles, where they would escape the notice of the press. They had to give three days' notice of their marriage and so they made the three-hour drive to Santa Barbara to register for their marriage, and then drove back to Los Angeles. Ronald Colman's wife Benita had bought the wedding ring, and when Larry and Vivien drove back there on 30 August, they were accompanied by their witnesses, Katherine Hepburn and writer/director Garson Kanin.

At the last minute it was realised that their three days' notice did not take effect until midnight, and so they, the witnesses and the judge had to wait, passing the time with a succession of drinks. At the stroke of midnight the ceremony began and Larry and Vivien were pronounced man and wife five minutes after twelve, on 31 August 1940.

Lady Hamilton was shot at General Services, a small studio in the centre of Hollywood. The budget was limited and the rental of the studio sound stages was relatively cheap. The screenplay was not finished and many scenes were being written by night and filmed the next day.

Alex's brother Vincent had constructed ship-bound sets which were rocked by an elaborate machine, giving the appearance that they were rocking to the motion of the sea. The simulated roll of the sea was far worse than Vivien had ever experienced on a real ship, and she quickly developed seasickness.

Then the Hays Office stepped in. It was required that all screenplays be submitted to the Hays Office before filming commenced so that the film industry's appointed censor could cut the film in any way it chose before it reached the screens. There had been no screenplay ready to show the Hays Office, but the film still had to be seen for it to receive the Production Code of Approval. Joe Breen, the head of the Hays Office, refused to pass the film, telling Korda that the film condoned adultery. Korda argued that the affair between Nelson and Emma was historical fact, to which Breen said he didn't care – they were still adulterers. A compromise was reached; Korda shot a scene in which Nelson confessed that what he was doing was wrong. But once the film was on release, Korda had that scene removed.

The Battle of Trafalgar was impressively staged, using full-size sets for medium shots and close-ups, and a fleet of miniature ships complete with firing cannons and sails that raised and lowered, all shot in the vast water tank at the studio. The resulting film was one of the best Alexander Korda directed, full of romance, extravagant backgrounds, a wonderful score by Miklos Rozsa, and a rousing climactic sea battle.

'It was Churchill's favourite film during the war,' Larry happily boasted. 'It said everything he wanted it to say without being overt.' And what Churchill wanted it to say was, Britain would never surrender to the invader.

It delighted most critics. Dilys Powell, of the *Sunday Times*, wrote, 'The death scene is finely done, a moving piece of acting. Laurence

Olivier's performance as Nelson, indeed, is within its conventions good throughout.'

Sight and Sound were not slow to spot that 'historically the film is worthless', but thought it 'a good entertainment film, with unusually good acting in all parts'.

But Larry was not just an actor working in an Alexander Korda film. He went to work in America for the British secret services.

16

England Expects

When he came to write his autobiography, Larry explained that he had felt that he and Vivien could not return to England at the outbreak of war simply because he didn't want to do so until they could be married, and that couldn't happen before August 1940 when his divorce from Jill would be absolute. And so they had remained in the US and embarked on *Romeo and Juliet*.

But David Niven remembered it somewhat differently. In 1978, he said:

Before I was able to leave Hollywood and return to Britain [to enlist] I was asked to remain in America to try and drum up support for the war effort. We were hoping America would join us, you see, but there was a lot of opposition to the very idea among many Americans, and it was to be a very secretive and really very difficult task because to do that very thing could result in one being arrested and charged. The isolationists in America were very strong, even though [President] Roosevelt was prepared to support us. So the British Government required people who could come and go at liberty in America and who could use their influence to increase support for the British.

I wasn't against doing that, but I wanted to get home and enlist and fight the war where it was happening. So I said, 'Why don't you ask Larry Olivier? He's dying to do something for the war effort, and it'll be a while before he gets home.'

I then put to Niven the obvious question that came to mind: 'And did they ask him?'

'Oh, yes.'

'Did he do it?'

'Larry isn't the kind of man to turn down that kind of request from his country.'

'But who asked you in the first place?'

'The British Embassy in Washington.'

'And they then asked Olivier?'

'Oh, yes.'

Niven explained further that the British Ambassador in Washington, Lord Lothian, had told him that he was needed in America to help to counteract the isolationists. That was when Niven suggested that Laurence Olivier would be a better choice. Niven managed to reach Europe on route to Britain, and in Paris met with Noël Coward, now working in naval intelligence.

'Noël tried to persuade me to return to America to work for naval intelligence,' Niven said, 'but I insisted I was returning to Britain, but I once more suggested that Larry Olivier might be willing. I believe it might have been Noël Coward who put Larry's name to Churchill. In fact, Coward told me that he personally asked Larry to assist.'

It may well be that Coward did ask Larry, but it was Alexander Korda, Churchill's man in Hollywood, working undercover for MI5 and SOE, who ultimately recruited Larry. This I learned from Noël Coward in 1972, before I knew anything of Larry's secret wartime work in America.

While discussing Coward's own contribution to the war effort and of the difficulties of getting full support from America in the first year of the war, and also discussing Laurence Olivier, Sir Noël suddenly said, 'We needed Larry, you know, because he was there [in America], and we asked, and he thought about it, and then it was down to Alexander Korda to tell Larry that Winston Churchill was not asking but telling him that his country expected him to do his duty.'

I suggested that this was a little like Nelson telling his men that England expects every man to do his duty.

'Well, that was the *point*,' said Sir Noël.

Sir Noël went on to say that Larry and Vivien remained in America and performed their *Romeo and Juliet*. Larry, then, was already working for a British Government secret agency before he started work on *Romeo and Juliet*, and he was able to use that production and his inability to marry Vivien as a good enough reason to remain in America.

Reluctant to tell me too much about it, Larry did say in 1979, 'There wasn't very much for me to do really other than tell my American friends how terrible the British were finding the war and that Germany would be invading our island at any time.'

But there was actually a lot more to it. When I pressed David Niven on the subject, he said:

> There were plenty of actors, writers, directors and producers in Hollywood who had connections to the American Government. Larry targeted those people specifically so that they, in turn, would try to influence their friends in high places. It wasn't as though Larry was going to change the course of the war, but it did put pressure where pressure was needed. And I believe, you know, that Roosevelt welcomed this pressure. But there were others who didn't.
>
> What was dangerous for Larry was that he could have been accused of being an agent. This sounds ludicrous now in the light of history, but before America was brought into the war, it didn't tolerate foreign agents. So this was a danger for Larry because he could have been arrested.
>
> And what was worse, if German agents had realised what Larry was doing, they would, I am sure, have gone after him.

It may seem difficult today, with America and Britain so close allies, to understand just why Larry's secret work could have been construed as being dangerous, and why it would also have brought him enemies among seemingly ordinary Americans.

During the 1920s, many Americans had come to feel that America's entry into the First World War was a mistake. Britain had long been regarded as the great enemy of American democracy, having fought a war with America (1812–15), threatened war over the Oregon Territory during the 1840s, and aided the south in the Civil War, while in the 1890s there had been serious tensions between America and Britain over Guyana–Venezuela.

The British had viewed American naval power with suspicion and, as late as the 1920s, the Royal Navy considered America as a possible adversary. Many Americans in the 1920s and 1930s were influenced heavily by their ethnic backgrounds. The British were hated by many Irish-Americans; the Irish Potato Famine of the 1840s had driven many Irish to migrate to America, and the fight for Irish independence throughout the nineteenth century was highlighted by the 1916 Easter Rebellion. During the 1920s, the terror of the IRA and the counterterror of the Black and Tans fuelled hatred and passions to a fever pitch. American politicians courting the Irish vote made inflammatory statements. The rise of Hitler and the forging of the Axis alliance between Germany and Italy generated anti-British feelings among German and Italian-Americans.

As the rise of Nazism made it increasingly clear that Europe was moving towards another war with Germany, there was a determination that America should avoid war at any cost.

The memories of the thousands of Americans lost in the previous war combined with a long-standing American isolationism resulted in the passage of a series of Neutrality Acts. Isolationist leaders opposed any kind of involvement in a European war and clashed with President Roosevelt, who was becoming increasingly concerned about the threat of the Nazi and Japanese military. The President was faced not only with the isolationist movement but also considerable anti-British feeling. Even celebrated pilot Charles Lindbergh spoke out in favour of isolationism, arguing that America couldn't win against Germany's Luftwaffe. Congress strongly opposed expenditure even for basic military preparedness.

Hitler feared America more than any other country, but was convinced that Britain could be defeated before America could be mobilised. Neither the Nazis nor the Japanese had any idea just how effectively American industry could be so quickly converted to war production, and Air Marshall Goering arrogantly stated, 'The Americans only know how to make razor blades.'

There were some Americans already preparing for the war, among them James Stewart. 'I just felt the war would inevitably involve America,' he told me, 'and it was important to prepare places where the Air Force could train its pilots, because there simply weren't the facilities to train them.'

So James Stewart, agent Leland Hayward, actor Johnny Swope and an aeronautics engineering expert called Jack Connelly purchased the Sky Harbour Air Service in Phoenix, Arizona, and transformed it into Thunderbird Field. They eventually set up two more training fields for pilots.

'Larry Olivier might have been a terrible pilot, but he was a true patriot,' said Stewart. 'He never actually said, "You know, isn't it time you Americans joined the war?" With him, it was more like, "We're doing the best we can and God knows the Nazis are going to invade and we'll all fight to the last man, but if we have to stand alone then that's what we'll do." And that made us think, "By golly, we can't just stand by and let that happen." And that's how it was with Olivier.'

On the face of it, what Larry was doing hardly seemed like the kind of work that either SOE or MI5 would have been active in. The mission of SOE was to encourage and facilitate espionage and sabotage behind enemy lines, and also to serve as the core of a resistance movement in Britain itself in the possible event of an Axis invasion. SOE was also known as 'Churchill's Secret Army' and was charged by him to 'set Europe ablaze'.

SOE was flexible in what it did and how it did it. But it wasn't in existence at the time David Niven was asked to remain in America, which was right at the start of the war. Niven, it would seem, was originally approached by naval intelligence, through Noël Coward.

However, SOE *was* in existence when Larry was in America performing *Romeo and Juliet*. It would seem most likely that Larry was working for what was originally a propaganda organisation within SOE called Department EH.

MI5 dealt largely with finding double agents who would transmit bogus intelligence back to the German secret service, the *Abwehr*. Larry was not in the business of training double agents, but then neither was Alexander Korda. Yet Korda was working for MI5 as well as SOE as a front for both agencies, and Larry was recruited by Korda. Larry didn't work as a paid agent in any sense. And although he was under orders from Korda, his boss was, ultimately, Churchill. As Korda was acting on behalf of MI5 and SOE, so too was Larry.

Jesse Lasky heard on the grapevine that Larry was 'drumming up support, and doing it with the British Government's sanction'. Knowing a little about the work Larry did when I interviewed Lasky in 1978, I asked him if he was aware that Larry had worked for either SOE or MI5.

'Nobody ever said it out loud, but there was a feeling that by the time Olivier and Vivien were working on the Nelson film that both Olivier and Alexander Korda were more than just British film-makers producing a movie in Hollywood that we all knew was a marvellous and clever story about British patriotism, but also that these two men were clearly some kind of official ambassadors for the British Government.'

Lasky knew that a number of prominent Hollywood stars voiced support for Larry.

Cary Grant was British and I believe he was very helpful to Olivier in finding the right people to talk to. There was also Tyrone Power and Clark Gable. These were not just the superstars of their day, you must understand. They were men of considerable influence. I know there were others also, and not all of them would have necessarily influenced politicians, but they could and did have substantial influence at their respective studios, and the power of the studios at that time should never be underestimated.

There was a lot of support for Britain among the studio heads. Many of them were Jews and were afraid what Hitler would do. Once the Nazis had conquered Britain, they would turn their attention to the United States. So I am sure that there were plenty of people in high places in Hollywood who secretly gave support to Olivier and Korda. I never actually heard that either Korda or Olivier worked for MI5 specifically, but I do know there were some isolationists in the motion-picture industry who disliked them and tried to rally some kind of opposition to them, so I suppose it is very feasible that they may have been some kind of secret operatives for the British Government, because there was so much concern and even active opposition by the anti-war movement against Korda and Olivier.

For instance, letters would be sent to studio heads asking them to boycott Laurence Olivier and Alexander Korda and also Vivien Leigh. Now it's interesting that despite the huge success of *Gone with the Wind*, Vivien didn't really get to work in Hollywood very much at all, and neither did Olivier. That might have been their own choice. But the major Hollywood studios should have been *begging* them both to come and make movies for them after the war. I always felt that there was something more *political* about all that.

And after all, Alexander Korda *was* called to appear before the Senate Committee.

That happened in 1941, following the release of *Lady Hamilton*. There were people who had been urging the American First Committee, an organisation set up to keep America out of the war and which attacked the film industry in Hollywood for making pro-British films, to press isolationist senators to investigate Olivier and Korda. This made Larry unwelcome in some circles. Korda was subpoenaed to appear before the Senate Committee on 12 December 1941. He was worried, as well he might have been, that he would be condemned as a British agent. He had reason to believe that by this time the Germans had compiled enough information on his covert activities and passed them on to the Senate Committee.

The hearing never took place. The Japanese attack on Pearl Harbor on 7 December brought America into the war, and any accusations made against Korda were redundant. But before that happened, both Korda and Olivier were in danger.

'The Germans weren't stupid, although we might like to think they were,' Niven said. 'They had a tremendously efficient intelligence network. I'm terribly sure that little escaped their notice, and they had their own spies in the film industry. Unhappily, there were some Americans who were misguided enough to support the Nazis. I know that Larry had his life threatened.'

When I asked Larry about this threat to his life, he dismissed it, saying, 'We were *all* in danger. I am sure I wasn't popular among the Nazis of New York and Los Angeles – oh, yes, there were Nazis there, working in the theatre and in films. Personally I would have liked to have had them all shot, but, well, the American Government wasn't up to executing the people who weren't, at that time, their enemies.

'It was a very painful situation for the British people who were in America and we all felt hugely embarrassed that suddenly our American hosts were not very keen to have us there at all and many of them couldn't decide exactly which side they were on. There were areas of America which were largely populated by German immigrants, such as Milwaukee, and so those areas were enthusiastically pro-German and therefore anti-British.'

Larry might have been evasive, but Noël Coward gave a very frank if brisk statement to me in 1972: 'Oh, yes, Larry was in danger, all right. We got wind of this and warned him. The Nazis would have killed him, no doubt.'

And it would appear from what David Niven and Jesse Lasky Jr said that German agents did close in on Olivier.

'I am convinced it was Samuel Goldwyn who got wind that something was in the air and Larry was in danger in New York,' said Niven. 'It was a tense and difficult time for him all round. He told me he was desperate to end the run of the play as it was costing him a fortune which he would never make back, and he had some problems with Vivien – but those two dear people *always* had problems – and then of course there was this threat from Nazis.'

To clarify, I asked Niven, 'Do you mean the threat was immediate?'

'Oh, yes, I am sure. That's why Goldwyn and some of the other top brass made sure he was kept safe.'

'How?'

'They all had offices in New York. I expect some kind of security was arranged. All very low key, but obviously effective.'

Jesse Lasky Jr said he only later became aware of all this when he was working for Cecil B DeMille. 'DeMille was the super-conservative of the American film industry. He loathed the Nazis and he believed God was waiting for America to pull its finger out and get into the war. So he personally contributed [financially] to hire professional guards to protect Olivier and Vivien Leigh. After all, there was the threat of death, of kidnap, of sabotage.'

I asked Lasky what kind of people would have been hired as guards.

'They would have been *professionals*. Mercenaries, I suppose you might call them. Probably ex-policemen, former agents, maybe even a little Mafia in there. Believe me, Hollywood knew how to pull strings and how to pay for it. And it wasn't out of any great love for Olivier. He had barely made two films in Hollywood. There was great respect for him as an actor, but more than that there were enough important – *very* important – people who believed in what he was doing.'

This, though, was in New York. Larry had to return to Los Angeles to film *Lady Hamilton*. Security was arranged there also. His guards were invisible, but not so invisible that they couldn't deter enemy agents. 'I doubt if Olivier ever saw one of them and knew what they were about,' said Lasky.

I asked Larry, in 1981, if he ever knew about all this security. He was reticent and typically evasive. 'I can see why some people wouldn't have liked what I had to say. I was just saying what any British patriot would have said. Not that I think there were many of us there at that time. Most of us, like Niven, had got home to enlist. I was hoping Ralph [Richardson] might be able to get me into the Fleet Air Arm, but otherwise I was too old to enlist. The other expatriates in that part of the world were merely *professional* Brits. They were largely character actors who talked a lot about "home" but who had lived in California for a decade or two and had no intention of returning to England. They'd play cricket and talk, and appear outwardly to be very British. But they were caricatures and frankly I despised them.'

Larry had cunningly avoided my question. I persevered.

'I didn't have a bunch of armed guards around me at any time,' he said. 'That would have been ludicrous, not to mention suffocating. Besides, the danger didn't come from being in America but when we left America. *That* was when we were in fear for our lives.'

I never could get Larry to admit that his life was at risk in America. But he did let it slip that there was danger when they left the US. German intelligence, it turned out, had decided to put a tail on the Oliviers as they voyaged back to Europe. The plan was to kill him.

17

Lisbon

The filming of *Lady Hamilton* was completed in just six weeks – an amazing feat for such an ambitious film. Despite interference from the Hays Office, the film was seen by the American public as *That Hamilton Woman* in 1941. The joint star pulling power of *Gone with the Wind*'s Vivien Leigh and *Wuthering Heights*' Laurence Olivier brought audiences flocking to see it. The picture sparkles with their own loving chemistry as well as their individual brilliance, and remains in my opinion by far the best of Larry's pre-*Henry V* films.

Filming over, the Oliviers were free to return to England. But before they did, Vivien flew to Vancouver to see Suzanne, who had been enrolled at a convent school. It had taken a year for Larry and Vivien to get their children out of Britain. Larry wrote in his autobiography that the delay was due to their decision to tour *Romeo and Juliet*. Olivier and Leigh could afford to spend $96,000 (from their earnings for *Gone with the Wind*, *Wuthering Heights*, *Rebecca* and *Pride and Prejudice*) producing *Romeo and Juliet*, but not spend it bringing their children over from Britain. Larry told me, 'It was just plain bad judgement. It was one of those ideas that seemed good at the time.'

But I think there is another reason. When Larry agreed to work secretly for Alexander Korda in his own endeavours for MI5 and SOE, that put Larry at risk; he might have decided to hold off from bringing his and Vivien's children to the United States because that would have put them at risk also.

The risk was still there when the children were brought over, according to Jesse Lasky Jr.

'When Vivien Leigh went to see her daughter in Vancouver, the press somehow got wind of the visit, even though she was travelling as "Mrs Holman". To answer their questions about why she was travelling under an alias, somebody put a story out that this was because of the fear of kidnap threats. That, of course, made headlines. The kidnapping and subsequent murder of Charles Lindbergh's little boy (in 1932) was still fresh in people's minds.'

But was there a real kidnap threat against little Suzanne Holman?

'The Mother Superior at the convent believed there was,' said Lasky. 'She insisted that Suzanne be removed, so Vivien had to remain in Vancouver until she was able to place Suzanne in another school.

'The kidnap-threat story may have been just a ruse to try and explain why Vivien was visiting her daughter in secret. Even Suzanne's real identity had been kept safe and I am sure even the Mother Superior didn't know that she was the daughter of Vivien Leigh. But nothing would have created more publicity that telling the reporters that the secrecy was to due to kidnap threats of all things.'

The so-called ruse was a double bluff. It was easy to believe that Vivien would have feared for her daughter because of the Lindbergh kidnapping. But there was a very real fear of kidnapping, which had nothing to do with the Lindbergh case and everything to do with Larry's secret work for Korda/MI5/SOE.

In America, protection was arranged for Jill Esmond and Tarquin, but up in Canada Vivien had nothing but Suzanne's anonymity to rely on. So when explaining Vivien's reason for secrecy, the press were immediately provided with a realistic explanation that gave no clue to the real threat that came from Nazi agents and the reason for it.

By alerting everyone who read newspapers to the threat of kidnapping, that may well have dissuaded enemy agents from attempting anything. Suzanne's schooling thereafter was kept secret, and Vivien did not go to see her daughter again until the war was over for fear of revealing Suzanne's whereabouts. I expect some kind of protection was offered by the Canadians.

If Larry and Vivien had thought that the danger had passed by the time they boarded the *Excambion* on 26 December 1940 to sail for the port of Lisbon in neutral Portugal, they were wrong. And they were quickly made aware of it.

The ship was American but the captain, although an American

citizen, was German. Olivier wrote that he and Vivien 'endured the most apprehensive voyage I have ever known', and that 'we could not rid ourselves of the fear that all was not well'. His fears, he said, were confirmed when on New Year's Eve the captain made boisterous toasts, including *'Deutschland uber Alles'* – 'Long live Germany'. There were only 23 passengers on board, but many of them responded with *'Heil Hitler'*. The ship was carrying Nazis. But not all the passengers were the enemy. At the table where Larry and Vivien sat was a US naval lieutenant who wore pilot's wings. Larry raised his glass and said to the lieutenant, 'To the American and the British naval air services'. The American replied, 'I prefer, "To all pilots trying to get home".'

Olivier did not elaborate on why he felt so fearful, although it isn't difficult to see how being on a ship captained by a German and carrying a number of Nazi passengers would, considering Larry's activities in America and the times they lived in, concern him. He did write that there was a 'constant nightmare' that the ship could be boarded, as some ships were at that time, by sailors from a U-boat and all non-Germans carted away for imprisonment in Germany.

This was a ship that had Nazis on board, and Lisbon was a known haven for agents from all sides. For the Oliviers, it was the only way to make their way back, ultimately, to England. But for Nazi agents, it was a direct route from America into Portugal, where the *Abwehr* operated in relative safety. Larry knew that there was nothing to stop the captain or any Nazi agent from sending a signal to a nearby German U-boat to come and arrest the ship's non-German passengers.

I once asked Larry if he ever felt that any of the Nazis on board seemed a direct threat to them. He said, 'They *all* felt like a direct threat. Under those circumstances one becomes terribly paranoid and we felt that eyes were upon us all the time.'

Would any of them have recognised Olivier, I wondered?

'I see no reason why they wouldn't have,' he said.

I pressed the point, and asked if there was anyone on board who might have had their eyes on him because of his secret work in America.

He was evasive as usual and said, 'My work was hardly a secret.'

I told him I was referring to his 'patriotic' work. He sighed heavily and replied, 'Telling friends that I hoped America would help Britain was not a secret.'

And yet despite his determination not to confirm his secret activities, he told me that he did remember one passenger who seemed to always 'be there, wherever we went. So we stayed inside our cabin for most of the time.'

When pressed further, he did say he felt he and Vivien were being watched closely. 'But that is paranoia,' he added. 'And we did arrive in Lisbon in safety after all.'

But once there, he was not as safe as he would have readers of his autobiography believe. He wrote that Lisbon was 'rammed with spies as a pomegranate is with pips' and described how 'there was a Mata Hari behind every palm tree', adding that behind every pillar in the hotel 'men would pause, say something in an undertone and move casually on'.

He wrote that all this 'was really funny'.

But that conceals the terror he experienced. David Niven said that Olivier told him that he believed there were agents on the liner who were out to kill him, but having failed to find the opportunity to kill him, they had disembarked at Lisbon. No sooner had Larry noticed that the agents were still around, they suddenly disappeared.

'The terrifying thing for Larry was that there would be other agents now assigned to bump him off and he wouldn't know who they were,' said Niven.

I asked Niven just why Nazi agents would want to kill Laurence Olivier. He said, 'Because it would have been a propaganda coup. Larry was no threat to the Nazis in America, but the news that one of Britain's great actors had been assassinated would have made everyone realise that nobody was safe, no matter who they were.'

Still unable to grasp this, I suggested that the Nazis could have killed any famous British person. Niven told me:

They did. They shot down Leslie Howard in a plane. They shot down Glenn Miller in a plane. That kind of thing made the citizens of Britain and America sit up. It had an effect on morale. These people were loved by millions. Don't underestimate the advantage the enemy has when the Allies lose someone they most love. But what the Nazis didn't understand was the tenacity of the Allies. That only made us more determined.

So Larry Olivier was a good target, not least because he had made himself unpopular with the isolationists, among who were Nazi supporters. I don't think he actually quite realised what a spot he had put himself working for Korda and SOE. When he talked to me about it – only the one time – he said he felt sick realising what he had been through. And I felt sick too. We were sitting in his house having had dinner and we were having a brandy I suppose, and talking about the war, and Larry said, 'What was the scariest moment of the war for you?' and I said, 'All of it.' And he said, 'For me it was that bloody voyage from New York to Lisbon.' And at that Vivien got up and rushed to the bathroom and threw up. So we all felt terribly sick. While Vivien was out of the room, Larry said to me, 'David, how could I have put Vivien through that hell?' And I said, 'Larry, because you – and Vivien – knew you were doing the right thing.'

He always thought that was his most important contribution to the war because although he tried to see action, he was never allowed to. So even though it made him and Vivien and me sick, he said to me, 'You know, David, my boy, I am really so very glad I did it. Even though we went through sheer bloody hell on the way to Lisbon and while we were in Lisbon,' because they were still trying to kill him, 'I am so happy to know I did *something*.' And he felt he had nothing to be ashamed of, because he *was* rather ashamed of a lot of other Brits who remained in America and did nothing.

Olivier wrote little of his time in Lisbon in his memoir. He said that he went to see the Air Commodore who was Air Attaché at the British Embassy where he presented a letter of introduction he had from Group Captain Adams, who had been a test pilot of American aircraft. He wrote that the Air Commodore was sympathetic and promised to get them on a plane to Britain in the next two or three days.

The Oliviers still had to survive until then and they remained inside their hotel room, waiting for news of their flight back to Britain. But they weren't entirely without the means to defend themselves in the event of enemy agents finding them. Larry had acquired a gun, probably from the Air Commodore, so Niven thought.

'Lisbon could be the deadliest place on earth if you were a target,' said Niven. 'Nobody knew who was who or on what side. Larry and Vivien signed in at their hotel as Mr and Mrs something or other and remained there. They had all their meals brought up, and each time there was a knock at the door, Larry was ready with his gun in case the bellhop happened to be someone who also had a gun.'

'But weren't Larry and Vivien two of the most recognisable people in the world?' I said to Niven.

'Larry was a master of make-up, and he put on some nose-putty and a moustache or beard, probably at the embassy, and he looked that way when they arrived at their hotel. Vivien would have kept her hat low and her coat collar up, and she would have just stayed right out of sight whenever room service turned up. They saw just an older-looking man with a large nose and whiskers. You know, Larry would have made an excellent James Bond – in real life, I mean.'

When word finally came that there was room on a plane for them, they checked out of the hotel and headed for the airfield. They might have thought the danger had passed, but that was not the case. Halfway home the cockpit caught fire. Larry at first thought they had been hit by enemy fire, but it turned out that the pilot had fired off the recognition signal but had forgotten to open the window. He and Vivien had survived the dangerous crossing by ship, a terrifying time in Lisbon, and now they were in danger of dying in a burning aircraft. Fortunately, one of the pilots acted quickly, rushed for the fire extinguisher and put the fire out.

Finally they landed at Bristol during an air raid. They hurried from the plane into the passengers' lounge, which, as Olivier said, made for an insufficient shelter. Outside, anti-aircraft guns fired upwards as bombs rained down. Larry and Vivien sat nervously waiting for the air raid to finish, and when it did, they finally felt they were safe.

But they were not yet home. They had to spend the night in a hotel that was missing one wall knocked out by a bomb. The freezing wind swept through the whole hotel. Finally they arrived – although Larry never said whether it was by car or train – at their home, Durham Cottage in London.

'When we got home,' Larry told me, 'the relief was so intense that we both sat side by side, holding each other's hands, unable to speak, and then we both just cried. Despite everything with Vivien . . . well, we had been to hell and back already.'

There was, right up to 1981, something I was dying to ask Larry, and finally I did.

'Why won't you be more open about what happened during the war – in America, and on the ship and in Lisbon?'

He smiled and said, 'My ego is too great to reveal all my secrets. It serves my ego to keep things to myself. My ego is fed gluttonously by *me* knowing and nobody else.'

18

Filming the Bard

The Oliviers returned to their beloved Durham Cottage where old friends came to visit, including Ralph Richardson, Jack Hawkins and John Mills. Hawkins, a second lieutenant in the Welsh Fusiliers, would grin at Larry, knowing he'd escaped the relative safety of America to come home and possibly get bombed or shot down if he managed to get into the RAF, and tell him, 'You are a silly bugger!'

One of Larry's first social events was the marriage of John and Mary Mills. 'When I first started courting Mary, we would go to the theatre with Larry and Vivien and then go to supper,' Mills recalled. 'They were wonderfully warm towards Mary and I think they found her just as enchanting as I did. When we got married (on 16 January 1941) we had only family and just a few close friends there, and Larry and Vivien were there. They were two of our very best and most beloved friends.'

There was film work for Larry: a cameo in *49th Parallel* for Alexander Korda, the story of Nazi submariners stranded on the coast of Canada who make their way to America. Larry played a French-Canadian trapper the Nazis shoot en route.

Ralph Richardson was now a naval commander working in the admiral's office at Lee-on-Solent. He helped Larry to get into the Fleet Air Arm as a lieutenant and was stationed at the naval barracks HMS *Kestrel* at Worthydown, near Winchester in May 1941. His job was to help to train air-gunners by flying them about in an old Walrus bi-plane for an hour or two.

To entertain his fellow officers, he performed perfect imitations of the CO and the chaplain. Even in war, Larry couldn't help but entertain, and pretend to be other people. Inspired by Shakespeare, he was seen striding to his aircraft, loudly proclaiming, 'Those friends thou hast, bind them to thyself with thongs of steel.'

HMS *Kestrel* was also used by the army to train its artillerymen. Soldiers were required, when on naval grounds, to treat naval officers as their superiors. This fact was lost on a certain Gunner George Munn – who just happened to be my father – and his companion who had been posted there to practise on the ack-ack guns.

One night, returning to base from drinks in town, Larry passed these two soldiers, who failed to salute him.

'You there,' Olivier called. The soldiers halted. 'Don't you salute naval officers?'

'We're not sure if we're supposed to,' replied Gunner Munn.

'When you're in naval barracks, you always salute officers.'

'Yes, sir!'

'Very well, let's not make a fuss about it. You'll know next time. Goodnight.' Lieutenant Olivier took his rank very seriously. And he would have been delighted if I had been able to tell him this tale, which I only learned from my father several years after Larry died. For me, it is another coincidence – and a most wonderful one – that connects me to Olivier.

Richardson had appointed Larry as parachute officer and would often come to see how he was getting on. Richardson noted that 'his manner was naval, was quiet, alert, and businesslike, with the air of there being a joke around'. He found Larry's parachute section faultless and noted how he had got 'such a hand of the work', and was able to introduce Richardson to every Wren and seaman by name.

Larry had found a bungalow to live in, and Vivien joined him whenever she could; she was still a working actress and was having success in a play, *The Doctor's Dilemma*.

The Ministry of Information decided to make use of Larry's greater talents as an actor, and asked him to make two films intended to enhance the British cause. The first was *The Demi-Paradise* with Larry playing a Russian scientist who arrives in England just before war breaks out and finds his new country to be inhospitable until he discovers love with a beautiful, young woman. The point of the picture was to help the British like the Russians, who were now their allies.

In many respects, this was the same thing Larry had done for the British Government in America, but this was a lot safer. I am of the opinion that this work, especially the choice of second picture, was a reward for Larry.

That second film, it was decided, would be *Henry V*. In between takes of *The Demi-Paradise*, or in the evenings and at weekends, Larry thoroughly enjoyed himself planning *Henry V* with set designers Paul Sherriff, Carmen Dillon and Roger Furse.

Larry originally had no intention of directing *Henry V* himself. 'Olivier asked me to direct *Henry V*,' Wyler told me. 'I said to him, "I won't do it, but you can. If it's Shakespeare it has to be you." I couldn't have directed it as well as Larry did. He created a masterpiece of cinema. And he was the one who told me that Shakespeare couldn't be done on the screen.'

Larry talked to me at length about how he made *Henry V* when we met on *Sleuth*, and I had gone there seeking wisdom about film directing. Larry was understandably proud of his achievement with *Henry V*, and also with *Hamlet* and then with *Richard III*, but this, his first directorial effort, was literally his baby.

Although credited as producer as well as director, Larry was interested only in what happened in front of the camera and not behind it. He told me, 'I was lucky to find Filippo del Giudice, an Italian interned by us for the first few months of the war. He produced the film and kept all the finances in check and left me free to have artistic control.

Del Giudice actually had his own film company, Two Cities Films, which also made *The Demi-Paradise*, so that film and *Henry V* seem to have been part of a package; presumably the Ministry of Information had persuaded del Giudice to co-operate. J Arthur Rank, the British film financier and distributor, also invested in the production. Larry was interested only in the artistic side of the film, and left all other matters to del Giudice.

Larry loved the challenges the play presented as a film: He told me:

The main problem I had was to find a style so that Shakespeare actors could do their stuff but still be acceptable to a cinema audience. I wondered at first how to begin the film. In the play Shakespeare complains about the confines of the Globe Theatre. He uses the Chorus to narrate and comment, showing his frustration that the Globe audience wasn't in France. I wondered how to present the Chorus. Have him as a voice-over perhaps? I realised I had to put him where

Shakespeare put him – in the Globe. The play was telling me the style of the film.

And so we have an Elizabethan actor challenging the very unruly audience to use their imaginations. And that would challenge the film audience, I felt. So I set the first few scenes in the Globe to get the audience used to the language, and enjoy the comedy of Falstaff, Nym, Bardolf and Pistol. I, as Henry, would be an actor waiting in the wings. I was getting the film audience to become restless and feel confined in the Globe, and then we leave the theatre, and Henry is saying, 'Now sits the wind fair, and we will aboard. And we're off to France.'

Despite opening up the film cinematically, the sets remained little more than cardboard cutouts, but Larry had his reasons.

'It was important that what the eyes saw didn't quarrel with what the ears heard. The dialogue is still poetic gobbledegook to some, so I wanted them to have not a crumbling Kenilworth stone but something artificial, something unreal, and yet even pretty. This was a romantic tale of a heroic mediaeval king.

'It's really my designers [Paul Sherriff, Carmen Dillon and Roger Furse] who were the geniuses behind the look of the film. I wanted the costumes and sets based on mediaeval illustrations with strange per-spectives – sometimes no perspectives at all – and bright colours. And that was how we got our style.'

Larry prepared his film meticulously. He couldn't afford to shoot miles of film, so he worked out every shot, every movement, every angle, and every cut. He wanted, wherever possible, to shoot in one take. He set himself an enormously difficult task as a first-time film director.

Most of the film was shot at Denham Studios over sixteen weeks. The battle sequence had to be filmed in Ireland where there was more countryside and fewer telegraph poles. One hundred and fifty Irish horsemen and five hundred Irish footmen worked on the battle for six weeks. The results were spectacular.

Larry's biggest disappointment was being unable to get David O Selznick to agree to allow Vivien Leigh to play the relatively small role of Princess Katharine on the grounds that such a small part would 'devalue' his new star.

When I first met Larry, on the set of *Sleuth*, I felt sure he was spinning me a yarn when he told me, 'I taught my horse the speeches. When the horse heard me say, "Be copy now to men of grosser blood, and each them how to war," he broke into a gallop. Every time I cried, "Saint George", his ears pricked up.

'After we finished the film, Arthur Rank wanted to give me a bonus and asked what I would like, and I asked for my horse. So I got the horse and kept him at Notley (the house Larry and Vivien would move to after filming) where I rode him at every opportunity. Sometimes I attached him to a trap and whenever we were expecting guests, we would take the trap to the station to meet our guests because petrol was rationed, and it was all very elegant.'

He told me about the day he collected Noël Coward, who complained that the trap didn't go very fast, so Olivier told the horse, 'Once more unto the breach . . .' and the horse began to gallop.

When I met Coward in 1972, I asked him about the story, and he said, 'Oh, dear God, yes, his horse knew Shakespeare. When Larry wanted it to go faster, he told it, "Once more unto the breach, dear friends," and the horse was off like a shot.'

John Mills also had a story about the horses from that film:

When Larry was making *Henry V* he invited Vivien, Mary and I, David Niven, Angela Baddeley and Bobbie Helpmann to ride the horses he was using in the film. We all lived close to each other at that time, very near to Denham Studios where we all seemed to work quite a lot and where Larry's horses were being kept.

They were magnificent horses. I was a little anxious about how I would cope as I wasn't a very experienced horseman, but we all mounted and Larry led the way out of the studios and down the road. It was all going fine until we reached the open fields when suddenly the horses, with no warning and no prompting, just reared up onto their hind legs and wouldn't come down again. Myself, Vivien and Bobbie fell off. Larry, Mary and David, who were all excellent riders, stayed on.

Larry looked down at us and said, 'I'm terribly sorry but they have been taught that an open stretch of countryside in front of them that meant "Action".'

I said, 'Larry, please tell us how you say to the horses "Cut".'

He said, 'Why, Johnnie, you just say "Cut" of course.'

And knowing all that, Mary and I joined Larry and Vivien every Sunday until Larry had completed *Henry V* and I became a pretty good horseman because of it.

The film was a triumph when released in 1945. The critics were quite bewildered by it, but they knew it was something special. Ernest Betts of the *People* wrote that Olivier 'deserves credit for undertaking the most ambitious film of our time. But it is also the most difficult, annoying, beautiful, boring, exciting, wordy, baffling picture yet made.'

Time said that it had 'been brought to the screen, with such sweetness, vigour, insight and beauty that it seemed to have been written yesterday, a play by the greatest dramatic poet who ever lived'.

The film had cost £474,888 to make, an unheard of sum for something as risky as Shakespeare, and it didn't actually make a profit until 1949, but that was not unusual with any film. It played for 46 weeks in New York, the longest any British film had managed to last in American cinemas, while in Britain it ran for five months as the Carlton, Haymarket. More importantly to Larry, it established him as not just the best-known Shakespearean actor in the world, but the first director to ever successfully transfer Shakespeare to the cinema. And he had done it all virtually on his own, under his own artistic control.

For his efforts, he won a special Academy Award in 1946 for 'outstanding achievement as an actor, producer and director in bringing *Henry V* to the screen'. The film also won the New York Critics Award of 1946.

All of this was vitally important to Larry. Few actors have ever had that much control over their films. But he *had* to do it that way. Absolute control, or as near as you can get to it, can be a characteristic of a victim of a sexual crime, and I believe that had much to do with driving Larry in that direction. The terms he used – such as 'the indignity of being raped by a New York stage director', and 'You don't want others fucking with you. I'll fuck up my own life, laddie' – are sentiments I recognise.

Over the next few years, Olivier and Richardson became increasingly fed up because they were forbidden from taking more active roles in the war. Larry spent some time touring military camps with his own one-man act designed to lift soldiers' spirits and generally whip up a suitable amount of patriotism. He would begin with a poem about Sir Henry Havelock, whose heroic exploits included putting down the Indian Mutiny. Larry then launched straight into *Henry V*. He said, 'By the time I got to "God for Harry . . ." I think they would have followed me anywhere.'

In 1944, Tyrone Guthrie asked the Sea Lords to release Olivier and Richardson to help him lead the Old Vic Company. Lord

Lytton, chairman of the Vic's board of governors, wrote to the Admiralty, pointing out the indispensability to the theatre of Richardson and Olivier, and how important they could be to the rehabilitation of the Old Vic, which he hoped the Admiralty would consider as nationally important.

As it happened, Richardson and Olivier had both been responsible for a number of damaged and written-off planes, and the Admiralty were only too happy to let them become civilians again.

19

The New Old Vic

Tyrone Guthrie, Ralph Richardson and Laurence Olivier began to revive the Old Vic Company, but not at the Old Vic itself because the roof had been damaged by bombs. It was the new Old Vic, based at the New Theatre in the West End of London.

Richardson and Olivier were basically allowed to choose what plays they wanted to do, and each would support the other. Richardson chose *Peer Gynt* to open with, which Guthrie directed. Then they would perform *Arms and the Man*, again with Richardson in the plumb part, as Bluntschli, and Olivier as Sergius, a part he hated. Then would come *Richard III*, with Olivier as Richard and Richardson in the supporting role of Richmond. Richardson chose *Uncle Vanya* to follow, in which he would play the main part, with Olivier as Astrov.

Larry was wondering how much of an impact he could make in *Richard III* which was, as he put it, 'rather a stale cup of tea; every actor-manager throughout history had played it'.

They needed to warm them up, and did so by taking *Arms and the Man* to Manchester, where Larry learned an important lesson that he felt I, as an aspiring actor, should know about:

> I was Sergius in *Arms and the Man*. Ralph had what was unquestionably the better part. One night Tony Guthrie came to see it, and as we walked back to our hotel, he said, 'Hmm, yes, liked you very much.'

I said, 'Thank you very much.' I wasn't happy and he could tell.

He said, 'What's the matter?'

I said, 'You know, Tony, if you weren't so tall I'd hit you for agreeing to the play and making me play that part.'

He said, 'Don't you love Sergius?'

I said, 'Are you out of your mind? How can you love a stupid fool like him?'

Tony said, 'Well, of course, if you can't love him, you'll never be any good as him, will you?' And I thought about that, and I realised he was right. You have to *love* whoever you play, even if you don't like him. You must love a character for his faults and everything that you might not like about him.

Peer Gynt opened at the New Theatre and played from April through to August. The new Old Vic Company was off to a good start. *Arms and the Man* followed, and then *Richard III*. Shakespeare forsook historical accuracy for dramatic effect, coming up with the tale of how, after Richard's military skills have helped to put his older brother Edward on the throne of England, the jealous and resentful Richard seeks the crown for himself, and conceives a lengthy and carefully calculated plan using deception, manipulation and outright murder to achieve his goal.

The play and the role filled Larry with dread. He told me:

I really didn't want to do *Richard III*. I didn't know the play very well, and Donald Wolfit had been playing it for years and had made the part his own.

I set about studying the piece, which is always my first task on a play. I had to find the character. I formed a picture of him in my mind. I knew I wanted to look like the most evil thing that ever lived. I based the make-up on an American theatre director called Jed Harris, who was easily the most loathsome man I'd ever known. Disney based the Big Bad Wolf on Jed Harris. I felt that this was my revenge on him.

But Richard of Gloucester wasn't just a villain. He was also at times a hero, and also a comic. He has to make the audience like him for all his villainy. He wins them over with his superbly dry sense of humour.

He has to be able to woo Lady Anne so he must be attractive too, somehow, and the only way I could think of doing that was to make him totally unrestrained in every way, so that when Richard looked at Lady Anne, she couldn't look at him; she had to turn her face away. And when she looked away, my Richard spent the time devouring her most intimate region, between her waist and upper thigh. By God, that was shocking. But it was right for my Richard. I had to make him *my* Richard.

Getting the right vocal effect was as important to Larry as getting the right look. 'The idea came to me of the thin reed of a sanctimonious scholar. It was thin and sharp as a blade, but powerful. It was perfect for the villain, the hero and the comic I was looking for. He was the perfect hypocrite. And it wasn't difficult to pitch. That sound helped me probably more than the look to formulate the character. He had venom coated with honey. He could demonstrate his sophistication and his wit, but beneath it all lay a sharp barb you did not want to get caught on.'

I mentioned how it appears to be his *Richard III* voice that all the mimics used.

He laughed. 'It is the voice the mimics think is really mine. When everyone, from comedians to young actors, copies me, they copy Richard. I am flattered, I suppose. But, really, actors, if they want to copy me, should find another of my voices. Or else they should keep it below the surface; they always go over the top with it.

'Some actors can do perfect impersonations of me. Michael Jayston is one. He does a marvellous impersonation of Ralph and Johnnie as well. Anthony Hopkins does me very well too.'

I have heard Michael Jayston perform his Larry impression, and also his hilarious Ralph Richardson and John Gielgud. Jayston told me, 'I found myself in a lift with Olivier and somebody else who said, "Oh, Larry, Michael does a wonderful impersonation of you. Go on, Michael, do it for Larry." So I was made to do it for Olivier, and he seemed to enjoy it.'

Anthony Hopkins actually provided Olivier's voice for a scene restored to *Spartacus* for which the soundtrack had long been lost. It's a subtle, believable impersonation, unlike the many *Richard III* imitations.

I also learned from Larry that you could 'play around' with Shakespeare to some extent.

When I was adapting *Richard III* I included parts of the end of *Henry VI Part 3* with Richard's opening soliloquy. Instead of it lasting the usual minute, it lasted for five or six minutes. And halfway through the opening I could tell I was in control of the audience with it, for when I said, 'Can I do this and cannot get the crown?' the audience made a sort of gasping sound, and I knew that whatever it was, and I never quite knew what *it* was, it had worked, and the audience was mine.

There comes a certain smell when you know you have a success. On our first night I was in the wings and I said to Nicholas Hannen, 'Do you smell it? A funny smell, like oysters.' He said yes, and a little later I said to Diana, 'Do you smell it too?' and she said, 'Yes, yes, I do.' It was everywhere. I knew I had seduced the audience as well as Lady Anne, and for an actor there is nothing like it in the world.

But it seems that Larry was not convinced of success on the opening night, according to John Mills who said:

On the night of the first performance of *Richard III*, Mary and I were just getting ready to leave for the theatre when Larry phoned us and said, 'You're coming tonight, aren't you, Johnnie?'

I said, 'Yes, of course we are. We can't wait. Good luck and we'll see you after the show.'

He said, 'Well, when you get here, come and see me in my dressing room before the show.'

I said, 'Come and see you before the show? But surely you don't want us —'

And before I could say any more, he said, 'But I *do* want. It's very important.'

After he hung up, I said to Mary, 'Why on earth does he want to see us *before* the show? Before *that* part?'

It just didn't make any sense. So we got to the theatre half an hour before curtain, and we went straight to Larry's dressing room where he was pacing up and down in full make-up and costume. He had the beaked nose and the long black hair and the hump on his back. He said, 'Sit down, my darlings.' Before we could say a word, he said, 'Now just listen to me. I want you to know that you are going to see a bloody awful performance tonight. The dress rehearsal was a disaster. I dried up at least half a dozen times. It's a bloody dreadful production and I just want you to know that I am terribly sorry because you are in for hours of boredom.'

Well, we tried to say all the right things we could think of and then we hurried out to the pub by the stage door and had two large drinks to prepare us for the terrible evening that was ahead of us.

Then we got into the theatre and found our seats. We were both so nervous and worried. The curtain rose, there was silence, and onto the stage limped Larry as Richard III. You could have heard a pin drop. The audience expected so much, and we were sitting there mortified with our fingers crossed.

Larry glared out at the auditorium, opened his mouth and gave the most inspired performance I have ever seen. His smile froze the blood and scared the audience. And he did things that night he had never done in rehearsals, and the rest of the cast had a heightened sense of anxiety, which added a feeling of spontaneous energy to the incredible drama that is already in the play. I tell you, anyone who saw that first night of *Richard III* were bloody lucky and I am sure none of them have ever forgotten it, because I certainly haven't. It was pure magic. And that's what Larry does in theatre. He performs a kind of magic. And maybe a part of that magic was to get us into his dressing room so that he would get in the right mood. I never knew if he really meant what he said.

I asked Larry if he meant what he told John Mills.

'Oh, I meant every word. Every actor has his own demons. I was convinced by mine that this was the end of me. I wanted Johnnie and darling Mary to know it before the rest of the audience did.'

So what happened?

'It is something you can't explain. There are times when an actor, while always keeping control of his performance, also loses himself a little and you do things you never did before that turn out to be wonderful moments for both the actor and the audience. They may never be repeated again. If you try to find them again, you overreach and you fail. So you just let them come, like angels, and they chase the demons away, and you remember every time it happens why you love to act upon the stage.'

While *Richard III* was still in rehearsals, Vivien became pregnant. Larry was elated. But a month later she miscarried. A week after that the play opened, and it is more than likely that Larry's despondency over how well he would do in the play was due to his depression over the loss of what would have been a baby boy.

Richard III was a phenomenal success, running from September 1944 to April 1945. In his book, *On Acting*, Olivier told a curious story about how, after the success of the opening night of the play, he returned to his hotel room and was writing a letter to Vivien when he heard a noise outside his window. Larry looked out and saw Richardson, the worse for drink, climbing up the drainpipe. Larry told him to get down before he killed himself, and Richardson descended to the ground. He then arrived at Larry's hotel room by more conventional means, pushed Larry, picked him up – 'like a baby', as Larry put it – then strode across to the balcony and held him over the edge.

'Ralph, I think we'll all look very silly in the morning,' Larry said as calmly as he could. Richardson said nothing. Larry asked, 'Why don't you pull me back?' Still no reply. 'I'm beginning to feel really nervous.'

After another pause, Richardson carried him back into the room and put him down. Larry wrote that he saw in Richardson's eyes that for a brief moment that Ralph had wanted to kill him.

Then Richardson left, and when they met the next morning, Larry said to him, 'Ralph, that was a rather near one, wasn't it?'

'Yes,' said Richardson, 'we were both very foolish. It was a double fault.'

Larry had no idea why he was at any fault.

Terry Coleman, in his authorised biography of Olivier, cast doubt on this story, which does seem far-fetched. But when I was in the company of Richardson and Gielgud in 1975, Gielgud suddenly said to him, 'Why did you try to kill Larry?'

I hadn't heard this story back then and couldn't believe my ears.

'Oh, I was just annoyed with him for being so smug,' Richardson replied.

'You tried to *kill* Olivier?' I asked.

'Oh, just a moment or two when I felt like throwing him from a great height.'

And that was all I could get out of him. So Larry's bizarre tale of how Ralph Richardson nearly threw him from a hotel balcony appears to be true.

Deciding it was time for a new home for himself and his frail Vivien, he bought Notley Abbey, at Thame, midway between London and Stratford-upon-Avon. It was a grand old house, partly in ruin, and it cost him a small fortune to have it rebuilt. Notley Abbey became the home of the Oliviers at the height of their marriage and careers, although they continued to spend time at Durham Cottage.

Uncle Vanya followed and was a great success for Richardson. After that Larry decided he wanted to direct a play, and he chose *The Skin of Our Teeth* for Vivien. Actually, what he really wanted to do was give Vivien the measure of his protection, and directing her seemed a good way to do that. He was, he said, 'the best director for Vivien. I knew how far I could get her to reach. And how to get her there. Another director could bully her, and I wasn't having any of that.'

He wouldn't let the critics mistreat her either. An incident occurred that brought a rare glimpse of Larry's anger. He was, in fact, uncharacteristically violent. 'There are times when I am overcome by anger and can scare myself to death at the violent streak that can suddenly rise in me,' he said. 'It is only on a rare occasion, but one occasion was when I struck one of our most respected – or maybe I should say disrespected – critics. On the opening night [of *The Skin of Our Teeth*] James Agate couldn't be bothered to take his seat before the curtain went up because he was too busy in the bar. I caught him as he was returning to his seat. The curtain was up. The play was under way. I felt an anger rise in me, and I raised my hand and slapped him round the face. I think there are many actors and directors who secretly admired me for that.'

While *The Skin of Our Teeth* played and kept Vivien occupied, Olivier, Richardson and the Old Vic company went on an ENSA tour of Europe with *Arms and the Man* and *Richard III*. The war in Europe had just ended and the war in Japan was soon to be over.

While away, Larry received news that Vivien had become ill with tuberculosis, but he was unable to get home for a further three weeks. When he finally got back, he took her to Scotland to recuperate. But in doing so, he missed vitally important rehearsal time for the next season, which consisted of *Henry IV Part 1*, *Henry IV Part 2*, *Oedipus* and *The Critic*. The last two plays were a double feature, and Larry was left with only four weeks to rehearse them all.

He was ready to play Hotspur in *Henry IV Part 1* when it opened at the New Theatre on 26 September 1945. John and Mary Mills were among those who went to see as many of Larry's opening nights as they could.

Sir John told me:

We saw Larry as Hotspur in *Henry IV*. With Larry, you never know what he is going to look like because he finds a staggering look for every part. He is a master of make-up. I don't know of another actor who is as artful and as creative as he is. Lon Chaney could do it, but I think Larry does it best of all.

He walked on to the stage and he just took your breath away. He was just so sensational. His costume was simply gorgeous, and he had a golden red wig that was sensational enough, but when it came to his soliloquy he stood in a single spotlight that made his hair and his whole look totally and utterly staggering. He left a few beats before starting in on his speech to allow the audience to take in the vision, although the man sitting next to us said in a rather loud and embarrassing voice, 'Oh, here's old Ginger again!'

But Larry didn't miss a beat and gave a superlative performance. And ever since then we have always sent him first-night telegrams that say, 'Oh, here's old Ginger again. Love Johnnie and Mary.' Larry has always thought that a grand joke. He can take his work seriously but not always himself, you see.

Then came *Oedipus* in the title role as well as playing Mr Puff in Sheridan's *The Critic*. That double bill, which became referred to as *Oedipuff* was, Larry admitted, his attempt to try and 'top himself'.

May and June of 1946 was spent in New York as the Old Vic Company played *Uncle Vanya, Henry IV Part 1, Henry IV Part 2* and the double bill of *Oedipus* and *The Critic*, all to great acclaim and success. But there was little money in it, which wouldn't have mattered to Larry if it was not for the fact that he was paying £3,500 a year alimony to Jill, and he was only earning £60 a week at the Old Vic – and that was only when he actually acted.

Looking how best to capitalise on himself, he set up Laurence Olivier Productions – LOP – in May 1946. LOP was there to provide any kind of service to theatre, film, market gardening, landscaping and even as a broker. He and Vivien were the only shareholders. As well as exploiting their talents for film and stage, they were also able to farm the land at Notley and subsidise the upkeep of that house. All expenses for their London house, Durham Cottage, were paid by LOP because it was necessary for when they were working in London, thus making any bills legitimate business expenses.

In time, LOP produced plays and put actors under contract, and actors under contract could be loaned out to other producers for a fee. LOP grew to be a considerable going concern. It continued to operate until 1972, but by then much of Larry's work, and Joan Plowright's (his third wife) was managed by another company he had founded, Wheelshare.

The season ended in triumph in New York for the Old Vic Company, and they took a break before starting again in September. During the break, the board of the National Theatre invited Richardson, Tony Guthrie and Olivier to merge the Old Vic with the

National Theatre Company. Larry called it 'a marriage between the NT and the Old Vic', and suggested 'they were the groom and we the bride'.

Richardson had some doubts, telling Olivier, 'It'll be the end of us. It won't be our dear, friendly, semi-amateurish Old Vic any more. It'll be of government interest now with some appointed intendant swell at the top, not our sweet old friendly governors eating out of our hands and doing what we tell them.' He predicted they would not stand for 'a couple of actors bossing the place around any more'. And he warned, 'We shall be out, cockie.'

Accepting their fate, Olivier and Richardson agreed that they should no longer both be in every play the Old Vic produced, since being in everything and going everywhere together was proving exhausting.

There were even some signs of small cracks in their association when the directors of the Old Vic met to discuss their new season. Richardson had always wanted to play King Lear. But again he didn't put it forward, so Olivier announced he would like to play and produce *King Lear*.

'It was pure villainy,' Larry said. 'I didn't really want to play Lear.'

Larry offered to swap parts with him, but Richardson declined.

The friendship survived that hiccup because, said Larry, 'Ralph is my most dearest friend. We have always been rivals in the best sense of the word, and we ran a theatre company together, the Old Vic, which was the best around at that time.'

I asked Larry in 1978 why he hadn't wanted to play Lear, a role that was, in the minds of many of the great actors, *the* part to play.

'Because I was still almost a wee laddie [he was 39 years old] and Lear is an old, old man. The problem with Lear is, when you have the strength to play that man-killer of a part, you're too young, and when you've reached the right age, you don't have the strength any more.'

I asked how important it was for him to direct *King Lear* as well as play the part.

He said, 'Oh, I had the audacity to think I could direct it better than anyone else. I might have done better if I had left that task to someone else. But really, Michael, when you're about to play what you feel is the most important part of your life, you don't trust anyone else to get it right. You can only trust yourself.'

In 1981, I came back to that question, and he said, 'We are all abused in some way or another. Lear was abused by Goneril and Regan [Lear's two daughters who professed to love their father but only because he was giving them each a third of his kingdom]. He didn't know that Cordelia [the third of his daughters] really did truly love him. And he disinherited her. I knew a little about how that must have felt, to be abused by those who claim to love you.'

It was also a matter of the control he had. Once he had tasted that kind of control, with his film of *Henry V*, there really was no going back. He needed, in 1946, to establish his control over his stage work, and no actor can have greater control than to direct at the same time. Directors can be bullies and blinkered and know a lot less about the character than the actor playing him. That can open the way to being verbally abused by an egotistical and tyrannical director, and for someone who has suffered one of the worst forms of abuse, that kind of treatment becomes unacceptable and intolerable. It can happen in all kinds of jobs. I have experienced just that in many areas of my work.

Many saw Larry as an egotistical ham. I saw – and see – him as an incredibly creative artist with a touch of genius and a whole lot of insecurity. He *had* to be good at what he did, and he *had* to be liked and even loved for his work. It wasn't ego that drove him but survival. His success may have fed his ego, but his success was driven by survival.

1946 was seen out by the incredible success of *King Lear*, first at the New Theatre in London, and then at the Theatre des Champs in Paris. In 1947, however, Larry didn't appear on stage at all. He was too busy making his next film, *Hamlet*.

20

Knighthood

1947 didn't start too well for Olivier when Ralph Richardson was knighted in the New Year's Honours list for his services to the theatre. Frankly, Larry was depressed that he had not been included; he felt he had done just as much as, if not more than, Richardson considering that he had become a success in Hollywood and, most of all, had created one of the great achievements of the cinema with *Henry V*. And he had also put his life on the line for his country, although that was not something he would publicly admit.

He had planned to return to Hollywood; success on the London stage did not bring financial rewards, and he needed the money. He had been considering a film of *Cyrano de Bergerac*, again stepping somewhat on Richardson's toes, and he wanted to do the film with Vivien, who was still recovering from tuberculosis. But Filippo del Giudice had been trying to persuade him to make another Shakespeare film.

'There's no doubt the money I would have got in Hollywood would have done me well,' Larry told me. 'But the idea of doing another filmed Shakespeare was too tempting.'

In January 1947, Larry decided he would make a film of *Hamlet*. He made that decision on the day Richardson was knighted. I think Larry was saying to those who make such decisions, 'Right, I'll bloody well show you.'

Hamlet was to be a very different kind of film to *Henry V*, which he had seen as being 'not quite a film, not quite a play'. *Hamlet* would be very much a film, and he chose to shoot it in black-and-white, not to save money, but because he wanted to use the black-and-white camera's ability to shoot deep focus, which meant that he could shoot characters in the foreground, in the middle ground and in the background in one shot, and all would be in focus. He wanted to have a shot of Hamlet in the foreground, seeing Ophelia a long way down the corridor, sitting on a wooden chair with love clearly showing in her eyes – all in focus. He was only guessing that this technique would work, but work it did, with the skill of his director of photography, Desmond Dickinson, to show him how.

To play Ophelia, he chose a young actress, Jean Simmons, who at the age of only eighteen had already appeared in eleven films, including the 1945 film version of *Caesar and Cleopatra*, which had starred Vivien Leigh. So she was not completely unknown to the Oliviers.

But Jean was not a Shakespearean actress. 'I did Shakespeare at school, but I just wasn't interested at all,' Miss Simmons told me (on the set of *Dominique* in 1977). 'So *Hamlet* was my first Shakespeare. I worked with a marvellous woman, Molly Terrain, who coached me.'

I asked her if she had been apprehensive about performing Shakespeare, and she replied, 'Apprehensive? Yes. But you don't say no to his lordship.'

She remembered being surrounded by so many experienced Shakespearean actors such as Basil Sydney, Felix Aylmer and Anthony Quayle. 'It was very exciting and they were all marvellous to me. While Larry was busy doing something else, they would try and explain what things meant. I was a bit out of the league.'

She had just undergone some mild cosmetic surgery, having her teeth filed down, and this was the cause of frustration for Larry that resulted in Jean bursting into tears on the set. 'I'd just had them done,' she said, 'and there was one scene when every time I took a breath the cold air touched a nerve and I couldn't say my lines properly, and Larry did not understand, and he was furious because it was very late and he wanted to get on with the shot. And I burst into tears. And then somebody told him what it was, and he was super and he was so upset that he had not understood.'

Hamlet, released in 1947, garnered reviews that ranged from pleasing to raves, as did Larry's performance in it. 'Laurence Olivier leaves no doubt that he is one of our greatest living actors,' said Milton Shulman in the *Evening News*.

'A man who can do what Laurence Olivier does for Shakespeare, and for those who treasure or will yet learn to treasure Shakespeare, is certainly among the more valuable men of his time,' wrote James Agee in *Time*. 'This [*Hamlet*] in every piece of casting, in every performance, is about as nearly solid as gold can be. The most gratifying thing in this film is to watch this talented artist, in the height of his accomplishment, work at one of the most wonderful roles ever written.'

The American Academy of Motion Picture Arts and Sciences awarded the film Oscars for Best Picture, Best Actor to Olivier, and two to Roger Furse, one for his art direction and the other for his costume designs. Curiously, Olivier didn't win Best Director, although he was nominated; that went to John Huston for *The Treasure of the Sierra Madre*.

Larry remained proud of *Hamlet* the movie: 'I think the film stands up after all these years. I am still very proud of it,' he said in 1978.

It was during the filming of *Hamlet* that Larry received a letter from the King offering him a knighthood and asking if he would accept it. He did accept, but only after writing to Noël Coward, basically asking for his approval; Larry knew that a knighthood had been withheld from Coward because of his sexuality.

On 8 July 1947, at the age of forty, he became the youngest ever actor to be knighted. Apparently, both he and Richardson felt a pang of guilt that they had received such an honour and John Gielgud had not.

Gielgud told me, 'Both Ralph and Larry were kind enough to write to me and apologise for their knighthoods, which was really very sweet of them.'

Knighthoods for actors were, back then, rare. There's no doubt that Larry received his because he had achieved so much on stage and on film. But I wonder if there was also a nod towards his secret work during the war, and when I suggested this to David Niven, he said, 'People get honoured for all kinds of things the public never know about.'

Larry was not saying one way or the other. I know – I asked, and got no response, just a mischievous grin and a slight flicker of the eyebrows.

21

Bipolar

In 1948, at the request of the British Council, Larry and Vivien accepted a request to tour Australia. The tour came complete with a very attractive financial offer, which the Oliviers needed. From March to October, Larry and Vivien performed in *The School for Scandal*, *Richard III* and *The Skin of Our Teeth*. During the tour, Larry received a letter from the Old Vic's board of governors that it had decided that he and Richardson were no longer required following the 1948–49 season. He could do nothing about it until the long tour was over.

As if that were not bad enough, he injured his knee, which had been weakened by the constant limp he affected as Richard III, and was also suffering from exhaustion. Part of it was to do with his work, but much of it was due to Vivien's increasing habit of wanting to stay up for hours each night and well into the morning. They didn't know it, but her bipolar disorder was taking hold of her.

There was another problem. Larry and Vivien had always been a passionate couple. But Larry was not getting any younger, he had a bad leg, and the work was wearing him out. He didn't have the strength to do the work *and* perform in bed for Vivien. This frustrated him as much as it did her; his sexual drive was usually high. Suddenly, he had lost interest.

All of this was going on when into their lives came a young Australian actor, Peter Finch. They saw him and the company he was a part of performing a play by Molière, in a factory of all places, with the workers as their audience.

Peter Finch said in 1972 (as I sat with him and Anthony Quayle):

It was John Kay [who was a director of the company] who had the idea of inviting the Oliviers. I thought he was mad to even think of inviting them. We had a tin-pot company and were performing in a glass factory to workers who probably never saw a play before. I told John that we just weren't good enough to perform in front of the Oliviers, for God's sake. We argued and I said I didn't want any part of it.

So John went ahead and contacted the Oliviers and they said they would come, and when I heard this I told John he would land us all in deep shit.

But after the performance, they both said how good they thought the play was and how good they thought I was in it, which was marvellous for the ego. But that's all you expect. So I was shocked when Larry said to me that when I came to England I was to contact him and he'd find me a job. And that was the making of me, and if John Kay had listened to me, I would never have met the Oliviers and never made it and . . . ! Oh, and there would never have been so much heartache and heartbreak.'

The heartbreak would come because of the infamous affair between Finch and Vivien, whose illness was worsening.

Larry had no problem telling me, in 1976, what he thought of Finch professionally: 'Peter Finch was a brilliant actor, and I knew that as soon as I saw him performing in a factory in Sydney. He had that special quality some actors have that makes them star actors. You couldn't help but watch him. And he was a natural clown. We were rocking with laughter at his performance, which was perfect in technique and timing. I knew immediately that he could become one of the great and truly gifted actors of our time.'

Considering all that was about to happen, this might be thought of as being remarkably generous of Larry, but despite the personal woes that afflicted their lives with Vivien at the centre of it all, Larry always liked Finch, but didn't love him; in fact, deep down, he probably hated Finch. But all that was yet to come.

At the end of the Australian tour, and during a visit to New Zealand, Larry had his injured knee operated on. When they boarded the ship for home, he was stretchered to the dockside, placed in a cradle and hoisted by a crane on to the ship. Vivien's impatience with her infirm husband grew, and she began to flirt outrageously with a young man in their company. Larry begged her not to be so obvious and cause them all humiliation.

He seems to have taken it very calmly, as though he were not surprised. Perhaps, by then, he had begun to realise that Vivien's behaviour was irregular but also that it was understandable if, being unable to get satisfaction from him, she should look elsewhere. But this was not, I feel, due to any excessive understanding on his part, but more a case of his own insecurity and also an inability to do anything about it. Many men would have laid down the law. Larry never did, even when things grew worse. He was almost compliant, subdued. He was, slowly, entering into a strange state of limbo, becoming unable to control the one person he truly loved. She was the one person he would allow, until it became too intolerable to bear, to emotionally rape him – which is how the sexually abused victim tends to think.

But for the time being, on that voyage home, Vivien, realising how she was behaving, promised not to do it any more.

Peter and his wife Tamara arrived in England in November 1948. Finch recalled, 'Tamara found us a small, cheap flat in Notting Hill Gate, and I went job-hunting. I phoned the Oliviers' house and was told they were in America and would be back in a couple of days. I thought I wouldn't be hearing from them again, but then a day or so later some flowers arrived from them with an invitation to go and have a drink at their house.

'So we went round to their house in Chelsea, just for half an hour, and then they had to dash off to some dinner. Larry said to me to go and see his agent and told me to keep in touch. And I thought, "Oh well, nothing is going to happen."

'Not long after, Larry told me he had a play he wanted me to read for.'

Finch was working on a film when he got a call from Larry. 'Larry said the script of a new play was being sent to my home that night and he wanted me to read it.' The play was *Daphne Laureola* by James Birdie; the star of the play was to be Edith Evans.

Finch recalled: 'Cecil Tennant [Olivier's manager] personally brought the play around and he told me to be at the [Wyndham] theatre on Tuesday for an audition. I turned up and so did a lot of other actors. Standing on that stage was very intimidating, looking out into the dark and not being able to see who was sitting out there. I knew that Larry was there, and so were Vivien and also Edith Evans.

'There were two chairs on the stage, and I was called out and asked to read a scene with Edith Evans's understudy. Then a voice – "When you're ready." So we did the scene, and then Larry said, "Thank you very much, Peter. Will you wait just a minute, please?"

'You could hear these hushed voices. I didn't know what was going on. The next thing I knew was a rich voice of a woman calling my name, and then I saw Edith Evans looking up at me, and she said, "I shall look forward to seeing you at rehearsal on Tuesday."

'Larry had already gone, but he phoned me later and said, "You'll be under contract to Laurence Olivier Productions." And then he said, "I'm so glad you came and read for us and that you'll be joining us for a while," as though I was doing him a favour, which was typically gracious of him.'

The play opened on 23 March 1949. During its run, Tamara gave birth to a daughter, Anita. At the christening, at which the Oliviers were Anita's godparents, Larry turned up at the church with a script under his arm. Finch recalled, 'He said to me, "Let's go down to the crypt for a while because I want to talk to you where there is quiet," so down we went to the crypt and he said, "I have this new play for you, *The Damascus Blade*." I said, "Couldn't this have waited until after the christening?" And he said, "I have you in mind for this play, but if I should happen to see another and think on a whim that he looks the better prospect, I might not even get to tell you about it. You have to grab these things when the moments are there or everything moves on at such a pace that you are left behind. Now, do you want to read this or not?" And I said, "Yes".'

The Damascus Blade opened in Newcastle on 13 March 1950. In the leading role was Larry's close friend John Mills. 'I liked Finchie very much and we became lifelong friends,' John Mills said. Yet despite their friendship they remembered the fate that awaited *The Damascus Play* quite differently, and also Olivier's part in it.

Finch said, 'Johnnie Mills wasn't happy in the play and it wasn't getting good notices wherever we played. I was just glad to be working but Johnnie was worried about the effect the play would have on his career if it bombed in London. So Johnnie called Larry and begged him not to bring the play to London. I know that he wanted this play in London because it was a good part for me and I was under contract to him. And he'd invested a great deal of money in it and had directed it, but Johnnie had been his friend since way back and so Larry reluctantly cancelled the London run as a favour to Johnnie.'

John Mills recalled it differently:

When Larry became an actor-manager and took over the St James's Theatre, he chose a play for me to do called *The Damascus Blade*. This was too good to be true for me because Larry was not only the best actor in England and probably the world, but he was also a wonderful director. Larry started rehearsals having worked out every single move and every little piece of business on each line. I prefer to have a little more freedom when blocking a play, but he was the director and so I applied myself to his style.

When we opened in Newcastle, Larry came to the opening night and the house was jam-packed. But by the end of the first performance we knew that the audience didn't like it. Mary and I went to supper after the show with Larry and also Roger Furse, who had designed the sets, and I said to Larry, 'You know, Larry boy, I just don't feel the audience has any sympathy for me. Somewhere I lost them and they didn't give a damn about the character.' So we went over and over the play while we had our supper and we decided we should make some cuts in the dialogue.

The next morning we met for breakfast and Larry read the review in the local newspaper. He hated the play. Larry said, 'OK darling, that isn't the greatest notice we've ever had, but it's clearly not his cup of tea. So don't worry about it. He's probably just on loan from the sports page anyway.' And we laughed and cheered up.

But everywhere we went [Edinburgh, Glasgow and Brighton] the reviews were bad and the audiences just didn't take to it. We were due to take the play to London to the St James's Theatre. Larry called me in Glasgow and asked how the performance went, and I said, 'Well, Larry boy, pretty much the same as before – they just don't like it.'

Larry then said, 'OK, listen, Johnnie. You are my dearest friend and the last thing I want to do is bring you into London with a flop. Would you be very upset if we simply accepted defeat and called it off?'

I said, 'My dear Larry, I would be most relieved. We've done our best and we just can't make the bloody piece work and I don't think we ever will.'

He said, 'All right, Johnnie, you and Mary come down to Notley Abbey next weekend and we'll drown our sorrows in the cellar and dream up something else to do together.'

Well, we managed to accomplish the first but failed to do the last, and now I will never get the chance to actually act upon the stage with Larry.

I asked Larry which was the truer version and he said, 'Nobody makes up my mind for me. I make up my own mind. I cancelled the engagement in the West End because it wasn't good enough. Johnnie wasn't happy in it, and the critics didn't like it, and neither did the audience. I don't recall whether Johnnie asked me to cancel it or not, but the decision was mine.'

Larry completed his commitment to the Old Vic by performing *Richard III* in January 1949, and then directing the double bill of *The Proposal* and *Antigone* in February at the New Theatre.

In the spring, Larry and Vivien were at their Durham Cottage, just finishing a meal on the small winter-garden porch, when Vivien suddenly announced, 'I don't love you any more.'

He was unable to speak. She explained there was no one else and that she loved him now like a brother. He wrote, 'I felt as if I had been told that I had been condemned to death.'

He wrote how a close friend told him he 'should have kicked her out, or upped and outed' himself. But Larry admitted that he simply couldn't grasp what was happening. He wrote how he couldn't bring himself to disillusion people, and so he kept it all bottled up. Vivien had suggested they carry on as if nothing had happened, and he complied. He was doing exactly what she wanted. Maybe this was her illness, or maybe just a matter of convenience for her. But he did what she wanted him to; he was unable to resist her. He even accepted her invitations to make love, but, he wrote, 'I never looked to be happy again.'

He was powerless to resist Vivien, as he had been powerless to resist the priest. He had been beguiled by both and, whether he was aware of it or not, I believe he was reliving that abusive experience. He had loved Father Heald, and he loved Vivien Leigh. He was, literally, unable to resist them, even though it brought him misery.

22

The Cleopatras

Larry could do nothing but throw himself into his work. He directed Vivien in *A Streetcar Named Desire* at the Aldwych Theatre in London. He was still hard at work on maintaining the career of a woman who didn't love him, and who had a hold over him that he was unable to break.

His one great strength, apart from his talent and his stature in the theatre, was his determination to be his own manager. His own career was the one thing he could still hope to control in a life controlled by an unloving wife who also happened to be his acting partner. But he could never have complete control of his own career while he was still doing exactly what Vivien wanted him to.

Following *Venus Observed*, *The Damascus Blade* and *Captain Carvello*, all of which he directed only, he went to Hollywood to make *Carrie* for William Wyler. Vivien was already there, making the film version of *A Streetcar Named Desire*, a role that would bring her a second Oscar for her performance as Blanche du Bois.

Larry was now only too happy to work the Wyler way, and making the film was a happy experience. He played a restaurant manager in Chicago who falls for a small-town girl, Carrie (Jennifer Jones), and becomes so infatuated with her that he steals $10,000 and abandons his family to run away with her to New York. She finally leaves him, in poverty, for a stage career.

There seemed to be something about the story that reflected his real life. Maybe that is why he was so good in it. Dilys Powell, writing in the *Sunday Times*, said, 'Wyler has delicately caught the tragedy of a man's downfall and decay; and Sir Laurence Olivier's acting is a triumph of autumnal sensibility.'

LOP was expanding in all directions, allowing Larry to focus on something other than his failing marriage; something he was trying to pretend wasn't happening. But still he had to live and work with Vivien – his own decision – and he and his manager Cecil Tennant, as well as designer Roger Furse and Tony Bushel (who was a long-time trusted friend), met in Paris with their respective wives, to discuss what Larry and Vivien should do next on stage.

They decided on Shaw's *Caesar and Cleopatra* with Larry as Caesar and Vivien as Cleopatra, and Shakespeare's *Antony and Cleopatra*, Vivien again as Cleo and Larry as Mark Antony. They would alternate the plays, first in England, and then in New York. Larry decided not to direct *Antony and Cleopatra* but hired Michael Benthall to do it, although Larry did give Vivien one valuable piece of direction. 'Darling, do me a favour,' he told her, 'just try and lower your voice a whole octave.'

He had taught her, when they did *A Streetcar Named Desire*, how to lower her voice just enough to make the difference. (This was something he taught me also – 'Your voice is very light and a shade too high, lad,' he said when I delivered my Antony speech to him in 1979. 'You can train yourself to bring the voice down an octave and even two, like this,' and he showed me how.)

Shaw's *Caesar and Cleopatra* is considered Shaw's first great play. It opens as Julius Caesar's armies arrive in Egypt to conquer the divided land. He meets the young Cleopatra who, having been driven from Alexandria, hides at night between the paws of a sphinx. He persuades her to accept her position as co-ruler of Egypt with Ptolemy Dionysus, her brother.

Shaw's Cleopatra is a spoiled and vicious 16-year-old girl who becomes a mature leader, while his Julius Caesar is a lonely, austere man, as much a philosopher and teacher as a soldier. Shaw wanted to show that it wasn't love but politics that drew Cleopatra to Caesar, stressing the political relations between the Roman and Egyptian conquerors.

Antony and Cleopatra embodies the love story of its title characters. Shakespeare's Cleopatra is a mature temptress and arguably the greatest female role he wrote, and one Charlton Heston told me was, in his opinion, impossible to play. 'I've seen all the great Cleopatras,' he told me in 1999 (he was helping me with my own production of that

Laurence Olivier and Valerie Hobson star in *Q Planes*, 1939

Olivier with Ronald Coleman-type moustache as he appeared in *The Yellow Passport* (aka *The Yellow Ticket*) in 1931, with Elissa Landi

Olivier as the Roman general Crassus, alongside Tony Curtis in *Spartacus*

The amazing transformation into *Othello* for the film version, in 1965

Laurence Olivier in *Henry V*, 1944

Hamlet – Felix Aylmer,
Laurence Olivier, Basil
Sydney, Eileen Herlie
and Jean Simmons –
1948

Left: Olivier's second film as a director, *Hamlet,* in 1948

Below: Romeo and Juliet – Vivien Leigh and Laurence Olivier

Taking London by storm, Olivier and Vivien Leigh as *Caesar and Cleopatra*, 1951

Above: Blacked up again, to play the Mahdi in *Khartoum*, 1966

Left: Olivier's first filmed Shakespeare, *As You Like It*, in 1936, as Orlando

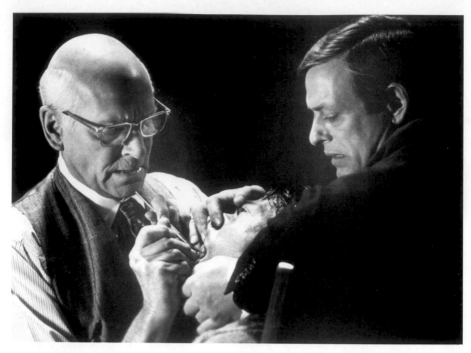

Above: Olivier tortures Dustin Hoffman in the
dentist's chair in *Marathon Man*, 1976

Below: A now legendary screen partnership; Olivier and Michael Caine in *Sleuth*, 1973

play), 'and believe me, as great as the actresses were who played her, none of them succeeded.'

Which naturally prompted me to ask him, 'Did you see Vivien Leigh play Cleopatra on stage?'

He replied, 'I saw her in both *Caesar and Cleopatra* and *Antony and Cleopatra* on successive nights. She was very good in the first as a child Cleopatra, and Larry was very good as a doddering Caesar, which he underplayed perfectly. But in the Shakespeare part, she was inadequate as the mature queen of Egypt. I noticed that Olivier played Antony as flatly as possible to give her some space to soar, which she was unable to do.

'That really was a loving thing for Olivier to do for her, to give her that space. He was, after all, establishing himself at that time as the actor of his time, if not the century. It was a *husbandly* thing to do. I understand that. But it wasn't right for the play. So, no, Vivien Leigh was not, in *Antony and Cleopatra*, a great Cleopatra.'

Larry, though, was convinced Vivien was superb in both plays. 'She was the best Cleopatra ever,' he said. Certainly the public loved seeing the Oliviers in the two great plays, and they ran through the whole of 1951, first in Manchester and London, then in New York from December 1951 to April 1952.

Laurence Olivier Productions was busy providing or producing work for many, including Orson Welles, who in October 1951, put on *Othello* at the St James's Theatre for LOP. Playing Iago to Welles's Othello was Peter Finch, who recalled, 'Larry came to see *Othello* and after the performance he told me I was giving a dying inflectional fall at the end of my lines and this was taking all of the meaning out of the poetry. He told me, "You must learn to use your diaphragm like an opera singer does when you do Shakespeare, or the poetry sags with a lot of unnecessary pauses for breath." I said, "You mean I need more puff." And he said, "You've got all the puff you need, you just need to control it." And he was right. I was bloody awful as Iago.'

Larry, though, didn't think Finch was bloody awful. He even admitted, 'I was terribly jealous because, you see, when I see an actor playing a part well that I have played, I am always jealous. When watching someone play what I like to think as *my* part, I remember that character and know him, and I can't be objective about someone else's interpretation.

'It was the same when Charlton Heston came to me, asking me to direct his film of *Antony and Cleopatra*. I *had* to turn it down because

I couldn't have directed him as Antony. I wanted to play the bloody part myself. As it was, Chuck's Antony is as good as I have seen anywhere.'

In February 1952, he somehow found time to direct *Venus Observed* by Christopher Fry. Rex Harrison, who starred in it, told me:

> We opened in Philadelphia, and I accepted the part on the condition that Lilli [Palmer] was in it also. Larry was happy to go along with this because he only really wanted to act with *his* wife [Vivien] as well, and he was at that time in New York with Vivien doing the two Cleopatra plays. He didn't need to get involved with our play but he really put himself out, travelling by train each day from New York where he was doing the Cleopatras each night, to Philadelphia to direct the play and supervise and he really made the producer's job a lot easier. He was so full of enthusiasm and he said to me, 'Rex, I played this part in London, but it is yours now, and I want you to be bloody good in it, and I know you will be.' I felt that was a very generous gesture and one that was sincerely meant.
>
> We didn't agree on every aspect of the role. He felt strongly about some aspects, I felt strongly about others. But he didn't bully me into doing anything I didn't agree with. In fact, he encouraged me to make the part my own, and he was really very helpful and was a marvellous director.
>
> After the play moved to New York, Larry began to feel the play wasn't working so well in the huge theatre we were in. It's really a very intimate play and should be performed in a small theatre, but we were in this huge barn called the Century Theatre. Larry got so desperate that he wrote to Christopher Fry and very eloquently asked him if the more difficult bits of the play – the parts that really didn't keep the audience's interest – could be cut. But even without the difficult bits, the play didn't work there and we were, frankly, a disaster.

Before they left England to do the two *Cleopatras* in New York, Larry became aware that Vivien was unusually nervous, behaving like a frightened child. She needed his protection and he was glad to give it. It made him feel like he was in his rightful place.

Then in New York she deteriorated. He would find her in the bedroom, sitting on the bed and wringing her hands, crying in terrible distress. She was inconsolable, so he persuaded her to see a psychiatrist, who prescribed some intensive therapy. But she refused it. Larry tried to change her mind, but she was so insistent and so distressed at the thought of further appointments that he relented.

Her bipolar disorder was beginning to overtake her. What amazed Larry so much, in due time, was how she was able to disguise her symptoms from everybody else. But he began to recognise there were times when she was desperately low, and other times when she was flying high. He just didn't understand why. And she didn't have the capacity to be able to see it in herself. It would all get much worse before it could ever begin to get better.

23

Bloody Finch

When the *Cleopatras* ended their hugely successful run, the Oliviers returned to England, by which time Vivien appeared to have recovered, much to Larry's relief. He made his one and only musical film, *The Beggar's Opera*, playing a dashing highwayman in this adaptation of John Gay's operetta. He wanted to actually sing rather than have a professional singer dub him, so he took singing lessons and was very proud of his achievements. Peter Brook directed; it was his first film, and Larry produced it in partnership with Herbert Wilcox. During the filming of one of the duels, Larry injured a calf and the production was set back a month. The film was not a success, in fact it was Larry's first film flop in some time.

He and Vivien were offered a film by Paramount called *Elephant Walk*, with some filming to be shot on location in Ceylon (now Sri Lanka). Larry was still deep in post-production on *The Beggar's Opera* and declined. He wrote in his autobiography that Vivien was enthusiastic to do the film and told him that if he wouldn't play the male lead, she knew for a fact that Peter Finch would.

Olivier wrote, 'The penny dropped, and it dropped with the knell of a high-pitched chapel bell.'

Vivien had taken a shine to Finch. Larry felt helpless as she and Finch flew out to Ceylon in January 1953. All he knew for sure was that for a while he had some peace in his life, and he relished it. It was to be the calm before the storm.

But the events as remembered by Olivier in his autobiography were not as they were recalled by the producer of *Elephant Walk*, Irving Asher, who told me in London in 1975, 'Olivier felt the script was poor, but Vivien liked it. So I asked Olivier if he could suggest someone for the role, and he took me to see Peter Finch in a play, *An Italian Straw Hat*, and I signed him straight away, right after the performance, even though I couldn't tell how well he would do as a screen actor, but I trusted Larry's judgement. The film was a big break for Peter Finch and that was all down to Laurence Olivier.'

It didn't take long for the people working on the film to realise that something wasn't right about Vivien's behaviour. Dana Andrews, who co-starred in the picture, told me on a visit he paid to London in 1974, 'I could tell that something was wrong with Vivien early on in Ceylon. She was full of energy – too much energy, I thought. She never wanted to stop – working all day and then she and Peter wanted me to go to a party when I had work to do the next day, and Vivien would say, "You old stick-in-the-mud," and off she and Peter would go. Oh, he was infatuated with her. We could all see that. I like a drink, but they were drinking heavily.'

Asher recalled, 'By the last week in Ceylon, Vivien didn't know what she was or where she was. She had an attack of hysteria where she was uncontrollable. It shook everyone. She was following Peter around and calling him "Larry". It floored Peter.'

When talking to Peter Finch about his time on *Elephant Walk* (sitting that day at the studio with Anthony Quayle), he said, 'I had no idea that Vivien was ill.'

Quayle said to him, 'You can't have missed it, Peter.'

'Look, Tony, I was probably too drunk most of the time to realise that Vivien wasn't drunk as well. She was just sick. Very, very sick.'

'I knew Vivien well enough to know that you couldn't help her when she was having one of her highs,' said Quayle.

Finch responded, 'I didn't know what to do. She would break down in floods of tears for no reason. Then she would become Blanche from *Streetcar* and recite her lines. I tried to keep calm but I was panicking because I knew we had a lot more filming to do and she was not going to make it.'

The time came for them to return by plane to Hollywood to film at Paramount Studios. Irving Asher recalled, 'We had only just taken off when Vivien became hysterical and we had to have her sedated.'

Finch admitted he was making a terrible mess of everything. 'I had stupidly fallen in love with Vivien, but I finally knew it had to end and

I tried to tell her that, but she was determined to have me for herself. And she wasn't letting Tamara stand in the way. And then it got terrifying.

'Vivien threw a big party for me to meet all her Hollywood friends. And she just suddenly went for Tamara with a pair of scissors. She had to be physically restrained. After that she broke down and left.'

'She tried to kill her?' asked Quayle.

'God, yes!'

'Didn't anyone have her arrested?' I asked.

'You don't arrest Mrs Olivier on a charge of attempted murder,' said Finch.

'But for God's sake, Peter, she tried to kill your wife,' said Quayle.

'But she didn't know she did,' said Finch. 'On the set she couldn't remember a thing. It was like her memory had been wiped.'

I asked him, 'You mean about what she did to Tamara?'

'Yes. And everything. She couldn't remember her lines, and I went over her lines again and again, but it was obvious she was not going to work again. I wish I had known she was ill from the start.'

'Would that have stopped you falling in love with her?' I asked him.

'To be honest, any man would have fallen in love with her. She had a magic quality. She was beguiling.'

'That's very true,' said Quayle.

'So you don't think there was any way you could stop yourself?' I asked Finch.

'Oh, bloody hell, I could have if I'd tried. I didn't want to try. I was flattered. But it went too far. And in the end she wouldn't allow even me to help her, or anyone else, and that's when they called for Larry to come for her.'

While they waited for Larry, Vivien became hysterical, and Stewart Granger and David Niven both tried to calm her at her house, but it was an impossible task. Said Stewart Granger, 'We spent most of the day and the whole of the next night trying to get her to swallow a couple of pills to sedate her enough to allow a couple of nurses to take her to a clinic. But Vivien managed to gradually empty the bottle of sedative pills into the swimming pool.

'She stayed awake all night watching television – naked! Finally a nurse came, and I had to hold Vivien down on the bed while the nurse injected her with a sedative. I hated being so rough with her, and as she lay there she looked up at me and said, "And I thought you were my friend." It cut right through me.'

Larry flew into Los Angeles to collect Vivien and to discover that she and Finch had been having an affair, although he wasn't surprised. Perhaps because he knew Vivien was ill, or perhaps because he was simply unable still to tear himself from her, so strong was the power she had over him, he somehow bore the humiliation of everyone else knowing that Vivien and Finch were lovers.

She was kept in her residence, tended by nurses, while Larry consulted with psychiatrists. Danny Kaye came round to help, and he and Larry had to hold Vivien down while she struggled against the nurse who would inject her. Vivien swore at them, bit and scratched them, until she finally relaxed.

Larry was able to get her on to a plane and back to England, where she was admitted to Netherne Hospital. She was heavily sedated and slipped into a long sleep, allowing him time to escape for a while to Naples to rest. He returned to find Vivien in the London Clinic, being treated by Dr Freudenberg, who had treated Larry's sister Sybille. Vivien had received shock treatment, although Dr Freudenberg informed him that there was no known cure for manic depression.

Larry always felt he had somehow failed Vivien. 'She was terribly ill,' he told me in 1979. 'I should have known. I should have been there for her.'

'But how could you have known?' I asked, not understanding much about her illness back then.

'I just *should* have,' he said.

Larry never stopped feeling guilty about what he saw was his failure towards her. She had told him she didn't love him any more, and he was finally beginning to feel that Vivien was no longer the woman he had fallen in love with, and his love for her was now much less than it had been. He felt he failed her, but he didn't abandon her.

I asked him why he felt he couldn't leave her.

'How could I?' he said. 'What else was there to do?'

He was not in control of his feelings or his basic common sense. That wasn't down to love – he was no longer in love with her as he had been. That was a feeling of helplessness to break out of the trap he was in – and that is very much a characteristic of sexual abuse.

When Vivien felt well again, they began work on *The Sleeping Prince* by Terrence Rattigan. Larry played the Prince Regent of Carpathia who meets and falls in love with a chorus girl, played by Vivien, while in England for the coronation of George V in 1911. The play was a big success, touring through October 1953 and then playing at the Phoenix Theatre in London from 5 November to 3 July 1954.

During the play's long run, Larry and Vivien became involved in a crisis that threatened the career of their friend, John Gielgud. On 21 October 1953, Gielgud – now Sir John Gielgud – was arrested in Chelsea for soliciting a homosexual act in a public lavatory. Arraigned the next morning, he pleaded guilty, apologised to the court and was fined ten pounds. An *Evening Standard* journalist was in the court that morning, and so the case was made public.

Publicly humiliated, Gielgud worried about how audiences would react the next time he appeared on stage. He was scheduled to open in N C Hunter's play *A Day at the Sea*, which he was also directing, at the Royal Court in Liverpool, so Gielgud's friend and colleague Binkie Beaumont, a highly influential West End theatrical producer, called upon Ralph Richardson and his wife Merlier Forbes, Larry and Vivien Leigh, and actor Glen Byam Shaw and his wife Angela Baddeley to a meeting to discuss what should happen to save Gielgud's career. They all agreed that the play should go ahead, except Larry, who suggested the play be postponed for three months. Vivien accused him of always being jealous of Gielgud and suggested to all that Larry's opinion should be discounted. It was agreed that the play should go ahead as planned. In the event, the public supported Gielgud and the play was a huge success.

This has been seen as another example of Olivier's attempt to sabotage Gielgud's career. But it was merely a matter of Larry's caution. 'John was a public figure and should never have been so misguided to put himself in that position. It was playing with fire, and he got burned, and I was afraid that ultimately the public might finish the job by incinerating him at the stage. I was only too happy to discover that I was wrong.'

Besides, Larry, along with Richardson, were instrumental in lobbying for Gielgud's knighthood, which they knew very well had been denied him because of his sexuality. They urged Winston Churchill to back them in 1953, and subsequently Gielgud was knighted in the Coronation Honours list in June 1953, before the crisis occurred.

But still there was always an edge to the relationship between Gielgud and Olivier. Sir John recalled, 'When I went to stay for the weekend it was always at Vivien's invitation, never Larry's. I felt he was always keeping a close eye on what I was doing next. I remember when he suddenly asked me, "Not thinking of another *Lear* by any chance, old boy?" And of course he had it in mind to do it himself.'

In 1954 Larry did no plays so he could make his third great Shakespeare film, *Richard III*. He cast Richardson as the Duke of Buckingham and offered Gielgud the role of the Duke of Clarence. Gielgud was insulted; the Duke was effectively killed off in the first half-hour of the film. He told me, 'It was such a minor part that it hardly seemed worth the time it would take. There is far too much waiting around doing nothing when shooting a film. I get paid only for doing nothing in between takes. The acting I do for nothing.'

Somewhat grudgingly, Gielgud accepted the part of Clarence.

Filming in the new wide-screen process VistaVision, and using the one camera available to him, Larry filmed the battle scenes in Spain during September 1954, with the next thirteen weeks spent at Shepperton Studios.

Richard III was as different from *Hamlet* as that film had been from *Henry V*, and it established Larry as the greatest director of filmed Shakespeare (today it might be argued that he has been superseded by Kenneth Branagh or Franco Zeffirelli – I enjoy all three for different reasons, but Olivier was the pioneer).

'Sir Laurence's own performance as Richard is dazzling,' wrote Paul Dehn in the *News Chronicle*. 'It embalms in celluloid one of the greatest Shakespearean performances of our day,' wrote Alan Brien in the *Evening Standard*. Milton Shulman of the *Sunday Express* called it 'a more exciting *Richard III* than anything that the stage has ever done or is ever likely to do'.

Larry was nominated for an Oscar for Best Actor but lost to Yul Brynner for *The King and I*. But he did win the British Academy Award, and the film also won the British Academy Award as Best Film and another as Best Film From Any Source. While Larry was busy filming *Richard III*, Vivien made *The Deep Blue Sea* with Kenneth More. Larry kept up the appearance of one deeply in love, while Vivien made no great pretence about her feelings. Kenneth More was convinced Larry loved her more than anything, and thought she was something of a 'bitch'. He told me (on the set of *A Tale of Two Cities* at Pinewood Studios in 1979), 'One day Larry came to the set to see her. He was so much in love with her and I felt he was completely smothered by her overpowering personality. He was convinced she was the world's greatest actress but I could see that while she had great beauty, she was not the world's greatest actress.

'He had brought her a beautiful aquamarine ring which he lovingly pressed into her hand. I thought to myself that this was just the most beautiful gift a man could give to a girl. But she barely glanced at it and just said, "Oh, darling, how lovely," and put it into her handbag.'

While men had once found it hard not to love Vivien, they now, it seemed, found it hard to even like her; at least that was Kenny More's experience. 'She was really a rather strange person. She was incredibly beautiful but she had the personality of a man, I always thought. She told the kind of risqué funny stories that men tell, not ladies. This made her personality somewhat overpowering, as was her beauty.'

It may be that her illness was making her the 'rather strange person' More found her to be. What seemed to be true was that she could switch from being a bitch to being the most charming woman in the world. This, I am sure, had more to do with her illness than her real personality.

Her behaviour – or rather her illness – became more extreme when, in 1955, she and Larry were in Stratford for that year's Shakespeare season. At her invitation, Peter Finch turned up and was welcomed at Avoncliff where the Oliviers were staying.

Larry always maintained he liked Finch. But Gielgud told me, 'Every now and then Larry would utter, 'Bloody Finch! Bloody Finch!'

24

A Very Dark Place

'I was summoned by Vivien,' Finch told me.

'And why did you obey?' I asked.

He thought long and hard, and eventually shrugged and said, 'It was Vivien. What else can I say?'

The love affair between Vivien and Finch resumed. 'I was so stupid,' said Finch. 'I was really an outcast in Stratford. I wasn't a member of the company and nobody really wanted me around then. But Vivien wanted me there.' And what Vivien wanted, she got, despite how Larry might have felt about it. But Finch admitted he had an ulterior motive for being there. 'I suppose, to be honest, I was also thinking that Larry could save me because I was broke and needed work. I'd signed a contract with Rank which I hated doing, and I think I just wanted Larry to save me.'

Anthony Quayle, who was present, asked Finch, 'But didn't you stop to think how Larry felt about having you there?'

'Of course,' he replied, rather haughtily. But then he mellowed instantly and added, 'But Vivien was just too irresistible.'

The season opened with *Twelfth Night* with Larry playing Malvolio and Vivien as Viola. John Gielgud, who directed the play, said:

I think our friendship, such as it was, really suffered when I directed him and Vivien in *Twelfth Night*. Larry and I didn't agree on many things, which was difficult enough, but there were also the terrible problems he and Vivien had within their marriage. Vivien was very ill by then, and I believe she had only recently had electric shock treatment.

It was most unfortunate for Larry that Peter Finch was still carrying on with Vivien. I did love her very much, and I said to her, 'Don't you think it would be better for you and Larry if you stopped your love affair with Peter Finch?' and she replied, 'Not at all. I don't love Larry any more, so what would be the point?' So I said, 'Then why don't you divorce him?' And she said, very sweetly, 'But if I did that, I would never get to play such wonderful roles in such wonderful plays, and I would be reduced to making the same kind of bad movies over and over again.' I wasn't at all sure that was the best reason to stay married, but I could understand it.

So Larry was very tired from the strain on their marriage and also from making his *Richard III* film.

Gielgud was also only just recovering from the trauma of his arrest. 'So we were, all in all, a rather unhappy team,' he said. 'I was most concerned when Larry announced that he would play the part of Malvolio with a long nose and strange hair, and then he began rehearsing the part as though he were playing what I thought was a very camp hairdresser, with a very funny voice. I begged him to change it.'

Larry related that Gielgud phoned him at Notley Abbey in the middle of the night and said, 'I've got it. Just play him very, very Jewish.' Larry complained about being woken at such a time with such an idiotic suggestion, to which Gielgud responded, 'All right then, play him very, very *not* Jewish.'

Gielgud didn't recall that phone call, but did say, 'I am afraid I thought Larry's Malvolio terribly vulgar. I tried to help him, but he resisted all my suggestions and he strongly objected to my criticisms. I also had the feeling that he re-directed Vivien Leigh after I had finished rehearsing her.'

I asked Gielgud why he allowed Olivier to override him, and he replied, 'Because I am unable to intimidate. I am too timid. I avoid quarrels because I always want to be happy in the theatre. Larry is not always an easy man. He is feared and respected and inspires enormous devotion and enthusiasm in his company. I always hoped to do the same, but I am a coward, you see.'

All this, as well as the crisis in Olivier's marriage, resulted in a performance that was something less than anyone expected from Olivier, as W A Darlington noted in the *Daily Telegraph*, 'What might have been a great occasion became merely a fairly good one.'

John Barber of the *Daily Express* felt that Olivier had peaked: 'Olivier was a great actor. But since his gleaming, viperfish Richard III and his fiery Hamlet he has lost his way. Now, at forty-eight, he is an ageing matinee idol desperately fighting to win back his old reputation while she [Leigh], at forty-two, is still a great beauty, but as an actress only good in a dainty, waspish way that seldom touches the heart.'

Then came *Macbeth*, with Larry as the Laird and Vivien his Lady. Gielgud said without hesitation, 'The finest Macbeth I have ever seen was Larry's at Stratford. When he made his entrance, he displayed a black soul; he was someone who had the idea of murder in his mind whether he knew it or not, before he had even met the witches. That was never something I got from the text myself, when I had read it, but it was an illustration of the creative brilliance of Larry to be able to see beyond the text.'

Kenneth Tynan, one of the most influential theatre critics, writing for the *Evening Standard* and the *Observer*, wrote, 'Olivier shakes hands with greatness here, but Vivien Leigh's Lady Macbeth is more niminy-piminy than thundery-blundery . . . still quite competent in its small way.'

Titus Andronicus, directed by Peter Brook, completed the season. This play is still one of the least performed of all Shakespeare's tragedies. It depicts a fictional Roman general engaged in a cycle of revenge with his enemy Tamora, the Queen of the Goths. It is certainly Shakespeare's bloodiest tragedy. One particular stage direction gives an indication of what the audience can expect: *Enter the empress' sons with Lavinia, her hands cut off, and her tongue cut out, and ravished* (Act II, scene IV).

Anthony Quayle said of it:

Titus Andronicus is one of the hardest plays to pull off, but I think that Peter Brook's production was one of his greatest, and in it Larry gave one of his greatest ever performances. It's not a performance that is talked about much, but it really was a triumph, and a terribly difficult one for all sorts of reasons. There was Vivien suffering terribly from manic depression throughout the run, and she had literally turned against the man she had loved most in the world, and now their marriage was in terrible trouble.

She was at times extremely hurtful to him on stage and off. There is a scene where Vivien as Lavinia has been mutilated, and Titus is speaking words of love and comfort to her. He brought a degree of emotion to that part which I'd not often seen in his performances. I was standing next to him, and I could hear Vivien cursing him with the most terrible obscenities you can imagine. The audience couldn't hear, thank God; she had a piece of bloodied gauze tied over her mouth. But I could hear it, and it was all aimed at Larry, but he didn't miss a beat.

It was sad to see Vivien so ill, and sad to see their marriage disintegrate, and it was sad that Vivien missed the chance to give a truly great performance. But apart from Vivien's failure in the part, I would say without hesitation that Larry as Titus is up there with the best of all the great performances, and it is without doubt one of the very best of all the tragic performances I saw Olivier give. And the production itself was one of the most remarkable achievements in theatre for a decade and maybe more.

Kenneth Tynan again aimed his critical arrows straight at Vivien, and not, it seems, without good reason: 'Vivien Leigh receives the news that she is about to be ravished on her husband's corpse with little more than the mild annoyance of one who would have preferred foam rubber.'

Larry knew that Vivien was no longer able to play the great parts. 'It was as if she had lost touch, all sense, of her craft,' he said.

The presence of Peter Finch at the Oliviers' house was not helping either Vivien's illness or her marriage – although the marriage was clearly over, even if Larry didn't want to let go.

Finch claimed he couldn't leave because he couldn't drive.

'Couldn't you have called a taxi?' Quayle asked Finch on that day we sat together in 1972.

'I could,' he agreed. 'I really could. But I felt literally unable to get away. I have this dangerous side to me that only wants to live for the moment, and that was the side of me that came out when I was with Vivien.'

They were all in a dark place. A very dark place. Larry found himself heading into a black cloud of despair, and yet he wouldn't let go of Vivien. After Stratford was over, he even invited Finch to Notley for dinner. He was the only guest.

After dinner, Larry asked Finch to go into the library with him where they could talk alone. Finch recalled, 'We stood in this bloody library, the two of us, Vivien off somewhere else and probably knowing what was going on, and neither of us knew what to say. So we stood in silence, and that made me start to giggle.

'Then Larry started giggling, and he began playing the part of the lord of the manor in a really funny way because he was trying to put me at ease. *He* was trying to put *me* at ease! All he really wanted to do was ask me to give Vivien up and to give him a chance to try and make their marriage work. I started playing the part of his elderly butler, a rather seedy old fellow who had served his lordship since birth. It was pure play-acting, and we ended up laughing hysterically until Vivien suddenly burst into the room and demanded, "Will one of you fuck me now?"'

'And which one of you did?' I asked.

Anthony Quayle quickly added, 'That's what I was going to ask!'

'Neither of us,' Finch replied. 'And Vivien wasn't at all happy that she wasn't fucked that night by either of us. That's the night I came to my senses and knew that I had to end it with Vivien once and for all. Larry had done more for me in my career than anyone. He was the kindest of friends and the most generous of employers I had ever worked for. So I said I would never see her again.'

Finch may have made a long overdue exit, but the end had come as far as Larry was concerned, and yet he couldn't make a complete break from Vivien. 'She was so ill, you see,' he said to me.

'Was that what kept you together?' I asked him.

'What else should I have done?'

Larry dealt with the problems by spending the next several years engaging in brief affairs. In his autobiography, he called these affairs 'acts of folly', and said that as well as being driven by a natural desire, he was also 'aware of an impulse of rebellion'.

He was, in essence, proving, if only to himself, that he could still be attractive and desired. He had a need to know that he could gain some control over his life, and he simply had to know that others might love him. Vivien clearly no longer did, and that shook and bewildered him.

Rex Harrison felt that Olivier had very mixed feelings about Finch. In 1982, he told me, 'Actors can be horrible people. Peter Finch was happy to steal Vivien from Larry. I suppose one could say Vivien allowed Finch to take her, but he was happy to be allowed.

'One Christmas [1954] Lilli and I were at the Oliviers' at the house in Notley for a party, and Peter Finch was there. They had fireworks which Larry fired off, and he aimed one right at Finch and at the last moment altered its direction. I don't know if Larry was really thinking for a moment of killing Finchie – who would blame him anyway? – or was just trying to give Finch a scare. But I looked at Larry, and I swear I could see murder in his eyes for a while.'

A year before Harrison told me this tale, I had been with Olivier for the last time, at Pinewood Studios for *The Jigsaw Man*. That was a time when Olivier was unusually honest with me about so many things. I asked him if he had ever contemplated murder.

He said, 'I would bet every one of us has thought that at some point in our lives. I know I have once or twice.'

In fun, I asked him who he had thought of killing. He smiled and said, 'Willy Wyler,' and then he fell silent, and finally said very softly, almost as a whisper, 'Oh, my dear boy – Finch.' His eyes welled up and I believe he really had considered killing Peter Finch.

Very curiously, Olivier and Vivien tried for a child in 1956. Rex Harrison told me, 'They did it because Lilli persuaded them to try. I thought it was a terrible idea, but Lilli thought that a baby would solve their marital problems. But Vivien miscarried.'

As if to show that he could work without Vivien, Larry chose to work with Marilyn Monroe, giving her Vivien's part in the film version of *The Sleeping Prince*, to be retitled *The Prince and the Showgirl*.

'Vivien was too old to play the showgirl on screen,' Olivier told me. 'On stage you can get away with playing younger parts, but on the screen the wrinkles and bags under eyes are there to see in close-up.'

'But why Monroe?' I asked.

'Because she was the biggest female star in the world, unbelievably beautiful in a rather tacky way, and undoubtedly sexy.'

I asked him if he thought he would have an affair with her.

'Ohhh, ohhhh . . . !' He almost cooed. Then he said, 'I thought she and I would be wonderful in bed. But – here's the thing, laddie – before we were halfway through filming I could barely bring myself to look at her.'

'That must have been difficult if you were directing as well as playing the Prince,' I said.

'I meant the way a man looks at a woman. At home I had Vivien giving me hell, and at work I had Monroe giving me hell.'

It all began so amicably. There was a meeting at her apartment in New York for her to meet with Olivier, Terrence Rattigan and Cecil Tennant from Warner Bros. She kept them waiting for an hour. 'I should have known immediately what trouble she would be,' said Olivier, 'but when she walked in . . . well, she had us all at her feet in moments. She won us over, and we were her slaves. I was sure we would have some wonderful times together . . . fucking. Instead, it was just fucking awful.'

Monroe flew into Britain to begin filming. So did Paula Strasberg, Monroe's acting coach; Monroe took Paula with her on every film she made.

Monroe was constantly late on the set, and Larry grew impatient. She was unable to rehearse and could only actually act when the cameras were rolling. But that sometimes took take after take after take until she got it right. Olivier fought to keep control of his temper. He would explain in detail what he wanted her to do and how she should do it, after which she would turn to Paula and ask, 'What's he mean?'

He was relieved when it was all over, by which time there was no love lost between director and star. But they agreed they needed to put on a show of affection for the cameras as he saw her off at the airport. Vivien was there also, and so was Monroe's playwright husband, Arthur Miller. Olivier kissed Monroe on the cheek. Vivien kissed Miller on the cheek. Monroe kissed Vivien on the cheek. Olivier remembered that it all looked like exactly what it was – a big act, and the newspapers knew it.

Released in 1957, the film was a flop. And yet it sparkles and delights, and Monroe is as good as Monroe can be, despite the troubles she caused Olivier, and he is a joy to watch. It's a film that, frankly, must seem better today than it did in 1957.

Nevertheless, Olivier felt his career was in decline and needed a boost.

25

Condition of Detachment

In 1956 Larry was invited to become a trustee of the National Theatre, and he was working on the script for a film of *Macbeth*. He scouted locations in Scotland and took his son Tarquin with him; he had never spent much time with him and was trying to make up for it. Tarquin was now at Oxford. Neither that relationship, nor the funding for the film, was working out. It would take a long time before father and son could really begin to enjoy each other's company.

Tarquin would go on to work in theatre, mainly as a producer, and to write books, notably *My Father Laurence Olivier*.

With *Macbeth* looking increasingly and inevitably unlikely, Larry went to see playwright John Osborne, who was riding high on the success of *Look Back In Anger*, and asked if he might write something for him. Osborne set about writing *The Entertainer* with Larry in mind for the role of Archie Rice, a strictly third-rate comedian who headlines a tacky music-hall revue in a seedy seaside-resort town. Archie can't face the fact that he's a failure and destroys everyone around him. Only his daughter loves him so much that she is blind to his flaws.

Dorothy Tutin played the daughter, and she and Larry began an affair. Before embarking on rehearsals and learning how to tap-dance, Larry and Vivien went to see *The Country Wife*, where he was 'entranced' by the young leading lady, Joan Plowright.

Joan Ann Plowright was born on 28 October 1929, in Brigg, Lincolnshire. Her father was a newspaper editor. Her mother

177

encouraged her to pursue an acting career, and she was trained at the Old Vic. She made her regional stage debut in 1951 and her London stage bow in 1954. Two years later, she joined the English Stage Company, where she was established in her most popular role up to that time, Margery Pincher in Wycherley's *The Country Wife*.

The Oliviers met the cast after the performance, and Larry 'had eyes for no one but Joan', as Olivier recalled in his autobiography. He was seeking out prospective lovers and throwing himself into his work to create what he called a 'condition of detachment from my marriage'.

'He would have done better to have simply ended his marriage,' Anthony Quayle believed. 'Of course Vivien was ill, but she was getting treatment, and most of all she didn't love him. And she made it clear, more and more, that she didn't.' We were talking in 1978, several years after we had sat with Peter Finch when he talked openly about Larry and Vivien.

The Entertainer brought Larry some of the detachment he sought, pleasing critics and the public in an initial run of 36 performances at the new Royal Court Theatre in April and May of 1957. He would have continued, but he had a commitment with Glen Byam Shaw for a European tour of *Titus Andronicus*, which ended his detachment since Vivien was also in it. From May, they performed it in Paris, Belgrade, Zagreb, Vienna, Warsaw and then back in London in July.

Vivien became ill on the tour. She was flying high and partying endlessly. After the final performance in London she threw a huge expensive party that LOP had to pay for. She refused to allow anyone to leave, so Larry sneaked people out through the back door.

When I asked Larry if he ever felt like he could kill anyone and he admitted he could have killed Peter Finch, he added another name to the short list. 'Oh, my God, and Vivien!' And he nearly did, some time after the end of *Titus*, when she wouldn't let him sleep. He locked himself in a room while she hammered away on the door. 'I snapped,' he told me. He stormed out of the room. 'I grabbed her wrist, dragged her along the passage into the bedroom and threw her at the bed. She fell and hit her head on a bedside table, cutting her very badly near the eye. How close we can all come to killing.'

He was still seeing Dorothy Tutin, but Vivien found out and confronted her, telling her that if she didn't stop seeing Larry, she would kill herself and Dorothy would be known as a 'murderess'. The affair ended, but Larry and Dorothy Tutin remained good friends. In fact, Larry generally remained good friends with the women he had affairs with.

He returned to *The Entertainer*, which ran another 166 performances at the Royal Court before going on to Edinburgh, Oxford and
Brighton. Dorothy Tutin, unable to continue playing Archie's daughter,
was succeeded by Joan Plowright, and he promptly fell madly in love
with her.

John Gielgud had hopes in 1957 of working with Olivier. He told
me, 'Larry was very taken with the kitchen-sink school of drama when
Look Back in Anger opened, and he was really the first of the major
actors to undertake this new kind of work with *The Entertainer*, which
was really quite wonderful and he was wonderful in it. We discussed
doing Anouhil's *The Rehearsal* together at the Court, but I was unable
to undertake it when he was available. That is the problem with actors
who take leading roles. We are hardly ever available at the same time
to work together, so people assume that we have some kind of lifelong
feud which, of course, is ridiculous.'

After *The Entertainer* finished, Olivier accepted an offer from Kirk
Douglas and Burt Lancaster to appear in their joint production, a film
of Shaw's *The Devil's Disciple*, set during the American War of
Independence. Kirk Douglas and Burt Lancaster were the stars, and
also co-producers, but Larry, as General Burgoyne, stole the film from
them, an opinion echoed by Douglas: 'I thought Olivier stole that
picture,' Douglas told me in 1988 when he was in London to promote
his autobiography. 'He was brilliant.'

It doesn't show in his performance, but Larry was very depressed
over the deepening crisis with Vivien. On the set he kept getting Kirk
and Burt mixed up for real. Every time Olivier addressed Lancaster as
Kirk, Lancaster looked him straight in the eye and quietly said, 'Burt!'
Olivier jokingly told Lancaster he was having a nervous breakdown.
It's a wonder he wasn't.

'I really wasn't at all happy on the film,' Larry told me in 1981, 'but
Burt Lancaster was very patient with me and we didn't have a single
cross word. In fact, when it turned out they weren't at all happy with
what I was doing, it was Harold Hecht [the co-producer] who came
to me and said, "Can you put more Mr Puff into your general
please?" It was a miserable time in my life, and I couldn't blame Mr
Lancaster for that.'

Harry Andrews, who was in the film, told me that he thought
Olivier was 'treated disgracefully by the producers. Larry, who was the
most confident of all actors at that time, suddenly lacked confidence
for the only time I can think of.'

Kirk Douglas saw firsthand the problems Olivier had with Vivien.

Larry and Vivien were very hospitable. Vivien was heavier than she was in the days of *Gone with the Wind*, but her face was still the same. But she wasn't well mentally or emotionally. Her behaviour was really very strange. Everybody pretended not to notice. But one day we were in a restaurant, and Vivien said to Olivier, 'Larry, why don't you fuck me any more?'

We were all shocked! But Larry seemed to be lost somewhere else, as though he wasn't there. I am sure he *wished* he wasn't there. Then she started coming on to *me*, and I was really uncomfortable about that, but Larry was just ignoring it, like it wasn't happening. I am sure he must have been used to it. She was like the part she played in *A Streetcar Named Desire*. Very sexual, very bizarre. I just felt so bad for Olivier.

Larry was contracted to star in and direct the film version of *Separate Tables* from the play by Terrence Rattigan, which Burt Lancaster was producing. Vivien was also to be in it, but disagreements with Lancaster caused Larry and Vivien to pull out. David Niven took Larry's role, as a bogus colonel who molests women in cinemas, and won an Oscar for it.

I asked Larry if he really had wanted to work again with Vivien after all they had been through. He mused, and finally said, 'No!' And that may have had a lot to do with why he didn't do *Separate Tables*.

Larry was living with friends now, and Peter Finch was again attending on Vivien at Notley. It no longer bothered Larry; he cared only for Joan. He took off to Paris from where he wrote a letter to Vivien asking for a divorce. She wrote back saying she would give him one on the grounds of desertion. He returned to England and had dinner with her on her birthday, 5 November 1958. Apparently, they were determined to keep everything amicable, and he even agreed to buy her a Rolls-Royce. It didn't work out quite that way. Within days there were blazing rows.

There was further personal trauma for him when his brother Dickie was diagnosed with leukaemia. Dickie's wife Hester and Larry agreed not to tell him straight away, but Dickie was deteriorating quickly and it was Larry who told him he was going to die.

Larry went off to America to do a play for television, *The Moon and Sixpence*, based on the book by Somerset Maugham; it earned Larry an Emmy. But a day into rehearsal he received the news that Dickie had died. He returned home for the funeral, which was, at Dickie's request, held at sea. On board the minesweeper HMS *Shannob*, Hester, Larry, his sister Sybille and Vivien watched as Dickie's coffin was committed to the sea.

Larry had to return to New York to finish the TV play, and would then be spending several months in Hollywood filming *Spartacus*. So before leaving England he met with Joan so they could spend some time together before being separated.

While sad to be leaving Joan, Larry was glad to escape to America and leave his problems with Vivien behind.

26

Spartacus

'It was while we were making *The Devil's Disciple* that I gave
Olivier the book of *Spartacus*,' Kirk Douglas said. The book by
Howard Fast was a highly fictionalised account of the slave
rebellion led by the escaped gladiator Spartacus in 70 BC. Spartacus
and his army almost brought Rome to its knees but were ultimately
conquered by General Marcus Licinius Crassus after other Roman
military leaders had failed.

Douglas continued:

He read it and thought the role of Spartacus would be a great role for
him. He said he liked Howard Fast's idea of Spartacus as someone with
an almost divine aura about him who was called 'Father' by the slaves
and was looked up to. But Dalton Trumbo was writing a screenplay
which saw Spartacus as an animal when he was a slave who evolves into
an intelligent man who becomes a leader.

I told Olivier I wanted him to play Crassus. Then Larry said he was
interested in directing the film. Well, we at least had him interested in the
idea which, back then, was a long way from being an actual production.

Trumbo worked hard to finish the first draft of the script so we could
send it to Olivier as well as Charles Laughton and Peter Ustinov. Olivier
was enthusiastic but had quite a lot of reservations about it. Laughton
called it 'a piece of shit', but his agent told us he would do it. Ustinov
had a lot of suggestions about the script but said he was interested.

183

Then I got a letter from Olivier which said he had a contract to do a play [*Coriolanus*] at Stratford in June the next year [1959] and was unable to be considered as director but was keen to play Crassus if we could improve the part in relation to the other three major roles which were played by me, Laughton and Ustinov. Well, of course we could improve the part for Laurence Olivier.

Douglas and his producer Eddie Lewis succeeded in gathering a distinguished cast – Olivier, Peter Ustinov as the *lanista* Batiatus and Charles Laughton as the senator Gracchus. There was also a strong Hollywood contingent including John Gavin as Julius Caesar and Tony Curtis as Crassus's slave, Antoninus. A German actress, Sabina Bethmann, was playing Varinia, the wife of Spartacus. Universal, who were backing the film, insisted on Anthony Mann directing. Mann had made a lot of successful Westerns starring James Stewart for Universal but Douglas considered him the wrong choice.

Larry had high hopes for *Spartacus*. He told me, 'I thought it was a very bold enterprise Kirk was embarking on, and there was enough in the screenplay I saw to make me feel the part was worthwhile. I just thought there should be *more* of it. Any actor wants to have more.'

Peter Ustinov believed that Olivier had managed to enhance the script. 'Kirk Douglas sent us scripts which had subtle differences in to favour our particular characters which he wanted us to play. We discovered that no two scripts were alike. Laurence Olivier had arrived a week ahead of the rest of us and had already inspired a newer version of the script in which his role had grown somewhat in importance. He had tremendous confidence in his own powers of persuasion and it was always somewhat amusing to see him at work in the wings, getting his own way. When discovered, he would give you a mischievous wink and then he would put on a performance simply because he was being watched.'

Charles Laughton immediately had his nose put out of place, simply by Olivier's presence, according to Ustinov: 'I could see from the start there was no great love lost between Laughton and Olivier, the result of some animosity that I understood nothing about and of which I was never inquisitive enough to ask about. Charles Laughton was very vulnerable, but sort of aggressively vulnerable like a child making you see what a victim he was, which made him also very petulant, sitting around just waiting to have his feelings hurt.'

Larry brought to the film a simple rule he used for all the characters he played. 'Whatever part you are playing, even if you are only a spear carrier, you must believe the play is about your character,' he told me. '*Spartacus* was about Crassus as far as I was concerned. I learned to love Crassus. I understood why slavery was important to the Romans. I don't have to personally agree with it. And I understood why Spartacus was not only a threat to Crassus but why Crassus became so obsessed by Spartacus. He wanted to know what kind of slave could almost destroy the empire. And so Crassus had to destroy not just Spartacus completely, but also the *memory* of Spartacus. The *ideals* of Spartacus. To me, Crassus was not the villain of the story. Spartacus was the villain. Crassus was the hero. He saved the empire.'

After filming began with the opening scenes of Spartacus in slavery, Anthony Mann was replaced by Stanley Kubrick. Exactly why and who made the decision has never been fully explained (though many have tried – few agree on the facts).

Kubrick was unhappy with the casting of Sabina Bethmann. 'We had to replace the actress playing Varinia,' said Kirk Douglas. 'Kubrick didn't want her. She was very upset and was afraid of what the people back home would say, so Olivier told her, "Don't worry. Listen, I was going to play a part opposite Greta Garbo and she didn't want me so I was fired. It's no disgrace." That was very kind of him to say that to her.'

As he so often did, Larry created a nose for the part. 'I needed to get rid of that weak spot,' he told me, pointing at the top of his nose. 'I needed some Roman nobility.'

Ustinov wasn't impressed by Larry's make-up. 'He *had* to have a false nose. You can see the join at the top if you look very carefully,' he asserted (I have never been able to see it). 'I think he imagined that it was going to look very Roman although I imagine there were Romans with hooked noses and snubbed noses and all kinds of noses.'

I engaged Ustinov in quite a debate about whether a false nose was any different to having your hair cut right to look more Roman, or to grow a beard as he did for his role as the Batiatus. The fact was, as it turned out, Ustinov failed to ever really warm to Larry. He said:

Larry is a wonderful companion. He arrived in Rome at the time his marriage to Vivien Leigh was breaking up and he was avoiding the press, so I met him at the airport and with help from the Italian authorities I whisked him away at high speed in my own car straight from the airport tarmac as he got off the plane all the way to my rented house.

In New York he and Joan dined with us even before their relationship was suspected. But, you know, in spite of enjoying his confidence and trust, I was never completely at ease in his presence, either on or off the stage. He seemed to know exactly what he was doing at all times, either in arrogance or in modesty, in gentleness or in strength, that I found myself unable to so much as bring down a mental guard in my own defence. My scenes with Larry in *Spartacus* were more in the spirit of a fencing match.

Douglas felt that Olivier quickly grasped the character of Crassus. 'When we first sent him the script he had thought of playing Spartacus. So then it became quite a challenge to get him to play Crassus. But once he knew that part was his, he began to understand the man.

'I think it is one of his most beautiful performances because he played this bisexual fellow but his deepest love was for Rome. I think that's the contribution that Olivier made. When Olivier talked about Rome, he made it seem like the most sensuous sexy woman. And he always had an undertone to whatever he was saying. It often meant two things and it was very subtle.'

Howard Fast originally wrote the screenplay but Douglas and Eddie Lewis binned it and gave the job of writing the script to blacklisted Dalton Trumbo. Trumbo had been one of the group of Hollywood writers and directors known as the Hollywood Ten who served a prison term for refusing to testify before the House Un-American Activities Committee about alleged membership in the Communist party. Trumbo served ten months and after being released was blacklisted by the Hollywood studios. He continued to write under various names. (Kirk Douglas was the first in the film industry to break the blacklist by publicly announcing that Dalton Trumbo was writing *Spartacus*.)

Very curiously, Howard Fast objected to the bisexual aspect of Crassus's character in Trumbo's script. When I talked to Fast by telephone in 1977, he complained, 'This was Trumbo's rather crude approach to left-wing decadence and to homosexuality. The question of whether Crassus was bisexual or not is of no importance.'

I argued with Fast that he was the one who wrote Crassus as a bisexual in his novel. It was a case of sour grapes, I'm afraid. The scene in question was the one that became known as the 'oysters and snails' scene because Olivier, as Crassus, tells his slave Antoninus, played by Tony Curtis, that liking men or women is like enjoying oysters or snails.

'When Olivier delivered that speech,' said Douglas, 'he really underlined all the subtlety of Trumbo's words. It was never overt, but it was there. That's brilliant acting.'

But the scene was cut before the film was released in 1960 and remained lost for the next thirty years. To Larry, the scene was essential to the story of Crassus. 'Crassus wanted to seduce his slave and he wasn't going to force himself upon him. He wasn't that kind of man. By cutting that scene, the audience never understood why Tony Curtis ran away. He ran away because he didn't want to be seduced, pure and simple.'

In 1990, the film was restored and the 'oysters and snails' scene put back in, with Anthony Hopkins providing Olivier's dialogue. Tony Curtis dubbed his own lines.

Curtis felt that one of the great experiences of his life was working with Larry. 'Olivier taught me a lot about acting,' he told me in 1974 at what was then his London home. 'He said to me, "Tony, clothes maketh the man." He taught me that you choose your clothes and you put them on and you finally become that character. He didn't just put on any costume that was given to him. He chose what was best for the character he was playing, and showed me how that helps to take the character into another dimension. I learned that from him and always used it. So he gave me tips of acting and I gave him tips on body building. I took him behind the set and said, "On your face." I hope he didn't think I was going to fuck him! Then I showed him how to do press-ups properly, and it helped to get him into good shape.'

Douglas was the executive producer of the film and the star, and he had Kubrick complaining that he wasn't being given artistic freedom, and Laughton threatened to sue Douglas, but never said why. Larry never had a bad word to say – to me, anyway – about Kirk Douglas.

Douglas recalled, 'We had all these top people, all these prima donnas. But Olivier was the easiest to deal with. As I recall, Olivier played the scenes as written. He may have suggested a change here and there, but he didn't try to change the script.

'I wasn't in any of the scenes between Ustinov and Olivier or Ustinov and Laughton or Olivier and Laughton. I just stood on the sidelines and watched, and actors are fans of other actors, and to watch those three great actors was really something.'

Larry insisted that he never disliked Charles Laughton. 'He was a wonderful actor. I admired him greatly. But he didn't like me, and I never understood why.'

Ustinov seemed to have the answer:

With Laughton in his state of mind, everything that Olivier did, even with good intentions, was misinterpreted. I was the catalyst of a row or a feeling of animosity that had gone on for a long time. Their whole careers had been eminently different. Laurence Olivier was living on a very tight allowance. He had not made a great deal of money back in England but had earned his reputation for his work. He had his old friend with him, Roger Furse, who designed all his films. They set up house together while we were filming *Spartacus*; they would make up their shopping lists and Larry would say, 'Do you think we can afford another packet of washing-up powder? No, that's going to cost money,' and they kept crossing things off their shopping list.

Laughton was a man who had made a compromise with a richer society which needed him intermittently because he also fell on hard times at one point and so he was playing American admirals in American B pictures, and I can think of no one less like an American admiral than Charles Laughton. But he'd made his compromises and had sold his soul to Hollywood and his favourite phrase was, 'Acting is whoring.' And then he fluttered his eyes to watch the effect such an outrageous statement might have. And he had a very nice house, a collection of pre-Columbian art and his nude Renoirs, and he floated on his pool like an iceberg that had gone topsy-turvy; he'd made his compromise. He was a Madam in his profession.

It was the exact opposite of Laurence Olivier. Well, he succeeded there, and Laughton succeeded in his way. Why there should be antagonism nobody knows except that I always thought in terms of a racing driver – Laurence Olivier was obviously in the lead but keeps looking in his mirror and there he sees Charles Laughton saying, 'I can overtake you whenever I feel like it.' And both were probably right.

I know that when we were near the end of *Spartacus* Olivier heard that Laughton was going to play *King Lear* at Stratford and he gave him a little hand-drawn map of the stage with spots from where you couldn't be heard, and he said, 'Do look out for those, Charles.' And Charles was very grateful. 'Thank you so much.' And then he looked at me and said, 'I'm sure those are the only spots from where you *can* be heard.' So it was that kind of relationship. It was absolutely hopeless, there was nothing one could do about it.

They had a scene in the senate when Olivier had to direct his speech to Laughton, who was sitting there looking noncommittal, listening but not looking at Olivier, and Larry said, 'I'm sorry, can I start this again? It would be easier to do this without Charles there.' And Charles's exit had to be seen to be believed. It was like an old cook who had been given notice, and out he went, and I am very sorry that nobody took a photograph of that because that was a real Roman exit from the senate. So you had that atmosphere all the time between the two of them.

For some reason, I was picked as confidant for both. Laughton was very sensitive to the influence Olivier was supposed rightly or wrongly to be exerting on Kirk Douglas, and he felt he couldn't carry sufficient weight to counteract this nefarious plotting he was convinced Olivier was engaged in, so he decided his best course of action was to sulk, at which he was very adept. He refused to act any of the scenes and so I was asked to try and find out what Laughton needed. What he needed, he decided, was to have his scenes rewritten, and so I rewrote the two major scenes I had with him. We rehearsed at his home or mine far into the night, and the next day we rearranged the props and furniture on the set to suit what we had engineered the night before to present a *fait accompli* to Stanley Kubrick, who seemed generally delighted with what we had achieved. The scenes were shot in half a day each.

Larry was aware Ustinov was rewriting scenes for Laughton. 'I wasn't concerned with what Charles Laughton and Peter Ustinov were doing. Peter wrote some very fine scenes. I didn't rewrite my scenes. I would ask for a word to be changed here and there because one single word in the place of another can make a tremendous importance. I would say that I was not troubled, but Charles Laughton behaved as if the world would end if he didn't get his own way.

'Actors are insecure people. We are the ones who are out there in front of an audience. We are the ones who will either reap the rewards or reap the whirlwind if it all goes wrong. So we are by nature temperamental. We need to be encouraged and maybe even mollycoddled. I am in competition with other actors. That is the way everyone gives of their best. I want to challenge the actors I work with. If they can see me out-acting them, they will, if they are of any worth, raise their game. And when we are done, we can tell each other how marvellous we all were. I want to be the best I can be, and that will often mean I want to be better than everyone else. I won't settle for being less than I should be.'

According to Ustinov, this kind of dedication was sometimes excessive: 'Olivier had made a tremendous study of ancient Rome. He liked to know the background to everything he did. Consequently he rode his horse without a saddle and without stirrups because he read somewhere that the Romans had neither.

'It led to all sorts of complications because even when engaged in a big close-up with an extremely sensitive lens he wouldn't do anything else but sit on a horse with no saddle. And every time the horse moved an inch Kubrick was forced to say "Cut! Larry, won't you sit on a step-ladder or something solid because the camera is so close to you the audience won't know if you're on a horse or not." And Larry said, "Dear boy, I feel I *have* to be on a horse," and this went on and on until after take twenty-five Larry said at last that he would sit on a ladder, and then unfortunately he fell off the ladder and had to have medical attention.'

And Ustinov experienced the competitiveness of Olivier at firsthand:

One of my first scenes with Olivier, which was cut and probably for good reason, had me running up to him as he sat on his horse, and he insisted I grab its bridle to keep it from cavorting among the mass of prisoners of war. I had to gaze up at him and say, 'Divinity, if I identify Spartacus for you, will you give me all the women and the children?'

He followed this with the most enormous pause. His eyes disappeared up under his half-open lids, he licked his lips, pushed his tongue into his cheeks, dropped his head – I think he was conveying a comic irony at the quirks of destiny – then hardened into the mould of mortal divinity, looked off into the distance as if staring into his destiny, changing his expression from one of brutal nobility into subtlety, and finally delivered his line, which was 'Spartacus?' which he cried very suddenly, and then hissed, 'You have found him?'

I was so staggered by this amazing and lengthy pause that I expressed the very surprise I actually felt, and I gazed away over the prisoners, determined to give nothing away just yet, smiled furtively at some private thought, chased it away as though I was about to say something but changed my mind. I had seen in his pause vanity, power and menace, and now I was using my pause to portray impertinence, servility and insecurity, until finally I let an almost inaudible 'Yes' slip from my lips.

Larry leaned down from his horse and said to me, 'Dear boy, do you think you could come in a little quicker with your "Yes"?'

To which I politely answered, 'No.'

We looked each other in the eye and smiled. He enjoyed the competition. But Stanley Kubrick didn't, and the scene was cut.

The film was an incredible success and earned good returns as well as good reviews. 'It is Sir Laurence Olivier who you'll remember – as a cold-lipped Crassus whose pettish pulling at his necklace hints at effeminacy while ruthlessness looks out of those foxy eyes,' wrote Alexander Walker in the London *Evening Standard*.

The film earned six Oscar nominations and won four, for photography, for art direction, costumes and for Best Supporting Actor for Peter Ustinov, who recalled, 'When I won the Oscar for the best supporting performance in *Spartacus*, Larry sent me a cable thanking me for having supported him so well. It was a joke, of course.'

27

Tumbling to Disaster

Just a few days after finishing *Spartacus*, Larry was at Stratford rehearsing *Coriolanus*, which ran from July to November. Harry Andrews, who played Menenius in it, told me:

> That was a truly heroic performance by Olivier. He was, I realised, a nervous wreck because of his personal troubles. His work meant everything to him. He was fifty-two years old and looked very fit. He told me Tony Curtis had helped him to exercise, and he was able to display tremendous energy and vitality, as well as giving a magnificent performance. I think *Coriolanus* was a play he wanted to do because of his interest in Roman history, and it was very fitting because he had only just played the Roman general in *Spartacus*. He'd played most of the great Shakespeare roles and there were very few left he felt he had to do, I am sure.
>
> But as fit as he was he damaged his knee – an old injury from years before, and had to miss a few performances, and his part was played by Albert Finney, who was very much younger than Olivier, but he was very good.

The knee injury occurred while Larry was filming *The Entertainer* by day while doing *Coriolanus* each evening. He was travelling every day, to Morecambe Bay for filming, and then to Stratford for Shakespeare. It was all getting too much for him. But the chance to film *The*

Entertainer was something he couldn't pass up. It was during a whole day spent tap-dancing, right into the early evening, that Larry suddenly felt his knee cartilage snap.

He was back on stage as Coriolanus within a few days, and both the play and the film finished in November. When *The Entertainer* was released in 1960, the critics were generally not as impressed with his performance on film compared to his stage achievement. 'Olivier's performance is still impressive,' wrote Fred Majdalany in the *Daily Mail*, 'though not quite as sharp as it seemed on stage where it spiritually belongs.'

Writing in the *Sunday Express*, Derek Monsey called the screen's Archie Rice 'a justly celebrated performance', but felt that it was 'the poorest and least interesting thing which the Western world's most magical actor has ever perpetrated'.

Brendon Gill of the *New Yorker* thought Olivier's performance 'a flawless piece of acting'.

It was good enough to earn him an Oscar nomination, but he lost to Burt Lancaster for *Elmer Gantry* in the same year Ustinov won his Best Supporting Actor Oscar for *Spartacus*.

When *The Entertainer* wrapped, he and Joan, in need of a good holiday, went to a small village, Seine Port, near Paris, for some much-needed peace and quiet.

He was looking forward to performing *Rhinoceros* with Joan in April, but before that he directed a very difficult play, *The Tumbler*, a verse play by Benn W Levy, about an English farmer, Kell, and his shrewish wife, Nina. The farmer meets a young woman in a barn and they make love. She discovers later that he is her stepfather and the possible murderer of her father. Larry told me, 'I knew it was a challenge from the beginning because it is all in verse, you see, and that isn't easy for any actor to do.'

Charlton Heston, fresh from his Oscar-winning success in *Ben-Hur*, was cast as Kell. 'I chose Chuck Heston because he was one of the few American actors who was constantly going back to the stage in between films,' said Larry. 'He wasn't interested in being a movie star. He only wanted to be the best actor he could be, and I knew that he was an actor who took his work seriously, and was seriously good.

'It was obvious that *Ben-Hur* would make him into a star, and to have someone with star pulling power in the lead role of a play that is going to be bloody difficult to pull off can only help, because people will want to see it to see the movie star.'

When I asked Heston why he chose to do such a difficult and obviously non-commercial play, he simply replied, 'I was desperate to work with Olivier.'

I talked at length with Heston about *The Tumbler* and he gave me quite an insight into the problems that make for a difficult production – in fact a disaster, which *The Tumbler* undoubtedly was – but mainly it illustrates what it was like to be directed by Olivier.

After *Ben-Hur* was premiered in New York [on 18 November 1959] I suddenly got two offers that were both impossible to turn down, both from Laurence Olivier. He wanted me for a film he was preparing to direct on Charlemagne and also for a play he was directing for Broadway, *The Tumbler*. Well, you don't take any offer to be directed by Olivier very lightly, whether it's a film or a play.

I can't remember now why the Charlemagne film didn't come off but I think it was because of Larry's commitments to the National. But *The Tumbler* was definitely on. To be honest, I wasn't too sure if a play where all the dialogue is in verse could work, but if you want to be an actor worth your salt you can't dismiss anything Olivier wants to do. *The Tumbler* was a very, *very* difficult piece.

At the same time I got an offer to do a film with Marilyn Monroe. Now this threw up a number of dilemmas. First of all, I had my new house waiting for me and my family to move into in Coldwater Canyon in Los Angeles, and a film made in Hollywood would have suited us well. Also the money they were offering was almost too good to turn down.

But then there is still Olivier to consider, and in the end I felt I had to go with the play. The balance between commerce and what you might call art is very delicate. As an actor with any kind of pulling power, you sometimes do the films that pay well to allow you to do the kind of work that Olivier was offering me which an actor should die for.

So I chose *The Tumbler*. I went to London for the premiere of *Ben-Hur*, and then a couple of days later I lunched with Olivier for the first time. I wanted to call him Laurence, but he insisted I call him Larry. He kept calling me Charlton so I insisted he call me Chuck.

He knew that there were a lot of problems in doing the play and he said he didn't have the solution to all of them but that we'd work our way through it, and that to an actor, especially when it comes from Laurence Olivier, is irresistible. You know you can't play it safe every time, and Olivier made the whole enterprise sound excitingly dangerous.

I knew that if nothing else, I would learn more from doing that play and being directed by Olivier than from doing almost anything else. I even talked it over with Willy Wyler who was also in London for the premiere, and he agreed with me.

I didn't meet up with Olivier again until early into the New Year [1960] when he came to the apartment we had in New York to read the play. That was an exciting experience, reading with Olivier, and getting direction from him straight away.

In Heston's published journals, *An Actor's Life*, he wrote, '[Olivier] says I must be straighter. "Don't try for colour . . . don't try to be liked."'

The following day the cast gathered in Larry's suite at the Algonquin to read the whole play. Said Heston, 'When you have a director like Olivier, you have to do some backtracking from the time when you first read a play and you think how right you are for it, and then Olivier gives you marks to hit that make you realise that this is going to be harder than you first thought.'

Heston wrote, 'Larry's not yet opened with Levy the delicate question of necessary cuts. They'll help, but the acting problem is still a huge one. I must not worry about making Kell likeable because *he* doesn't worry about this: the disinvolved alienated man.'

In 1981 it was fun for me to sit with Larry and pore through the entries in Heston's published journals about *The Tumbler*, and to get Larry's response to them. He told me, 'It was apparent from the beginning that Chuck Heston was a gifted actor. He didn't care about whether he looked good just so long as he gave you what you wanted. He has exceptional depth for an actor who had made his name in films, and he was a good Shakespearean actor too. Better than Orson Welles was, in my opinion.'

Larry managed to persuade Benn Levy to cut some of the dialogue. 'It's always tricky telling a wonderful playwright that you feel he needs to cut his work. But I am of the honest and deepest conviction that it is the rarest of all playwrights who really know what it takes to bring off exactly what is needed to make a play work. God knows, none of us really knows that or we would never fail but, alas, that doesn't happen to anyone. But the delicate and sometimes ego-damaging collaboration between a director and the playwright might sometimes produce a surprising success. Sadly, *The Tumbler* is not an example of such a success.'

Before he knew what a failure *The Tumbler* would be, he and his cast kept working away at what he and Heston always knew would be a play against which all the odds were stacked. But the experience of working with Olivier, whom Heston clearly idolised, was something very special.

'I soon found we were much of the same mind when it came to acting,' said Heston. 'Some actors have to sit around talking and solving the mysteries of meaning and motivation and movement. But Larry shares my instinct that you solve those things by doing the scenes and not talking about them.'

When the cast met to block the first act of the play, Heston was surprised to find that Olivier used a model set with little figures of each of the characters that he moved around while reading all the text himself. 'It was the whole play performed by Olivier and these little dolls,' Heston said. 'It was easily the most pleasant blocking session I can recall. It goes much faster than standing around for hours, bumping into each other.'

With Larry's method of blocking, they ran the first act twice. Heston recalled that Larry's main comment to him was, 'Don't read for poetry. Keep it clean and unadorned.'

Two days later they ran the whole play for Benn Levy to see. It was, said Heston, 'a stumbling sort of run-through'. He said, 'I knew the play was hard to pull off and I had no idea if it would satisfy anything except this urge to be directed by Laurence Olivier.'

The next day, 14 January, rehearsals began in earnest. Larry impressed upon Heston that he needed to play Kell with an arrogant 'fuck you' quality. Heston said he knew Olivier was right, 'but it's tough not to blur it'.

Heston said, 'I broached the idea of supporting him in something, somewhere, sometime, and he reacted warmly to the idea.' Ironically, it turned out to be the other way around, with Larry supporting Heston in the 1966 film, *Khartoum*.

They spoke little of private things, and only occasionally would Larry suddenly mention the nightmare of his marriage. One day, without any prompting, he told Heston, 'Vivien is several thousand miles away, trembling on the edge of a cliff, even when she's sitting quietly in her own drawing room.'

Heston chose never to pry. A few times Larry flew back to London. Heston recalled, 'Some emergency would arise and Larry would cancel a rehearsal and fly home, and then get back a day later, somewhat distracted. I simply asked, "How was London?" And he simply replied, "Bloody ghastly." We were due to rehearse my suicide scene, and he said, "I don't think I'm up to working on this scene tonight, laddie. A bit close to the bone." Vivien, it turned out, had been threatening suicide. 'He went back at least another two times,' recalled Heston, 'the second time only days before our Boston opening, and when he got back he was exhausted and very gloomy. He made no hint that things were going any better with his marriage, although he surely seemed to be trying, I thought.'

Heston clearly didn't know that Larry was now in love with Joan.

Rehearsals proved both stimulating and frustrating, especially for Heston. 'Heston really had to carry the play,' Larry told me. 'The leading actor always does, which is a blessing and a curse.'

Heston wrote in his journals, 'I still don't feel the surge of confidence you need for any part. Olivier's helping immensely, but he hasn't yet dug into my guts, where the performance I hope for has to be.'

For Larry, the play and his life were both proving difficult. As usual, he devoted himself to the work, but Heston felt that Olivier was somehow not giving his very best. He felt desperate to 'somehow get at Olivier, or get him to get at me', as he wrote in his journal. 'He must *not* be satisfied with competence. If I'm ever to reach anything special creatively, it surely must happen with this part, this director.'

Almost thirty years later, Heston said, 'Well, I was asking a great deal, even of Olivier. That play was a terribly difficult piece in blank verse. Whether any actor could made Kell interesting, I don't know, but ten years earlier I think it is conceivable Olivier himself might have.'

Heston's spirits sank as rehearsals proceeded. He felt it was 'lacking in inspiration from my quarter', but was surprised at how well Larry coped through all this. 'He was unfailingly good-humoured and light about it, and everything he said to me added something more.' Heston believed he was not measuring up to his own standard and therefore couldn't possibly be measuring up to Olivier's.

Reading all this from Heston's journals, Larry reflected, 'I thought he was doing his very best. Heston has always felt that there has to be something *more*, and he's right, if you hope to be any good. But I have found that it is in the performance that something happens, not in rehearsals, and I think that frustrated our dear friend.

'We got to run the play before opening with a small audience of about a dozen or so, and I warned the cast that this would set us all back somewhat. It was *that* kind of play. I knew that Heston would be reaching for something that he would not yet find, if he ever did.'

Heston recalled the first run-through: 'I was tense – far too tense. The first audience you play to always shifts your focus to the wrong side of the proscenium. But we were prepared for this setback.'

The play opened in Boston on 4 February 1960 at the Shubert Theatre, with sets designed by Larry's ever-reliable Roger Furse. The reviews the next morning were split between very good and very bad. Heston recalled, 'I remember sitting in an empty room with Larry and a bottle of brandy. It was supposed to be the first-night party, but most everyone had left. I thought I would be very nonchalant and I said, "Well, Larry, I guess you learn how to forget the bad notices."

'He leaned over and gripped my elbow, hard, and said, "What's much harder, laddie, and far more important, is to learn to forget the good ones." He was right.'

Larry called for a full rehearsal, after which he treated his cast to champagne and lobster.

Heston was learning all he could from Olivier, and while they discussed acting, which Heston described as 'so intangible an art', Larry told him, 'Star acting is really a question of hypnosis: of yourself and the audience.'

Four days after opening, Larry rehearsed them through a new opening, but it did little to improve the play or to attract audiences. Those who came, Heston noted, consisted largely of movie fans. Two days later, the play's producer, Alfred De Liagre, decided that a major weakness in the play was the casting of Hermione Baddeley as Nina, the wife – he wanted to replace her with Jo Van Fleet. Larry objected.

The following day, 12 February, Heston was summoned to Larry's hotel suite; it had been agreed that Nina should be recast and the two favourites Larry had in mind were Martha Scott, who was pregnant, and Judith Evelyn. Heston favoured Martha Scott, having worked with her on *The Ten Commandments* and *Ben-Hur*. Larry agreed, despite the fact she was pregnant. That night she travelled up from New York to see the play, after which there was 'a long, long conference thrashing around the whole thing', as Heston recalled. The decision was then made: Martha Scott would replace Baddeley. Nobody got to bed before four in the morning.

'Of course, nobody had told Hermione before Martha Scott was chosen,' Heston told me. 'Thank God Olivier had to tell her, which he did the very next day before we started another rehearsal. He really had to concentrate all his efforts on Martha that day. She really was much better than Hermione, whose comic image coloured her role as it did everything she played. She was miscast from the beginning.'

Larry recalled, 'Hermione Baddeley was very good about it, really. I suspect she was relieved to be getting out of what was obvious to me by then a play that could not be saved except by a miracle, which we were not expecting. She even continued to play the part for the next few evenings until Martha Scott was ready to go on.'

Martha Scott finally went on eighteen days into the run and just a few days before they were due to open on Broadway. 'The play was better with Martha in the role with her particular chemistry,' said Heston.

Larry, to his immense credit, stayed with *The Tumbler* right through, never ceasing to try and find a way to make the play work. Just a day before they headed for New York he took out an ending to the second act that had been manufactured to make for a curtain, and put back in part of a new opening that had been dropped four days earlier.

'I don't know if *The Tumbler* would have ever worked,' Heston said. 'Olivier made a heroic effort with it. True, he was heavily burdened at the time with his disintegrating marriage to Vivien Leigh, and the replacing of Hermione Baddeley in Boston was an added strain on all of us.'

That the play was doomed to failure finally dawned on the company when the play opened in New York on 24 February. The party after the first night was dampened by the news that the reviews were going to kill it off prematurely. The next day the closing notice went up.

The final performance was on 27 February. It had run just four performances. 'A play is always a gamble,' said Heston, 'and maybe the dice were loaded against us in this one. I got the only profit from it: what I learned from Larry.'

In between the difficult rehearsals and more difficult performances, Larry took refuge at the home of Rex Harrison. 'Rex was a good friend and when I was directing *The Tumbler* he often invited me to dine with him,' Larry said.

Harrison told me, 'He was in the process of getting divorced from Vivien and he was throwing himself into his work but he needed to relax, so I had him over for some of the dinner parties I occasionally threw. We are very different kinds of people, Larry and I, but we are tremendous friends.'

Sexy Rex Harrison was no longer with Lilli and had a new girlfriend, as Larry recalled: 'Rex was seeing a young actress [Tammy Grimes] who would often be late, and one day she turned up and Rex told her to leave. He could be very hard on people, and the poor girl looked like she had been told to leave the country and never return. I said to Rex, "You can't throw her out like that. Be a good fellow," and so he allowed her to stay and then he bought her a Cartier watch and told her she had no reason to ever be late again.'

28

Divorce and Marriage

Following the disaster of *The Tumbler*, Larry returned to England and went to work on *Rhinoceros*, which ran at the Royal Court and then the Strand Theatre from the end of April to the end of July 1960. The joy of working with Joan turned into a nightmare as news broke of his impending divorce from Vivien. It was Vivien herself who had calculatedly leaked the news to the press from New York, naming Joan as Larry's new love.

The press parked outside Larry's flat but got no statement from him. So they besieged the Royal Court Theatre in London and were waiting for him and Joan as they came out of the stage door. He realised it wasn't a good idea for him and Joan to be appearing on stage together, fearing not only for their joint humiliation but also for her safety. So she was replaced by Maggie Smith when the play transferred to the Strand Theatre.

In July, Larry asked Kenneth More to appear in a sketch with him in the annual charity show *Night of a Hundred Stars*. More recalled, 'Larry and I were playing in drag in a sketch by Noël Coward about two middle-aged women who are stranded at a party because of fog. Larry was totally loving the experience of getting every laugh he could wring out of what was a very funny sketch anyway. Here was this wonderful, powerful Shakespearean actor, who was without doubt the greatest actor in the world, and he was having an absolute ball playing for laughs in drag. Into the bedroom come these two men and they were played by Jack Hawkins and Rex Harrison. The audience went wild.

'There were hysterics when we all appeared for our curtain call, and Rex presented Larry to the audience, and Larry went into the persona of a ballerina and did the most wonderful curtsey to the audience.'

None of this was below Sir Laurence Olivier, who lived only to entertain others. 'I have never lost that desire to make people laugh,' he said. 'It produced the most wonderful feeling of self-congratulation which naturally feeds my ego and my desire to be liked. And it always helps when I can bring my feminine side out.'

I wondered why Larry felt he needed to bring out his feminine side, and promptly asked him.

'Because it's in there, bursting to get out from time to time. You can't keep that kind of thing corked up all the time without some temporary release.'

That was one of the few times I knew Larry was flirting with me.

In August 1960, Joan went to New York to do the play *A Taste of Honey*. A week later Larry followed, to play the title role in *Becket*. Anthony Quinn was cast as Henry II and found it a somewhat intimidating experience, working side by side on stage with Larry. Quinn told me (in 1977 at Elstree Studios where he was filming *The Greek Tycoon*), 'I'd not worked as much on the stage as Olivier. I thought during the first week of rehearsal that Olivier was trying to shout me off the stage. He was so *loud* and I was struggling to get my voice even up to his level, and I was shouting, and finally the director Peter Glenville asked me, "Tony why are you shouting?" I said, "I have to shout because Olivier's shouting so much." And Glenville said, "Tony, Larry's not shouting. He's *projecting*." I said, "Well, what am I supposed to do?" and he said, "For a start, stop shouting. You just need to project more." So I took a refresher course in stage projection so I could match Olivier.'

Quinn, who was really rather arrogant in an almost lovable way, complained, 'When we first started rehearsing, he said to me, "I want us to be the best of friends." I said, "That's fine by me, Larry." But then I found that off the stage he was like a lost soul, somewhat sad, following me around like a sad dog.'

Larry quickly realised that the role of Thomas Becket was nowhere near as good as the role of Henry II. He told Charlton Heston, 'I cannot describe to you the black depression that seized me on the second day of rehearsal when I realised I had chosen the wrong part.'

When Quinn announced he was leaving *Becket* to do a film, Larry called Charlton Heston and asked him to come and alternate in the roles. But Heston was committed to filming *El Cid*. 'That was without doubt the biggest disappointment of my career, being unavailable to do that play with Olivier,' said Heston.

Larry played Henry II with Arthur Kennedy as Becket when it toured Boston, Toronto and back to New York again from March to May 1961. When Peter Glenville directed the film version, Larry was bitterly disappointed not to be cast. Richard Burton, who played Becket in the film version, told me in 1984, 'Olivier was magnificent on stage as the King. But, really, he was too old to play the King in the picture. Henry and Becket were young men. Glenville wanted younger actors, so he got me and Peter [O'Toole], and Olivier felt robbed.

'But there is nothing that can take away his success in the part in New York. He had the authority and the sense of irony and the sympathy the part requires. Playing Becket is easy. You only have to be self-righteous. That was too easy for Olivier, and no challenge at all.'

On 2 December 1960, Vivien Leigh had petitioned for divorce in London and was granted a decree nisi. During the tour, on 3 March 1961, the decree absolute came through; Larry and Vivien were no longer husband and wife. Vivien, by this time, had settled into a happy relationship with actor John Merivale.

On 17 March 1961, Larry married Joan in Wilton, Connecticut, and then they rushed back to New York for their respective plays. Larry was also busy making a film for television, *The Power and the Glory*, in which he played a drunken priest in a revolutionary-run Latin American state, hunted by the police.

It was thought, wrongly, good enough to release theatrically in Europe but, as the *Monthly Film Bulletin* noted, it bore all the hallmarks of a TV movie: 'There are signs of haste in shooting, the make-up is poor, the photographic quality hazy.' It was, for Larry, simply one of those times he worked for the money.

On 3 December 1961 Joan gave birth to a son whom they named Richard, after Larry's brother Dickie. Richard grew up to become a stage director and, inspired by his father, directed *Henry V* and *The Merchant of Venice* at the Globe in London.

Larry seemed to be settling into a life of idyllic stability. He had success as an actor with the best still to come, and he had a new wife and a baby son.

This makes it hard to understand why, while filming *Term of Trial* in late 1961, he had an affair with a new eighteen-year-old actress, Sarah Miles. She played a schoolgirl obsessed with her alcoholic headmaster, played by Larry. The irony is that while filming in Dublin and then in Paris, Larry was seducing Sarah for real. Even when filming was over, they continued to meet behind Joan's back on and off over the next few years. To protect his identity when they met at various arranged locations, he called himself 'Lionel Kerr'.

Could it be that Larry really hadn't found the happiness he was so desperate for? According to Olivier in his autobiography, he was 'blissfully happy with what I'd got' when his son was born. But beneath the skin, Larry was still unhappy and unsettled. His affairs during the final stages of his marriage to Vivien could be excused. But his affairs during the first years of his marriage to Joan are harder to understand. I was never able to talk about that to Larry as I had no idea when I knew him what he had been up to.

But I do believe there is more to it than him being a Lothario. I think it was even more than a mid-life crisis, with Larry desperate to be desired by young women. I think it was his never-ending need to be liked and loved that was an impulse he could not control. Reading Sarah Miles's own account in her memoir, it seems clear to me that Larry was doing what he did best – playing a part, and this one was of the older lover. He could play any part he liked, to suit the occasion.

Sarah's portrait, in her book, of the relationship she had with Larry is very touching. But reading of the games he played to bed her, the things he said to tease her, I find something very sad beneath it all. There is still the young boy, raped by a priest, desperate for something, although Larry clearly never understood exactly what that something was. It should have been closure.

Larry was able to clear all this from his mind when he wrote in his autobiography how, during the filming in Dublin, his wife and baby boy moved in with him into a house in Ballybrack in January 1962; they 'enjoyed a lovely life together for the next six weeks'.

The film was a disappointment. Critics felt he was unable to be convincing as a victim. The irony is that they never knew just how much of a victim he was.

Thomas Wiseman wrote in the *Daily Express*, 'His noble looks, his commanding personality and his natural authority are against him. He can play a king but he cannot play a mouse.'

They had caught him out; Laurence Olivier could never again be dominated or controlled. He was now controlling his own life. Or so it must have seemed to him. What he was fighting to do was *not* be a victim. And that's why he wasn't convincing in that film.

29

The Moor

Larry kept busy through 1962, directing a play he wasn't in at the Chichester Festival, *The Chances*, and two plays he was in, again at Chichester: *The Broken Heart* and *Uncle Vanya*. He was happy to just act in *Semi-Detached*, which played Edinburgh, Oxford and London where it ran 157 performances at the Saville Theatre.

At the beginning of July he was appointed director of the National Theatre Company and it was decided that the company would take over at the Old Vic in 1963. There was also to be a new National Theatre building, but the location was still to be determined.

To Larry's astonishment, in October 1962, one of the critics who had so often slated Vivien's performances and had continued to write harshly of his work at Chichester, Kenneth Tynan, suddenly wrote to Larry stating his admiration for him and of his enthusiasm for the National Theatre Company, and asking him to give him the post of his dramaturge. Joan persuaded Larry that it would be a good idea to have him at his side and make everyone see that Larry was thinking forward and anew with the National. And so Tynan began working with Olivier.

On 10 January 1963, Larry had one of his greatest desires fulfilled – to have a daughter – when Joan gave birth to Tamsin Agnes Margaret. Tamsin would naturally grow with the desire to be an actress; she went on to study at the Central School of Speech and Drama, and for a while she was a working actress. She was with her mother and sister Julie-Kate in *Time and the Conways* at the Old Vic in 1990. But she seems to have given up the stage to run a restaurant and be a psychotherapist. As such, she, I think, would understand her father's troubles as a victim of sexual abuse.

In 1963, Larry revived *Uncle Vanya*, in which Joan played Sonia, at Chichester, then directed but not did act in *Hamlet* at the Old Vic which was his first National Theatre production. He followed by again reviving *Uncle Vanya* for the National, and from then on he virtually devoted himself to the National, culminating in his astonishing, justly celebrated and probably greatest stage performance of all time, as *Othello* at the Old Vic from April to June 1964, and then again at the Chichester Festival that year.

It was Tynan who suggested that Larry play Othello. Larry argued that he couldn't play the part. Tynan told him, 'Of course you'll do Othello. You've done all the others. People will wonder why you're ducking this one.'

In the end, Larry couldn't resist the challenge.

Among the play's many admirers was Charlton Heston, who said (in 1979, on the set of *The Awakening*):

> I think it's true to say that Olivier's Othello is widely regarded not only as the best Othello in living memory, but perhaps of all time. I saw it, and I will put my name to that. No other actor alive could come near his Othello, and no other white actor would have dared.
>
> His Othello was great, which is an adjective that has worn out its value because we use it to describe anything remotely good. Olivier's Othello was *really* great.
>
> More than that, I've seen what you might call a few great actors and many very good ones give what you would accurately describe as unforgettable performances on stage and on film. But I've never seen any performance, on stage or screen, that could match Olivier's Othello.

Everyone involved, including director John Dexter, marvelled at the technical extremes to which Larry went, including blacking himself from head to foot, even the inside of his mouth, and teaching himself to lower his voice one or two octaves to reach for the bass voice he felt Othello must have.

On the final night, the audience gave a standing ovation, as it had done every night since it opened. Maggie Smith, so I was told (by Heston, in fact), knew how high he and all the cast had soared that night, and she wanted to make sure he knew it. So she went to his dressing room where he was sat slumped in a chair, sweat running through his make-up, a whisky in his hand. She said to him softly, 'Larry, you do know how good that was?'

He said to her, 'Yes. But I don't know how I did it.'

Heston told me, 'When we did *The Tumbler*, Larry told me, "Sometimes the gods blow in your ear and you can do no wrong." This surely happened to him on that final night. But to have come, as I am sure he did, to accept that he was the finest actor alive and that this was his finest performance and on the final performance to transcend all he had ever done in the part and to realise he had no idea how to reach that level again, must have chilled his soul. Because how do you reach that ever again? Civilians laugh when I tell them this. But actors shut their eyes in anguish. Acting, as satisfying as it can be, is also a hard mistress.'

In October, Larry began a marathon run – with breaks here and there for other projects – of Ibsen's *The Master Builder*, directed by Peter Wood for the National Theatre Company. Joan was in the early stages of pregnancy, and sadly she miscarried. Oliver pressed on with *The Master Builder*.

After opening in Manchester for three performances, then shifting to Leeds for five more, then another four at Oxford, *The Master Builder* played at the Old Vic from 17 November for 73 performances.

Somehow, in January 1965, Larry found time to direct *The Crucible* and then returned to *The Master Builder* for just three nights in Glasgow, followed by another three in Coventry. But something was terribly wrong. Larry began suffering from terrible stage fright. He would go on stage, be unable to remember his lines, and feel the theatre spinning around him.

People who aren't actors – 'civilians' as Chuck Heston calls them – don't understand stage fright. They think it's little more than an attack of nerves when you can't quite remember your lines. Larry tried to describe it in his autobiography: 'My voice had started to fade, my throat closed up and the audience was beginning to go giddily round.'

Even that does not sum up the full horror of stage fright. At least, not the kind that Larry was experiencing. 'Oh, Michael, I thought I would literally die every time I went on stage. I mean, *literally* die,' he told me in 1981. By then I understood what he was talking about, and today I understand a whole lot more of what was happening.

Much has been made of Olivier's legendary stage fright, even by Larry himself. He couldn't hide it. It continued when he returned to *Othello*, which he performed sporadically through 1965, in Moscow, Berlin, Edinburgh and Newcastle, and then once more in 1966 at the Queen's Theatre in London. Frank Finlay, who played Iago, recalled (when I interviewed him in 1977 on the set of the BBC's television version of *Count Dracula*), 'Larry had a terrible time, and couldn't be left on stage on his own. So I always made sure that when I had to leave the stage, I stayed in the wings downstage so he could see me there. That seemed to ease his mind. But he went through such terrible stage fright; I don't know how he found the strength to carry on.'

Larry wrote that 'everyone who had scenes with me had to know what was going on, in order to be able to cope in case of trouble'.

Stage fright appears to be a phenomenon experienced only by actors. Not true. It is, simply put, a panic attack. Anyone who has suffered from panic attacks will understand what Larry was going through. And I don't mean the kind of panic you experience because you suddenly remember you have forgotten to pay the phone bill or turn the gas off before leaving the house. It is an experience almost impossible to describe definitively. An inexplicable panic engulfs you, making your legs turn to jelly, your heart beat so fast you are sure you are having a heart attack, your head spin, your mouth goes pepper dry, and you have one overwhelming thought – *you are going to die*! These feelings are, for many, literally uncontrollable.

So stage fright is a panic attack that just happens to take place on stage. For others it might happen when they get on an underground train, or in a confined space – claustrophobia – or while they are outside – agoraphobia. They are all panic attacks, triggered often for no obvious reason, but once they happen, they will invariably be repeated in whatever environment or circumstance they occurred the first time.

For Larry, panic attacks were triggered by going on stage. Nothing could be more debilitating to an actor than that particular form of anxiety disorder. Once it begins, it seems impossible to ever find a way to stop it. And Larry suffered with it for the next five years.

He could never understand why. He felt that it began when, one night, as he was about to go on in *The Master Builder*, he thought to himself, 'I think I'm too tired to remember it.' And when an actor fears he will forget his lines, he invariably does. When that happened to Larry, on that night, he went into a full-scale panic attack, and as a result each time he had to step on stage he suffered the same terrible nightmare.

What I have learned, from my own experiences, is that panic attacks are often triggered by being unable to control that which is most important for you to control. For Larry, it was his whole life and career. He had fought to gain mastery of it, and he now had the added burden of trying to manage the growth of the National Theatre Company. He then feared he was losing control over his ability to remember lines.

I speak from miserable experience. My panic attacks started shortly after I was sexually abused. They were infrequent at first. But then, one day, sitting alone in a cinema, I had a full-blown panic attack, and I could never go to the cinema alone again. It gradually spread to other areas of my life. I had no idea what was happening, and the doctors were unable to explain it, until 1981 when a doctor finally told me I was experiencing panic attacks. I'd been having them almost daily for years, and each day I thought I would die. Lurking deep within my subconscious was that experience of rape, and something connected to it – possibly a loss of control – was enough to bring it to the surface and cause a massive panic attack.

I relate this only to explain what was happening to Larry on stage. I was able to tell him a little about it in 1981. By then he was over his stage fright – indeed, he was no longer appearing on stage – but he was so grateful for this knowledge. 'Oh, dear boy, if only you had been there to tell me,' he said. With some anguish he asked, 'Why didn't anyone tell me?'

Some people are predisposed to suffer panic attacks, though it doesn't mean they will. But for those who are, when an event causes it to happen, they are likely to find the horror repeating itself. I am convinced that for Larry it began when he was a boy at All Saints when or after he was sexually abused. He suffered his first panic attack – his first experience of stage fright, or stage panic as it might be more accurately called – when he sang his solo 'Trinity and Unity' during his last evensong at All Saints. In his autobiography, he wrote that even though he managed to relax and finish the song 'there was a pocket of slight doubtfulness, though, in my mind that was to lurk there, never to be totally dismissed'. It was waiting, like a demon, for the right time to strike again.

He had almost lost control of that early performance at All Saints, as he had lost control over his young life when he was abused. When he felt himself losing control during those years at the National Theatre Company, the phenomenon of panic attacks struck him again, more forcefully than ever, and it occurred, as it had the very first time so many years before, while performing to an audience.

If, in 1981, I had understood how his stage panic was a direct consequence of being sexually abused, I would have told him so. Or, I would have tried to. He deserved to know why he suffered what is a terrible psychological illness that manifests itself in such a horrifically physical manner.

The fact that Larry carried on, battling this illness for so long, might be considered a credit to his tenacity and courage. Or it might be that he was even more scared of *not* going on. I think the thing that kept him going and prevented him from retiring from the stage was a subconscious will to take control once more. He had fought all his life to be in control, and even though he was probably not conscious of it at the time, he was desperate to regain it. That is the effect sexual abuse can have on children when they become adults.

After one particularly traumatic performance of *Othello*, Larry asked Sybil Thorndike and her husband Sir Lewis Casson for advice. She told him, 'Take drugs, darling – we do.' So he did. He didn't say in his autobiography what kind of drugs – whether they were prescribed or not.

He then developed another problem. He kept losing his balance, a symptom of panic disorder, but this turned out to be caused by labyrinthitis, an inflammatory disorder of the inner ear. This condition produces disturbances of balance and hearing to varying degrees and may affect one or both ears. Fortunately a doctor prescribed him some pills and the condition cleared up. That was, at least, one problem solved. There would be worse to come.

During 1965 Larry added only one other play to his repertoire, *Love for Love*. He alternated that with *The Master Builder* and *Othello*, and in that can be seen the battle Larry had with trying to regain control over his work.

He was, perhaps, over his head somewhat as director of the National Theatre, but it meant so much to him. It was like his child, and he gave it everything he had. He even turned down the chance to be directed by his good friend Franco Zeffirelli, who was known for his great work producing operas and plays before establishing himself as a film director with *The Taming of the Shrew* in 1966. When in

London to direct Joan Plowright in *Filumena* in 1977, Zeffirelli told me, 'The first time I worked with Larry was when he asked me to come and produce *Much Ado About Nothing* for his new National Theatre Company at the Old Vic. I wanted Larry to play Don Pedro, which he would have been marvellous at, and I spent a lot of time trying to lure him, but he simply had too much administration work and already had too much other acting and directing work to take on Don Pedro. But it was wonderful for me because I got to know him, although we had met some years before when I directed *Romeo and Juliet* at the Old Vic [in 1960]. I may even have met him before that, but I have felt like Larry and I always knew each other.'

Larry was eagerly finding new talent to build his National Theatre, such as Derek Jacobi – to my mind, the only true successor to Olivier – who played Cassio in *Othello*. In fact, many of today's finest actors of Jacobi's age came from the National Theatre, such as Anthony Hopkins. Larry literally nurtured the talent that he discovered, as Zeffirelli noted: 'Larry really believed in giving his actors plenty of experience in all kinds of roles in all kinds of plays, and some roles would be large and some small. Michael York had a number of small parts in *Much Ado*, and I knew he had real talent. I asked Larry what he had in store for Michael, and he said he was letting him simmer for a while – playing almost walk-on parts for a couple of years. That's how Larry honed new talent. There was no thinking for any actor that if he played Hamlet he couldn't go back to playing smaller roles. With Larry a young actor would play Hamlet one month and carry a spear the next.'

As if he were not busy enough, Larry found time, during the summer of 1965, to make a film, *Bunny Lake is Missing*, for director Otto Preminger. With all else going on, Larry also squeezed in a film version of the National Theatre's production of *Othello*, filmed at Shepperton Studios with all the sets based on the stage production. The intention was to faithfully recreate the stage play for posterity, in Technicolor and Panavision. And I, at the age of just twelve, had the privilege of seeing a single day of the filming, under the direction of Stuart Burge.

I remember watching in fascination the lights being set, the camera being put in place, the hubbub and organised chaos that was all part of the filming process, which somehow all managed to turn into a few magical moments of actual filming. The takes on this were much longer than was normal – as I would only realise in later years from watching many other films being shot. Whole scenes were being filmed in one go, as far as I could tell, or at least great chunks of them were.

On that day I was mesmerised by Laurence Olivier, blackened up to look eerily like an African Moor, speaking dialogue I hardly understood. And yet I was held by the power of his performance. It was almost a theatrical experience as Larry was, indeed, re-creating his role as performed at the Old Vic. That was the first time I ever became aware of the magic of a great actor giving a great live performance.

For his filmed *Othello*, Larry was nominated for an Oscar. He didn't care that he didn't win. He told me some years later, 'The part is the reward.'

There was more film work. In December 1965, Charlton Heston fulfilled his long-cherished wish to act opposite Laurence Olivier. The film was *Khartoum*, an epic in Cinerama about the English General 'Chinese' Gordon, a devout Christian, who in 1883 was sent, unofficially, to evacuate Egyptians from the Sudan, but stayed to protect the people of Khartoum from the Mahdi, a religious fanatic who brought terror and destruction throughout the Sudan.

Larry was cast in the crucial but brief part of the Mahdi. Much of the film had already been shot on location in Egypt, but all of Larry's scenes were filmed on a sound stage at Pinewood Studios just outside London.

Larry told me in 1976:

I worked just for a few days on *Khartoum*, but it was really quite rewarding. And also frustrating. The screenplay [by Robert Ardrey] was very good. Chuck Heston was playing Gordon. I knew he could do an English accent because of *The Tumbler* but I felt sure I would be able to . . . ah . . . prove I was the better actor. And I would have preferred to have played Gordon. I was the right age; Heston was too young, and he was also too tall; Gordon was quite short.

I used the same kind of make-up technique I had used for *Othello* and had learned how to do a very good Sudanese voice, I thought. Some critics said it was just Othello again, but they know fuck all. The Mahdi also had to have a slight lisp. You can get careless about those things and overdo it, but it had to be there and the trick was to make it subtle.

So there I was, feeling highly pleased with myself, and then I saw Heston in his wonderful costume, looking far too tall really to play Gordon. But his make-up made him look absolutely dead right. He had worked on the hair and the moustache so it was authentic and not just a bit of greying up with some old moustache stuck on. It was the moustache of a Victorian aristocratic general in the British Army.

But I *knew* I had him beaten when it came to getting the accent right. We began our scene – and *then* I knew I was not going to find it so easy to be the best because he not only spoke with a believable English accent but he had taken the time to learn to speak impeccably, the way Victorian army officers did.

They only had two scenes to shoot. 'It was an excellent script with the kind of dialogue actors like,' said Heston. 'We made no changes to it at all, I recall. I must say, it was a memorable experience acting with Olivier. He is unquestionably a gifted actor; he and John Gielgud are probably the two finest actors in the world. I couldn't say who was the best. But since my favourite film is *Henry V*, then I would have a bias towards Olivier.'

Those two scenes between Gordon and the Mahdi, inventions in the script because the two men never really met, are wonderful to watch just to see two fine actors showcasing their special gifts.

When Larry saw the finished film, which was released in 1966, he was furious, according to his stand-in Patrick Jordan, who played the Mahdi in long shot for the scenes filmed on location in Egypt. 'Olivier was furious as we came out of the screening. He said, "That bloody American actor is better than me," and he didn't like it.'

Larry had admitted to me in 1976, 'I was really quite foolishly upset that I hadn't been asked to play Gordon, and even more upset that Chuck Heston was so good in the part. I should have been satisfied with what I did; I think I was good as the Mahdi.' Then, with a mischievous twinkle in his eye, he said, 'But I did so want to act him off the screen.'

A number of critics accused Larry of simply re-creating Othello for his characterisation of the Mahdi. Heston slammed those critics:

That is a ludicrous criticism. True, both parts were passionate Muslim generals. But Olivier's Mahdi was markedly different from his Othello, which I saw, so I know. Olivier's Mahdi was a far more controlled and even engaging man than Othello, who padded across the stage like a black panther with a rose in his teeth, awesomely persuasive. It was nothing like the Mahdi he created.

It was certainly daring of Olivier to undertake the part. He was no longer a young man but he worked himself very hard into sufficiently athletic condition just so that he could play the part in loose robes. He had his body stained from head to toe and polished with a cloth to give it a fleshly sheen so it wouldn't look like make-up, and it worked.

In July 1966, Joan gave birth to a daughter, Julie-Kate. It followed a difficult and potentially fatal three-day labour, and in the end the baby was delivered by Caesarean section.

Julie-Kate became a successful actress for a while, working at the Old Vic and the Royal Court. She became interested in film documentaries and began producing them for Channel 4 in 1989, and she also founded, in 2001, the Women in Theatre Company.

While delivering his final, and still panic-stricken, performances of *Othello*, Larry began rehearsing August Strindberg's *The Dance of Death*, in which he played an artillery captain living with his wife (played by Geraldine McEwan) on an isolated island off the Swedish coast. Here they argue constantly as she tries to convince him he is unwell.

It was, Larry said, 'a variation on the common love/hate relationship theme: it was ten per cent love and ninety per cent hate'.

The play was a great success and his performance was much admired. It also happened to be a very physically demanding role, but Larry stood up to these demands well; only stage panic threatened him and yet each night he was able to overcome it in a way that meant neither critics nor audience ever realised the nightly horrors he experienced.

30

His Lordship

On 22 May 1967 Larry turned sixty. Three days later he became acutely aware of a terrible pain in the area of his prostate. He *knew* it was his prostate, but he continued working, performing in *The Dance of Death* and rehearsing *The Three Sisters*, which he directed but did not perform in; Joan Plowright played Olga, Louise Purnell was Irina and Robert Stephens played Colonel Vershinin. It was after almost two weeks of pain that he finally saw a doctor. A week of examinations confirmed he had prostate cancer, and he was admitted as an outpatient to St Thomas' Hospital, under the name of Lionel Kerr.

His treatment was by hyperbaric radiation. He was placed in a large cylinder, which he described as a 'torpedo tube', and his prostate area was aggressively attacked by radium-soaked cobalt. The treatment was effective, but each session left him feeling weak and nauseous. But he continued to travel each day between Brighton and London to rehearse *The Three Sisters*.

On 7 July, he had his last course of treatment; that night Vivien Leigh died. Jack Merivale called Larry while he was in hospital to break the news. He discharged himself and went to Vivien's flat in Eaton Square in London. Merivale let him in, and then left him to be alone with Vivien.

Olivier wrote, 'I stood and prayed for forgiveness for all the evils that had sprung up between us.'

A postmortem established that she died from tuberculosis. Cecil Tennant attended her funeral, and on the way back he was killed in a car crash. Larry was devastated by the double tragedy.

He put all his thoughts and efforts into a tour of Canada with *The Dance of Death, Love for Love* and *A Flea in Her Ear*, through most of October and November. His doctors warned him not to tour, but he would not hear of it, although for once he was happy to cancel a performance of *Othello*. He was still unwell from the effects of the cancer treatment, but refused to give in to both that and the stage panics.

When he returned to England he placated John Gielgud, who had been upset, believing that Olivier had slighted him. Gielgud told me, 'I was a little hurt that Larry didn't invite me to perform or to direct in his National Theatre Company at the Old Vic until 1967.'

'I was always looking to find something John and I could do together,' Larry said to me, and he had thought he had found it in 1967 in Ibsen's *The Pretenders*. But that production had to be abandoned when Larry was struck with cancer. So he gave Gielgud Molière's *Tartuffe* as a star vehicle, followed by *Oedipus*.

In the autumn of 1967 Larry decided, after some persuading, to play the Soviet Premier in *The Shoes of the Fisherman*, which starred Anthony Quinn as a Russian priest released from a Siberian prison camp who goes on to become Pope. Larry's agent talked him into doing it when he got MGM to agree to pay $240,000 for three weeks' work in Rome. Larry finally accepted but insisted, in an act of one-upmanship over Quinn, that his name be billed last; he recalled that in music hall, the top artist was always billed last.

The Shoes of the Fisherman was released in America in 1968 but flopped. MGM finally gave it a London charity premiere in 1972, attended by Princess Anne (and me – we were not together!) and then promptly shelved the film. It didn't deserve that fate and was an interesting prediction of the time when a non-Italian would become a modern-day Pope.

While filming *The Shoes of the Fisherman* in Rome, he discovered Franco Zeffirelli was there making his film version of *Romeo and Juliet*. Zeffirelli recalled, 'He came to me and said, "Can I do anything in your film?"'

'So I said, "I would be delighted if you would voice the prologue. He was disappointed and said, "Isn't there anything more I can do?"'

'So I got him to revoice Lord Montague, who was played by an Italian actor who had a very thick accent [so] that it would have been dubbed over by someone, so there was no one better than Larry to do it. In fact, he dubbed many small parts and did some crowd noises in what was a hilarious variety of improvised voices. Nobody ever knew how much he was involved in the film. He can be heard all the time, but you would never know it was him.'

In February 1968 Larry performed in *The Dance of Death* in Edinburgh. During its run, he received a letter from Harold Wilson, the prime minister, asking if he would accept a peerage. Larry declined, feeling it would separate him from his colleagues through a form of class distinction that he abhorred. Wilson wrote a second time, and again Larry declined.

He was still unwell from the radiation treatment but insisted he continue with *The Dance of Death*, although he had to be replaced by Lewis Jones, and later by Anthony Hopkins, when he suffered severe abdominal pains and was rushed to hospital with acute appendicitis. He insisted that he be operated on back in London, at St Thomas' Hospital, so he would not be kept from his work for the National.

He arrived at St Thomas' just in time; the appendix was on the verge of bursting. The surgeon who operated on him also checked his prostate and was able to tell Larry that the cancer had gone.

A month after the operation, Larry was back performing *The Dance of Death* at Leeds and Oxford.

Larry told me with, I think, only a modicum of seriousness, 'The title of that play was like a bell ringing out doom over me, and I wasn't about to let the bugger get me.'

Back in London, Larry and Joan were invited to a dinner party at 10 Downing Street where Harold Wilson again broached the subject of a peerage. Again Larry declined.

Back at the Old Vic, Larry had a terrible shock when he discovered what Peter Brook had done to *Oedipus*. Following the final exit of Gielgud, being led off as the blind Oedipus, Brook had devised a finale that consisted of actors dancing up and down the aisles to a jazzed-up version of 'God Save the Queen'.

Larry begged Brook to amend the finale, and he did. This time, after Gielgud's final exit, a six-foot-tall phallus was hauled on stage.

Said Gielgud, 'Olivier and Brook had some terrible rows. When Larry saw the giant phallus on the stage he thought the Old Vic would be closed down by the police. They went into my dressing room and continued arguing so I left them to it. When I came back half an hour later they had gone but there was a huge crack down my mirror. I never found out which of them did it.'

Larry felt that Brooks's outrageous alternative ending was a personal insult to him as the director of the National, and also a body blow to his position of authority.

In the summer he played Field Marshal Lord Haig in the film version of *Oh! What a Lovely War*, which was Richard Attenborough's directorial debut. He then gave a cameo as Air Chief Marshall Sir Hugh Dowding in *Battle of Britain*. For both roles, Larry typically went to some trouble to get his appearances right. Guy Hamilton, director of *Battle of Britain*, said, 'Larry got some photos of Dowding and saw that he and Dowding were facially quite similar. Larry arranged to have his hair cut the way Dowding had it, and had it dyed the same colour. He also went to some trouble to imitate Dowding's slightly clipped diction. But it is not a flamboyant performance because Dowding was not a flamboyant man.'

He then made a film version of *The Dance of Death* in much the same way *Othello* had been filmed. But this was not to gain the praise and reputation of *Othello*. It was far too theatrical for a non-Shakespearean film version of a stage play, and critics were generally unimpressed.

Olivier also found time to appear fleetingly in an American telemovie, released in cinemas in Europe, of *David Copperfield*, playing Mr Creakle. His only stage performance of 1969 was in the National's *Home and Beauty*. He was so wracked by stage panic that he kept his name off the posters and out of the programme by billing himself as 'Walter Plinge', hoping that would keep the critics away.

In 1970 he revived *The Three Sisters*, this time playing the part of Chebutikin, with Alan Bates taking on the role of Vershinin, all as preparation for the film version, which Larry directed. Again, the critics were underwhelmed by this piece of filmed theatre. 'Many of the performances, among them Olivier's, are to be admired – but it does not belong to the cinema,' said Dilys Powell in the *Sunday Times*.

Early that year Larry met with Arnold Goodman, chairman of the Arts Council, who convinced Larry that by accepting a peerage, he could stand in the House of Lords and speak for the people in his profession. Joan told him, 'They obviously very much want you to have it; I think that perhaps you should take it.'

So, on 13 June 1970, Larry became Lord Olivier of Brighton.

31

A Two-handed Film

Both *Home and Beauty* and *The Three Sisters* on the stage had been a warm-up for what was to be the big one for Olivier – *The Merchant of Venice*, playing Shylock. Jonathan Miller directed, and set the play in the nineteenth century. Larry freely admitted that he based the look of his Shylock on George Arliss's portrayal of Disraeli in the 1929 film of that name. He decided that, rather than go for the traditional and stereotypical Jewish false nose, he would enhance his lips, which he noticed was a characteristic of Jews, by having a set of teeth made with an extra lower gum, producing an effective protrusion.

He played Shylock 138 times at the Old Vic from April 1970 to January 1971. He made a request to his fellow actors on the opening night not to look him directly in the eyes; he still suffered stage panic, and yet, somehow, between the first and last night of *Merchant*, he managed to overcome it once and for all.

Like any aspect of anxiety disorder, stage panic can be overcome, and sometimes it disappears for no apparent reason. It simply takes one panic-free experience where it would normally intrude, and it can disappear. Larry still didn't understand what had really sparked it in the first place, but he knew when it began. He wrote, 'It, I realised, with hindsight, had all started with my abortive soprano solo during the evensong of Trinity in 1921.'

He also made a decision that would have gone a long way to keeping further attacks at bay; he decided he was free to retire from stage acting if he wanted to. Beating his panic disorder was like a battle that had to be won. He had won it. He didn't retire, of course, but the thought was always there that he could if he wanted to. And that thought protected him from further attacks. That was *control*, which was essential to him in his life and work.

Kenneth Tynan came up with the idea for the National Theatre to put on the musical *Guys and Dolls*. It made good sound commercial sense and Oliver knew it. At the end of the financial year in 1970, the National had made its first loss, £100,000. He put it to the board of directors and they agreed, but on condition that Larry was creatively involved.

Larry called Garson Kanin and asked him to direct it. Kanin agreed only if Olivier would play Nathan Detroit. But towards the end of July 1970, Larry was ill with pleurisy, and before he had recovered from that, on 1 August he was back in hospital with a thrombosis in his right leg that made it so swollen and heavy that it was ten pounds heavier than his left leg. There was no choice but to postpone *Guys and Dolls*.

'Larry was so despondent when I said we had to postpone the show,' Garson Kanin told me in 1988. 'He just wanted to do it, thrombosis and all. But he was too ill to move, and he had to agree in the end. But he would have got up there and done the show and danced and everything. There's no stopping Larry.'

Still hoping to pull *Guys and Dolls* together, Larry was well enough for another film cameo, in *Nicholas and Alexandra*, an epic about the last Tsar of Russia and the fate that befell his family. The film seemed like a poor imitation of a David Lean epic, and only Olivier came out of it with any real credit.

'Only Sir Laurence Olivier manages to pierce the pantomime by inventing details of performance that trick us into feeling for a moment,' wrote Gavin Millar in *The Listener*. Critics were still awed enough by him to refer to him as 'Sir'.

He followed up with another film cameo, as the Duke of Wellington in *Lady Caroline Lamb*, which starred his former lover Sarah Miles. Her husband, screenwriter Robert Bolt, was making his debut as a film director. Larry only spent a few days filming but went to the trouble to get the right kind of hairpiece and false nose.

After his last shot on the picture, Bolt said to him, 'Thank you, Larry, your Iron Duke surpassed the character written.'

To which Larry replied, 'My pleasure, old boy.'

Kenneth Tynan came up with another challenging idea for Larry to do at the National, *Long Day's Journey into Night* by Eugene O'Neill. In fact, Tynan had been suggesting this since 1964, but Larry had always resisted playing an actor; O'Neill had written an account of his own explosive home life, fused by a drug-addicted mother and a father who wallows in drink after realising he is no longer a famous actor.

Long Day's Journey into Night ran from December 1971 through to September 1972, first at the New Theatre and then at the Old Vic. In 1971 the National made up the £100,000 it had lost the year before. But it was a blow to Larry when he was told that the board had decided to cancel *Guys and Dolls* at a meeting he complained been held 'behind my back'.

He felt betrayed and helpless to stand up to people he had thought were his friends and colleagues. As such, he felt it was time to step down as director of the National. The final stab in the back came on 24 March 1972, when he was told by Sir Max Rayne, the successful financier who was on the board, that a successor had been chosen as director; Larry had made it known he wanted to be involved in the decision, and had even put forward a name, Michael Blakemore; but once more the Board had met behind his back and a decision had been made. His successor would be Peter Hall, the eminent stage director.

In this stage of depression, Larry gladly accepted his first real leading film role in years. It was *Sleuth*, based on a two-hander and highly successful stage production by Anthony Shaffer. Larry's co-star was Michael Caine, one of the hottest names in films for the past ten years, and the director was Joseph L Mankiewicz. The film, as did the play, revolved around the meeting of two men, one an author called Wyke, played by Olivier, who has lost his wife to the working-class tradesman Milo, played by Caine. The film/play is a cat-and-mouse game in which Wyke murders – or appears to murder – Milo.

When in May 1972 I had the chance to go to Pinewood Studios to see Mankiewicz directing *Sleuth*, I jumped at it. My reason was simply that I wanted to meet Mankiewicz and talk about directing movies. Meeting either Olivier or Caine was not foremost in my mind. I was nineteen years old, and my only ambition in life was to be a film director.

When I reached the set, the two actors – there were just the two of them in this film – were not, as far as I could see, present. But Mankiewicz was, working with his director of photography Oswald

Morris. They were deep in conversation about something that I wasn't privy to, until finally Mankiewicz broke away and came over to me where we were introduced, and he proceeded to give me some of his precious time. And it was precious. Directors do not have time to sit and talk to informal visitors. But he indulged me as I asked him about one of the great sore spots of his life, *Cleopatra*, which led to him talking far more enthusiastically about his version of *Julius Caesar*, filmed in 1952.

And talking of *Julius Caesar* and Shakespeare prompted him to suggest that I speak to Laurence Olivier. 'Larry is really one of your country's greatest movie directors,' Mankiewicz said.

Mankiewicz thanked me for my interest in his work, hoped I'd have an enjoyable day, and got an assistant to take me to Olivier's dressing room. I couldn't tell from Larry's blank expression as he opened the door to be presented with this nineteen-year-old would-be-film director if he was delighted, horrified or just nonplussed. And yet he invited me in.

He was struggling to remember his lines and needed time alone to study them while Mankiewicz was setting up some complicated shot for which only Larry's stand-in was needed. 'They won't ask me to stand there for them, you see,' he told me with a gentle smile, 'because I'm a Lord, I suppose.'

I quickly told him that I had seen him before, when he was filming *Othello*, and this seemed to bring the faintest of smiles to him, and then when I told him that seeing the film version of *Othello* was my first experience of seeing Shakespeare, he seemed more pleased but said, 'My dear boy, you have simply *got* to come and see Shakespeare in the theatre to see it for real.'

So I pointed out that he had been something of a pioneer in bringing Shakespeare to the screen. 'Ah! Yes! There were others before me, but . . . !'

The 'but' that he never concluded was that he recognised he was the first not only to make Shakespeare adaptable for the big screen but also big box office. 'Mr Mankiewicz said I should talk to you about directing because he thinks you're one of the country's best film directors.'

'And what do *you* think?' he asked.

And that was a tricky one to answer, because I hadn't seen any of the Shakespeare films he had directed. But I had seen *The Prince and the Showgirl* and so, rather than admitting that I had seen neither

Henry V nor *Hamlet* nor *Richard III*, I said, 'I think David Lean is probably *the* best, but he's had a lot more practice than you.'

And with that, Larry laughed. The ice was broken, and we began to talk, and I began to learn, not only about directing films the Larry way, but also about Shakespeare. And at some point, I had to ask the question, 'What do I call you?' And that's when he told me to call him Lord Larry. And he decided to nickname me Eminem.

It was all he could do to keep himself from laughing each time I said, 'Lord Larry . . .' and then followed up with some question like, 'What were the advantages of filming in VistaVision?'

He appreciated my knowledge and enthusiasm about film-making, but finally he said to me, 'I have directed few films but many plays, and my advice to you is to direct in the theatre.'

And being the kind of young fellow who asked the first thing that always came to mind, I said, 'And how do I do that?'

He said, 'I will show you.'

It is only in retrospect that the power of that reply hits me. Laurence Olivier himself said that *he* would show *me* how to direct plays. At the time I was little interested in that prospect. And yet, although my work as a stage director has been restricted to small, regional theatre, I am proud that I learned most of what I know from Lord Larry.

But for now, Larry had a film to make, and he was struggling. 'It's getting harder to remember lines,' he said.

He was struggling, and yet he took time to talk to me. And so we talked, despite his desperation to study his lines, and I suppose, looking back, I would have to say that he might have even found me somewhat attractive. He made no overtures, and I never felt any kind of sexual threat from him. But I can look back and realise that he was, even in a subconscious way perhaps, affected by his bisexual nature and was, I am sure, flirting with me. All I knew back then was, I had his full attention.

A week or two earlier, just a week into filming, following two weeks of rehearsal, it had become clear that Larry was having some trouble, partly because he was insisting on getting all he was doing technically correct. Especially when it came to the filming of a snooker game in which Larry had to pot every ball while Caine looked on, getting no chance at all to use his cue.

Larry wanted to pot all the balls himself, even though Mankiewicz was going to insert shots of the balls being pocketed by an off-camera expert. So it really didn't matter if Larry failed, but he was determined to get it as right as possible. And as he went for each ball in turn, he would announce the colour of the ball about to be pocketed. This intense concentration was resulting in him sometimes forgetting to name the colour of the relevant ball, but worse, he was fluffing his lines a lot. Every time he dried, he stopped the take, saying, 'Oh, shit,' or 'Sorry, Joe.'

The scene dragged on. Mankiewicz kept his temper and broke the tension by relating a story of Samuel Goldwyn that had Larry laughing and then relaying one of his own Goldwyn tales.

Michael Caine, talking to me in 1976, said, 'Larry and Joe both worked for Goldwyn and each had their own favourite Goldwynisms. One time Joe told Larry that he needed a rewrite on *Guys and Dolls*, and when he showed the rewrite to Goldwyn, Goldwyn said, "I loved the rewrite. Now the picture has warmth and charmth." That made Larry laugh, and then Larry said that when Goldwyn heard that the atom bomb had been dropped on Hiroshima, he said, "That atomic bomb is dynamite." And that kind of thing really broke the tension whenever Larry had trouble with his lines.'

Anthony Shaffer was on set throughout, and became the target for Larry's frustration at times. He had a line: 'What does my insurance company discover when it swings into action, antennae pulsing with suspicion?' Technically pedantic, Larry spent some time explaining how 'antennae' would be pronounced if Wyke had learned Latin at an old-fashioned public school as Larry did. To Shaffer, it didn't matter. Mankiewicz didn't have a clue one way or the other, and finally Larry stormed off the set, telling Shaffer in passing, 'There's no such word as *pulsing*.'

Shaffer was heard to respond, 'It's going to be a long summer.'

All of this was behaviour that Larry regretted, as he would tell me later during a rehearsal he was directing at the National. 'I am quite embarrassed to have taken my own inadequacies out on others. I don't like my actors doing it to me, and I don't like me doing it to others.

'It was such a very hard part to do. Tony Shaffer is a very clever writer and I did him a disservice at times. He wrote the part as it should have been written – as an author speaking in the way that an author would like to speak, but doesn't. Those kinds of words that Wyke speaks are not the kind of words that spring to mind on the spur of the moment. It isn't very colloquial. So I found myself, as Wyke, having to find them.'

In a BBC TV interview on *Film Night* in 1973, Olivier talked about that problem and explained, 'Those long alliterative lists of things are always difficult to put in the right order, as they derive from the author's struggle for the *mot juste* and abound in literary references.'

So for Larry, the problem was making the very literate dialogue of Wyke sound like real speech. But his problem was also simply one of age messing with his memory. He also had the problems of the National to deal with.

'It was such a very long time between this and my last leading role [in *Term of Trial* in 1962]. And the National was keeping me very busy that I had no real time to commit the script to memory which, for me, is the only real way to do it.'

Michael Caine told me that he had nothing but affection and admiration for Olivier.

> I was in awe of him at first. Who wouldn't be? He was this great actor of the state, knighted, made a baron, and he had all this stage and film history behind him. So that was pretty intimidating at first. But then he was coming to me with the problems *he* had. I mean, *me*! And you quickly realise this is someone with human frailties as we all do, and as he began to worry endlessly about the script and his problems remembering lines, I found myself in the position of being the one who listened to him and giving him *my* advice.
>
> Two weeks before we started rehearsing, he sent me a letter which said, 'If you are wondering how to address me when we meet, I think it would be a great idea if you called me Larry.' I was still very nervous of meeting him.
>
> But when he came onto the set, he just walked straight over to me, ignoring Joe [Mankiewicz], and smiled very genuinely at me and shook my hand and said, 'What a pleasure, Michael. We meet at last.' And I said, 'Hello, Larry.'
>
> We had two weeks' rehearsal, which was wonderful to have on a film. On our first day I was amazed at the amount of energy he was putting into it. He gave me a very good bit of advice which was, always do the part out loud even if it is the very first time you read it, and make it as though you are playing it. I took his advice.
>
> But I could see he was struggling with what he was doing and seemed very dissatisfied with what he was doing. At the end of the day he left, and I stayed behind to talk to Joe, and he came rushing back in

and said like it was a big secret, 'Joe, I've got a great idea and I'll show you in the morning.'

The next morning he came bounding onto the set full of enthusiasm and produced a small moustache which he held to his upper lip and said, 'What do you think, Joe?'

Joe said, 'That will be fine, Larry, if you think it's necessary.'

Larry said, 'Oh, I do, because I suddenly realised what was wrong with me yesterday. I can't act with my own face. I always need some sort of disguise.'

So Joe said, 'Well, use it,' and from then Larry, with his moustache stuck on, was right into the part.

During the two weeks of rehearsal we had, he would come into my dressing room during breaks to run scenes. He wanted to memorise the whole script before we started shooting, which was very admirable and is the way you have to do it when you do a play. But this is film, and film is very different, and after we started filming, he would come to me worrying about what we had done the day before, and worrying about the scenes tomorrow. I told him, 'Just forget about yesterday's work and forget about tomorrow's scenes, and just concentrate on what we're shooting today.'

After just a few days of filming, we discovered from reading in the newspapers that Larry had been thrown out of his National Theatre Company, which he had been working so hard for over the years. This was a terrible blow to him. He would forget his lines. He seemed to be suffering a lot from loss of memory.

It would turn out that his loss of memory was partly to do with some tranquillisers he was taking to calm him down; a side effect was memory loss.

Caine told Olivier that because of the problems the loss of the National Theatre was causing him, he would never disturb him in his dressing room. But he told Olivier that he was welcome into his dressing room any time he liked.

'He'd come to my dressing room with something new he'd dreamed up to tell me about it,' Caine said, 'and I was watching Wimbledon on a television. He said, "What *are* you doing?"'

'I said, "Watching the tennis."'

'He was astonished at this and said, "You have a *television* in your dressing room?"'

'I said, "Yes. Don't you have one?"'

'He said, "No. I would never have thought of asking for one."'

'So I said, "Would you like to watch the tennis with me?"'

'He said, "Oh, yes, thank you, Michael," and he sat down and we watched it over the next week up until the Ladies' Final when Billie Jean King won.'

Larry said of Caine, 'He was a great leveller. I was really very jealous of his status as a film star.'

There were times when Larry displayed some of his greatest strengths. He could feign an old woman's accent flawlessly, as the script required, while setting a charge of dynamite. And, true to form, his moments of mere reaction were perfect examples of acting consisting largely of reacting. As Mankiewicz explained to me, 'You shoot reaction shots in close-up while the main speaker is off camera, and you film them and then simply edit them together. It's really very simple.'

When Larry gave a reaction shot, it was, Mankiewicz said, 'pure art. Pure genius. He could react to what was being said brilliantly. Michael Caine was not so good in his reaction shots, but I think he learned a lot watching Larry.'

Larry was modest about this particular ability. 'It comes from years and years of just doing it,' he told me. 'Michael had not been working at it as long as I, and I could see he would learn to do it better in time. Michael's great gift is being able to deliver his lines as though he were saying them for the first time and being utterly believable. And you can really ask no more of an actor than that. I have the greatest admiration for him, and the most tender affection. Without Michael, I might not have survived *Sleuth*. Another actor in his part might not have been so generous, so endlessly patient, so undeniably brilliant in the part – all at the same time. I consider *Sleuth* to be one of the best films of my life.'

The film was completed in time for premieres in New York and Los Angeles in December 1972, to qualify for the Oscars. Felix Barker wrote in the London *Evening News*, 'Wyke is not only wealthy, urbane, a connoisseur of mechanical toys and a master of the sardonic epigrams; he also provides Laurence Olivier with the best comedy role of his film career.'

'Olivier is quite brilliant,' wrote Cecil Wilson in the *Daily Mail*, 'bounding athletically up and down baronial stairways and cellar steps and impressing his own authority on glib lines.'

American critics were unimpressed by Olivier, though, and there seemed to almost be something of a backlash against him, not for his performance so much but for his stature. Stanley Kauffmann of the *New Republic* said, 'This is Lord O in Entertainment, and we are all supposed to rave at Greatness Unbending.'

Andrew Sarris said in the *Village Voice*, 'Olivier's vocal imitations are less accomplished than Peter Sellers's, but I suppose we are supposed to be overwhelmed simply because Sir Laurence deigned to do them.'

Olivier and Caine were both nominated for Oscars in 1973, and both lost to Marlon Brando in *The Godfather*. But Larry did receive the New York Film Critics Circle award for his performance. When the National Society of Film Critics awarded Al Pacino for *The Godfather*, Mankiewicz declared, 'To compare Michael Caine's performance, let alone Larry's, with Al Pacino's makes me despair not only of the so-called cinemas as an art but of the people who evaluate the cinema.'

Mankiewicz told me on the set of *Sleuth*, 'You don't really direct an actor like Olivier. You judge him and edit him. He's the most incredible "institution" I've ever directed. With fifty years of acting behind him, he's played everything in every way. You can't teach him anything new, but you can get a new combination from him with the same colours. I asked him what he would do at the National Theatre under Peter Hall, and he said, "What would you suggest, old boy? You see, I've played them all."'

32

Back from the Brink

Olivier continued at the National for a while as co-director with Peter Hall. In 1972, Larry asked Franco Zeffirelli to direct something for the National and invited him to be a guest at the Oliviers' home in Brighton so they could discuss what to do.

'Olivier was always a hero of mine,' Zeffirelli told me in 1977. 'He is, I think, the greatest actor alive. I loved his Shakespeare films; I was brought up on them, and I think he was intrigued by me because I was an Italian who had made Shakespeare films [*Romeo and Juliet* and *The Taming of the Shrew*] and those films had once been his domain.'

They decided on *Saturday, Sunday, Monday*, a comedy by Eduardo de Filippo about a large Italian family in Naples. The kitchen and dining table are the heart of this household. Food equals love. Eduardo de Filippo wrote his plays for his own company, which was, by Neapolitan tradition, an extended family, and so his work invariably was about the lives of Neapolitan family relationships.

Zeffirelli told me:

It was Ken Tynan who came up with the idea of doing a play by de Filippo at the Old Vic. De Filippo is very popular in Italy but was unknown in London, and I thought it would be a wonderful idea to do both *Filumena* and *Saturday, Sunday, Monday*. Joan asked me which of the two plays was the best, and I gave my honest answer, which is *Filumena*. So she decided we should do *Saturday, Sunday, Monday* first and if it was a success then to give them the better play. Larry was keen for Joan to do both the plays as she was perfect for both roles.

Larry and Joan came over to Pitano to prepare for the play [in 1972], and Larry was very busy absorbing all the gestures and manners of the people in the village.

Edward de Filippo came up from Naples to meet Olivier, and there were two great men engaged in conversation. De Filippo is one of the great figures of the Italian stage and there he was with Laurence Olivier, the great actor of any stage, and they were locked in a conversation that one moment was very formal and polite and the next they were like two theatre people engaged in bitching like they were masters at it.

When I asked Larry what he thought of de Filippo, he said, 'Boring old fart,' which meant that he liked him very much.

In 1973 Franco Zeffirelli arrived in London to begin directing *Saturday, Sunday, Monday*. He quickly discovered the delights and the pitfalls of directing the great Olivier. Said Zeffirelli:

We were rehearsing [in London] and he turned up with a book of Italian gestures. I have no idea where he'd found this book, but it had hand signs for 'I'm hungry', and 'I love you', and some less polite expressions. He said to me, 'Excuse me, Franco, darling, but as you are Italian, perhaps you could kindly help me by explaining what this gesture means.'

He was very good at using the gestures, but his accent was not so good. In fact, it was very bad, and it was infectious, and it spread through the company and everybody was sounding like comedic ice-cream sellers. So that had to stop. But the problem was, how do I do this with Laurence Olivier? How would I direct him? In a way I was too inexperienced to be daunted, but I also knew enough to realise that you didn't just charge in.

Larry was a great actor, and he could absorb ideas and transform them into whatever he wants – speech patterns and expressions. These are things he knows will work for him. What I had to do was trick him into finding in himself things he didn't know were there. The great and the terrible things about Larry is that he will praise you for your insight, bless you for your help, and then he'll do it exactly as he wants. He is a wonderful old fraud.

And so you have to stop him from overwhelming you, and I was able to find a way of directing him.

Olivier was, by habit almost, still losing himself in other personalities.

Talking about Zeffirelli, Larry told me, 'The thing about Franco is that he is a genius and you have to respect what he says.'

I had the privilege of watching Larry and Joan Plowright in rehearsal, sitting quietly in the dark. Larry had told me that I should direct for the stage, and to my surprise one day in 1973 I got a call from the National to come along and observe. By this time the rehearsals were well advanced, and Zeffirelli was making only subtle suggestions, each one seeming to delight Larry, who seemed eager for any extra nuance he could put into his performance.

The delight of that day was also seeing Larry and Joan on stage together. Their professionalism seemed to override their personal feelings, but every now and then there was the holding of a hand, or a hand upon an arm, or a kiss upon a cheek, and sometimes a little discreet conversation that I was too distant to hear. But it was a delight to observe.

When I had the chance to speak to Larry, I told him it was wonderful to watch but I didn't get much of a feel for stage directing from it, so he promised me I would come and see how he directed the next time he did it.

Saturday, Sunday, Monday played at the Old Vic from October 1973 through to February 1974, running for 42 successful performances. It was decided that *Filumena* would be the next de Filippo play, but that wouldn't happen until 1977.

In December 1973, Larry appeared in *The Party*, by Trevor Griffiths, for the National Theatre Company at the Old Vic. He played John Tagg, a communist from Glasgow. Although it was a supporting role, he had a twenty-minute monologue that took him four months to learn. He also perfected the Glaswegian accent.

Ill health was once again to take its toll on him, though. In February 1974 he began suffering with what he was sure was just a frozen shoulder, and so he took Valium during the day, to try and relax the stricken muscles, and Mogadon by night to sleep.

He continued in *The Party* until it came to the end of its run in March. It was his final appearance at the National, and would be his last in any play.

In the spring of 1974 he began directing his wife in Priestley's *Eden End*, and I was allowed up to his office. He showed me the model of the stage and set, and with great delight, like a little boy with his newest toy, he demonstrated how he blocked the play using little models of the characters to move around the set.

As he moved each character he delivered their lines in different voices. He was having fun, plain and simple. He still took time to talk about the serious side of directing, and explained to me in exquisite detail the miracle of blocking. 'It's thought to be a work of genius when some directors do it,' he told me. 'But it is just judgement. I would do it differently to Peter Hall or Tony Guthrie, and if my judgement is correct, the audience will love me. And of course, I always am, and of course, they always do.'

Some days later I was in a rehearsal room, watching Larry direct, and as they were in the early stages of the process, there was much talk and discussion as Larry and his cast worked their way through a scene. What impressed me was that there was no bullying, no raised voices and no egos on show, least of all from Larry.

'When you choose your actors,' he explained, 'you have made your decision to allow them to use what they have in themselves, and about themselves, to give you what you hope for. And then I will take what they have given me and mould it closer to what I want. Somewhere at some point, if we are all very lucky, we reach as close as we can for what I hope for. Then it is down to the actor to make it live for an audience.'

Eden End was his final production for the National. Of course, what he really wanted to do was get back on the stage again. But sadly, that was not to be. He had been forced into retirement as a stage actor by his failing health. And that frustrated him, not least because his two most notable peers, Gielgud and Richardson, were still going strong.

In August his shoulder was in severe pain again, and so were his arms. His fingernails became terribly sore. By the end of September his face was so swollen that his eyes were almost hidden.

He was referred to Dr Joanna Sheldon, a specialist in dermatology, who sent him to the Royal Sussex Hospital for blood tests that confirmed he had a rare disease called derma-polymyositis. Basically, his muscles and areas of his skin had become inflamed, and he had to be hospitalised for up to six months. He was treated with steroids, and with a few days the swelling in his face had begun to subside and he was sure his muscles were aching less. But the improvement was only slight and he continued to be extremely ill. He began to have difficulty swallowing and had to be fed through a tube directly into his stomach. Dr Sheldon even began to fear that Larry would not survive, and warned his son Tarquin that he might not last beyond another six weeks.

He was growing weaker. He could barely lift an arm. But in December, after eight weeks of treatment, he had turned the corner and Dr Sheldon became confident that he would survive. Joan lifted his spirits by urging him to write his memoirs. His sister Sybille came and sat with him and they talked about their early life. After those visits, Larry began work on his memoirs, writing by hand, despite his sore fingers. But by now something else had started to be of concern – his mind.

'I became like Viv,' he told me in 1976. 'I was manic. Out of my mind. And the thing is, I knew it but couldn't help it. And then I plummeted. I wanted to throw myself out of the window. I scared poor Joan to death. I placed an order for iron bars to be placed at the upstairs windows of our cottage.'

The window bars were never placed; Joan sent them back.

Nobody ever knew for sure what had caused this sudden but brief mental breakdown. 'It must have been the steroids,' Larry said. 'The dosage was reduced and I came back to earth.'

I have no idea what kind of effect steroids can have on the mind, but I do know the effect that recalling dark, hidden moments from the past can do. And that was what Larry had been doing. He had been recalling his life, and writing about it, and discussing things with his sister Sybille who was herself mentally ill. I doubt that he discussed the sexual abuse he had suffered, and he certainly didn't write about it. But it would have been there, in his mind and his memories, and it would have been enough, in his weakened condition, to have caused him to become lost for some days.

There was a brief spell when he seemed much better, eating scrambled eggs for breakfast, his first solid food in weeks.

And then came a relapse that was so terrible that he gave up the will to live. His fingers were so sore he could no longer write. There was, it seemed, nothing left for him to live for.

But Joan wasn't giving up. She asked her brother, David Plowright, programme controller at Granada Television, to come and visit him, and when he did, no doubt at her prompting, he told Larry he had an idea for a series called *Laurence Olivier Presents*, in which modern plays of his choosing would be produced. Plowright suggested Larry would direct maybe one or two and told him he would be in control of the whole project.

Larry displayed no interest at first. But two weeks later he suddenly became enthusiastic about it, and that was the turning point. From then on, he began to get stronger.

Speaking to me at Granada Studios during the recording of the second of that series David Plowright had devised in 1976, Larry told me, 'This series saved my life. David Plowright saved my life. I was dying. I know I was. I didn't want to live any longer. I had nothing to live for, and I felt that it was cruel of me to put Joan through agony any longer and that she would be better off if I could just pass away. And I was trying to do just that – and then my dear brother-in-law David gave me my life back. He literally brought me back from the brink.'

33

The Hollywood Legend

On Christmas Day 1974 Larry was allowed home for a few hours. Throughout January 1975 he slowly regained some strength. But he would never be strong enough to do anything like *Othello* or *The Dance of Death* again. Being immobile in hospital for even just a few weeks is very debilitating; being immobile for three months had wasted much of his muscle, and he had lost weight because of it.

Remarkably, he was strong enough to leave hospital and go home at the end of January. He immediately began discussing *Laurence Olivier Presents* with David Plowright. He still had very sore fingers, the tips of which were constantly covered in bleeding sores. Susana Walton, wife of composer William Walton, spent hours each morning patiently dressing his fingers.

He was now prone to all kinds of illnesses: the flu, sore throats and toothache. He was also worried about money; there was a lot less of it now that he wasn't working.

The proposed Granada TV series had given him a tremendous boost. But what he really wanted to do was act. And he was given that chance when he got to play Moriarty in an unusual Sherlock Holmes film, *The Seven Per Cent Solution*. Dr Watson was played by Robert Duvall, and Sherlock Holmes by Nicol Williamson. It took only three days to film Larry's scenes, but Pauline Kael, writing in the *New Yorker*, said, 'Olivier is in tremendously high form. His Moriarty, a prissy, complaining old pedagogue who feels persecuted by Holmes, is performed with the covert wit that is his speciality.'

Universal, who produced the film, were so uncertain of it they held it back from distribution until 1977.

Then came what Larry had been waiting for – a leading role in a major film. The picture was *Marathon Man*, to be directed by John Schlesinger, who personally called Larry by telephone and offered him the role of a Nazi war criminal in hiding. His fee would be $135,000. But there was a major problem; producer Robert Evans discovered that no one would insure Olivier for more than a week's work. So David Niven and Merle Oberon arranged for Evans to meet with members of the House of Lords, who in turn persuaded Lloyd's of London to bend the rules and insure Larry for six weeks.

Larry was rejuvenated; it was his first leading role since *Sleuth*. He persuaded Dr Sheldon to write a certificate to say that he was well enough to go to America in October. He received equal billing with Dustin Hoffman, who played an obsessive runner in New York who is drawn into a mysterious plot involving his globetrotting brother, (Roy Scheider), his European girlfriend (Marthe Keller) and Nazi war criminal Szell, played by Olivier.

For his role of the sadistic Szell, Larry shaved his thinning hair from the top of his head to give him a realistic-looking bald pate, and he wore large glasses with powerful lenses that magnified his eyes to tremendous effect.

The most famous scene in the film is the one in which Larry tortures Hoffman, who is strapped into a dentist's chair while Larry goes to work on him with the drill and no anaesthetic. It was said that a lot of people were put off from visiting their dentist for a long time after they saw that movie. Larry performed the whole sequences with great care, having learned how to handle dentistry tools expertly. He was inspired in the way in which he performed his torture by watching a gardener cut some roses.

There is a now legendary anecdote about Hoffman being unable to find the right motivation for a scene and the advice Larry gave him; it is worth repeating here, told to me by Larry himself.

'Dustin is a wonderful actor but like many of his generation [he is] too concerned with the bloody "Method". John [Schlesinger] was being entirely patient with Dustin as he held up filming while trying to figure out if he should take off a shirt, and if so how to. He said, "I'm sorry, John, but I just can't get the right motivation to do this," and so

I, who was eager to get on with filming before I died, piped in with, "Why don't you try acting, dear boy?" I mean, Michael, it really is the *only* way to do it.'

Hoffman probably didn't know that Larry was in terrible pain throughout production, especially in the torture sequence, due to his still very sore fingertips. Larry just wanted to get on with the work.

The film was a hit and broke New York's opening weekend record after *The Godfather*. After finishing *Marathon Man*, Larry remained in Los Angeles to see in the New Year of 1976. He met up with Sarah Miles and took her to a party where the guests, including Jean Simmons, Burt Lancaster, Dustin Hoffman and Kirk Douglas, all stood as he entered.

He returned to England and his Brighton home feeling rejuvenated. In March 1976, he went to Tunisia to appear as Nicodemus in Zeffirelli's TV series *Jesus of Nazareth*. The series was more like a major film epic than a TV production and boasted a cast of major international stars. Zeffirelli credited Larry with the success he had in getting such an impressive cast.

'Larry was just so eager to take a part because he really has such affection for the Biblical tale,' said Zeffirelli. 'He just wanted a part and wasn't worried if it was a small role and wasn't concerned about getting top billing and really wasn't going to argue about money. But what part was there for him?

'He said, "I can't be Pilate because I am too old for all that horse riding. I'm not Jewish enough to play Caiaphas."'

I said to Zeffirelli, 'Do you think he preferred not to play Caiaphas because he would be playing the man who was responsible for having Jesus arrested?'

'That is very possible. I think he liked the choice of Nicodemus who speaks for Christ at his trial. It was such a tiny part. But once news got around that Laurence Olivier was playing a small role which took maybe three days to film, other big stars were wishing to have roles.'

The cast included Peter Ustinov as Herod, Rod Steiger as Pilate, Anne Bancroft as Mary Magdalene, Michael York as John the Baptist, Christopher Plummer as Herod Antipas and Ralph Richardson as Simeon.

Larry's major scene was with Jesus before the Sanhedrin with Anthony Quinn as Caiaphas, James Mason as Joseph of Arimathea and Robert Powell as Jesus. But he complained to Zeffirelli that the director of photography, David Watkin, was taking too long to light a single scene. Larry was beginning to feel the strain of waiting in the North African heat that was made even worse by the arc lights.

Zeffirelli recalled, 'When Larry got to do his scene, he simply couldn't speak. His wonderful voice had given up on him and let him down at the crucial moment. It was really a terrible moment. I wrapped the scene for the night and we filmed it the next day and Larry was fine. But he came to me afterwards and said, "You know how much I love you but I must tell you that you are going to lose the picture if you do not fire the cameraman because he doesn't know what he is doing."

'But when we saw the rushes Larry was the first to admit that David Watkins's work was stunning. But he reminded me of how much he had suffered and then said, "Of course, it was nothing compared to the sufferings of our Lord."'

Zeffirelli also credited Larry with saving the day when Lew Grade, who was producing the series, came to visit the set and insisted that the script needed some cuts to prevent the series from running over schedule and over budget.

'I didn't know how I could ask these wonderful actors who had done the film for little money and little glory to cut back on their parts which were brief enough,' said Zeffirelli. 'We were filming the High Council scene, and Larry rose from his seat and said to me, "Darling, can I cut these two lines?"

'Taking their cue from him, the other actors also asked to cut lines.'

James Mason recalled to me, on the set of *Murder by Decree* in 1978 at Shepperton Studios, 'We could see Franco was desperate and we were experienced enough to find lines that you could do without. Larry was cutting his lines, Ian Holm was cutting his, but Anthony Quinn just sat in his throne as Caiaphas and said, "Well, Franco, I just don't see how I can cut any more of my role."

'So Larry said to Quinn, "Really, my dear boy, if you take another look and read it very closely, you'll find there is quite a lot you can do without." And then Larry whispered to me, "And *we* could do without too." We were really quite horrified at the way Quinn's strong American accent contrasted with the rest of us. And then Larry said, "Take your time, Tony. We can wait, can't we, Franco?" And Franco by now was looking delighted, but Quinn was very reluctant to cut any of his lines.'

Filming the scene finally got under way. Zeffirelli said, 'There were Larry Olivier and James Mason simply hanging their heads and wringing their hands every time Anthony Quinn said "Lord" because he said it with such a long drawl. Finally Larry said, "Tony, my darling, are you sure we are showing enough respect to our Lord if we pronounce him as 'Lorrrrd'? Why not try 'God' instead?"

'So Quinn changed it to God but it would come out as "Gaaahd". Larry and James just shook their heads and shrugged. And then Larry said, "Of course, no matter what we do on the set, in the end Franco has the scissors." And that is true. Larry knew as a director that you can do a great deal in editing.'

In May Larry was one of scores of major stars in the Second World War all-star epic *A Bridge Too Far*, playing a Dutch doctor caught up in events surrounding the disastrous invasion of Holland by Allied forces. His fee was $200,000 for six days' work. Then he was back in England where the National Theatre on the South Bank was, at long last, about to open. He also had his TV series to begin work on at Granada Studios in Manchester.

The first in the series was Harold Pinter's *The Collection* with Alan Bates, Malcolm McDowell and Helen Mirren. Bates, who I spent time with in Devon in 1977 when he filmed *The Shout*, recalled, 'Olivier insisted that we rehearsed for two weeks in London before moving to Manchester to record it. That was a marvellous way to work. It was almost like doing a stage production, which I would guess is how Larry wanted it.'

The second play was *Cat on a Hot Tin Roof*. It featured Natalie Wood as Maggie and her husband Robert Wagner as Brick. Larry played Big Daddy, and Maureen Stapleton was Big Mamma.

I went up to Granada Studios in 1976 to interview the cast. Natalie Wood was no longer getting plum roles in major films as she had in the late 1950s and early 60s, so I asked her how she came to do what was a major boost in her career. She said very simply, 'Well, Larry invited me to do it. I can't tell you how delighted I was that he should ask me.'

'Don't forget me, dear?' said Wagner, who sat alongside.

'Yes, he wanted you too, dear,' she told Wagner.

Larry told me, 'I asked Natalie because I had seen her in *This Property is Condemned* and *Splendor in the Grass* and I could see that she could handle this kind of a role.'

It was also, someone on the set suggested to me, because there was something about Natalie that reminded Olivier of Vivien Leigh. Robert Wagner, it seems, came as part of the package. Larry understood this; he had often chosen projects just so he and his wife could work together.

'Robert Wagner is a far better actor than the lightweight roles he usually plays would suggest,' said Larry.

Wagner found the technique of rehearsing for two weeks and then recording the show, doing one act at a time, very different to what he was used to. He was in the middle of filming his series *Switch* and actually persuaded Universal (who produced the show) to give him two months off to make *Cat on a Hot Tin Roof*. 'Television is usually so quick; you set up, you rehearse, you shoot, and you move on,' he said. 'This is a marvellous way to do TV, and Larry makes it interesting for everyone.'

Robert Moore, an American, directed *Cat on a Hot Tin Roof*, but Olivier's influence and authority was stamped throughout. 'It was the next best thing to working on stage,' Larry told me during the recording of the show. 'We are taping whole scenes with no breaks, no cuts.'

'How is your memory holding up?' I asked him.

'I seem to be doing reasonably well. On *Sleuth* there was just Michael [Caine] and I, but here we have Natalie and R J and Maureen Stapleton.'

'How are you getting on with Natalie and R J?'

'They are wonderful. I wish I had worked with Natalie sooner. She is greatly underrated, it seems to me. And Bob Wagner is wonderful.'

If this was just all merely mutual admiration for the sake of good publicity, it became something more as Olivier and the Wagners became firm friends. A year later, Larry was in Los Angeles to make *The Betsy*. 'Natalie and RJ were very kind to me,' Larry told me, 'often inviting me to have dinner with them.'

Natalie later told me (in 1980, when she had come to London to promote *The Last Married Couple in America* as well as speak at the National Film Theatre) that it was obvious to her, when recording *Cat on a Hot Tin Roof*, that Olivier was finding the part of Big Daddy somewhat 'difficult because he wasn't in good health'.

She found working with him both 'inspiring and intimidating'. She said, 'When we got to the scene where Maggie makes the claim that she is carrying Brick's baby, all Larry had to do was react, and he did it differently each time with each take. All he had to do was look at me, and he never did it the same twice. One time he looked, and he just looked and looked, and his look went on for so long that I began to feel quite faint. It was a moment in acting that becomes so real that I was responding to his reaction the way Maggie would have, and it was very uncomfortable. But it was perfect because it was the take that the director chose.

'Maureen [Stapleton] said something to me afterwards. She said, "Honey, when you've been looked at by Laurence Olivier, you *know* you've been looked at."'

In 1978, Larry looked back at the experience of making *Cat on a Hot Tin Roof* and said, 'I was let down by my health. I knew it at the time. But I wouldn't allow it to beat me down. I wasn't true to the character of Big Daddy as Williams wrote it. Inside I was. I wish you could have seen what was going on inside. But my body wouldn't allow me to convey all that.'

Of Natalie Wood, he said, 'She was nervous when we got to the dress rehearsal, and her nervousness added to the tension of the whole piece. Afterwards, she told me she had felt she let herself down because of her nerves, and I told her that a certain amount of nervous tension is the best thing for any actor. I had suffered in the past because I was too confident. She didn't believe me. So I told her how I had suffered terrible stage fright when I became too confident. You can be nervous and you can make sure you get it right, or you can be plain terrified for all sorts of reasons, and being nervous is better than terror.

'I don't know if that helped her or not, but when we started taping, she was as good as any actress could be in that part.'

Natalie felt that one actress who could have played the part was Vivien Leigh in her younger years. 'Vivien Leigh is my favourite actress,' she told me.

'Did you tell Larry?' I asked her.

'I did. He didn't say anything. He just looked at me, and there was something in his eyes that seemed to say, "I know what you mean." But he didn't speak the words.'

It took thirteen months to film the six plays Larry had chosen for Granada Television, and as soon as he had finished them, Larry went back to America to play the leading role in *The Betsy* as the elderly patriarch of a family-owned corporation. A series of flashbacks, to reveal the family's troubled past, featured Larry as a younger version of his character.

The film was based on a book by Harold Robbins that was a steamy bestseller, but the film was awful. So bad, in fact, that I asked Larry what induced him to do it. He said, 'Because I wanted to have one last attempt at a lusty, sexy part, and I figured that would be it.'

The only thing of interest about the film was to see how Larry, as frail as he was, transformed into a lusty forty-year-old. It also provided him with his one and only sex scene, which, frankly, was embarrassing, not because it was sexy but because it was so tasteless, and it was tasteless of Olivier to do it.

There was, ultimately, a very good reason for him to make *The Betsy*: the $350,000 fee plus $1,500 expenses and a share of the profits. But this was no mere mercenary act. Larry was on a roll, and he knew it, and while he had made a good living as an actor throughout most of his life, he had never been rich. And he still had to pay alimony to Jill, his first wife. But what really bothered him was that he had little to leave his children, or to pay for their schooling, and so he was making as much as he could in as short a time as possible, not knowing how much time he actually had left, for his family.

Newsweek commented, 'God only knows what the incomparable actor of the Western world is doing in a piece of hilarious idiocy like *The Betsy*. Taking away a zillion dollars, one hopes.' And that's what Larry hoped.

By the time he came back to England in August 1977, the eight weeks' filming had taken its toll and he was looking frail again, and then he became ill with kidney trouble. He underwent an operation and recovered, and almost immediately returned to Hollywood in December to make *The Boys from Brazil*. He played a veteran Jewish Nazi hunter who discovers an insane plot to resurrect Adolf Hitler and establish the Fourth Reich in South America. At the head of the Nazis is the infamous Dr Josef Mengele, played by Gregory Peck.

Peck told me in 1978, 'One of my lifetime ambitions was to work with Laurence Olivier. He was just beautiful – a darling. He was gallant, funny, easy to be with and not at all intimidating to me or the others.'

Larry was nominated for an Academy Award for his role of the Nazi hunter. But then, he was bringing class to everything he touched, as *Time* noted: 'One of the consistent joys of '70s movie going has been Laurence Olivier's game, witty performances in otherwise terrible films.'

He didn't get the Oscar, but he did get $725,000.

When he had finished his thirteen-week stint on *The Boys from Brazil*, Larry went to Paris for *A Little Romance*, playing a charming old Frenchman who befriends two teenagers in love, played by Diane Lane and Thelonious Bernard. Larry was, said *Variety*, 'a modern refashioning of the old Maurice Chevalier role. The prototypical lovable scoundrel, Olivier hams it up unmercifully.'

He knew as soon as he started filming that he wasn't physically up to it. And by the time filming was over, he was very weak. He came back to England, to his home, The Malthouse in Brighton, to recover. He was ready to go back to work in 1978, playing Professor Van Helsing in *Dracula*. It was produced by Walter Mirisch, written by W D Richter, directed by John Badham, and had Frank Langella in the title role. Langella had been playing in a stage revival of *Dracula* on Broadway since 1977.

Badham told me on the set of the film at Shepperton Studios, 'Getting Laurence Olivier to play Van Helsing was one of the best bits of casting in the film. English actors have a very strong tradition of respect for the text. Larry is very easy to work with in that regard.

Badham recalled how, on many occasions, Larry had a tendency to let his jaw drop open slightly. Said Badham, 'You look at him and suddenly he's standing there with his mouth half open. As politely as I could, I pointed out to him that he looked much stronger when his mouth was closed. So he obliged. It always looked better. But when we got to the library scene, he is watching Langella go out the window, and I see his mouth is hanging wide open. I said, "Sir, would you mind if we do it again, and try to keep your mouth closed?" He said, "Dear boy, I have just seen a man jump out of a window and turn into a wolf. I am entitled to have my mouth open." I said, "It's OK! You can do it! Sorry! Sorry, sir!" He had a great sense of humour, a very dry British wit that was kind of wonderful."

The film had been budgeted at $10 million and a generous sixty to seventy-day shooting schedule in 1978 and early 1979. Exterior locations were shot in Cornwall, with interiors filmed at Shepperton Studios.

I went to Cornwall to watch Larry filming on location. His fingers were still sore and he couldn't even shake hands. He was in pain much of the time but refused to show it. I asked him why he was working so hard, making virtually one film after another at that time. He said, 'They keep asking me, so as long as I like the work, I accept it. I can't stop now. I would wither and die.'

He didn't much care for the part or the subject, but he thought the shame of it was worth the $750,000 he was being paid.

I saw Larry again when they went to Shepperton to film interiors. He was sitting in a canvas chair on the sound stage, and he seemed very tired. He didn't recognise me when I went up to him. Then I said, 'Lord Larry, it's Eminem!'

'My dear boy!' he exclaimed. He stood up slowly and held both my hands, and I knew that had to be painful for him. We went to his dressing room and talked, and I was afraid it would be the last time I would see him.

Despite his sore fingers and his frail frame, he continued to work at a frantic pace, wasting his talents in 1979 in *Inchon*, an epic about the Korean War in which he played General MacArthur. It was filmed in South Korea and directed by Terence Young, with a cast of thousands and untold problems. Larry had worked hard to create the illusion of being MacArthur, from his physical appearance to the pattern of his speech, but his energy level during the making of *Inchon* was lower than ever. He told Rex Reed of the *New York Daily News* in 1979, 'I have very little adrenalin left. And I'm fading fast.'

Terence Young, while directing *The Jigsaw Man* in 1981, told me:

> We were all duped on that film. Larry, me, everyone who was a professional on that picture. I discovered halfway through filming that the money for the picture came from the Moonies [the Unification Church] and their leader, Sun Myung Moon wanted his name on the credits as the producer. I told him if he had his name on the credits, they would have to take mine off. I was having nothing to do with his religion. Not that the film had anything to do with his religion, but the idea was to make money for Moon. The Moonies took control of the film and added some black-and-white newsreel footage of the real MacArthur at the end. I told them that wrecked everything Larry had done in creating the illusion of becoming MacArthur. Then the Moonies decided to distribute the film themselves. Well, they didn't know what they were doing, and it opened in America and promptly closed and has never been seen again.'

I have never seen *Inchon*. Few have. But it was described by *Newsweek* as the worst movie ever made. At least Larry was well paid, receiving a million dollars, plus $2,500 a week expenses over six weeks.

But there was one thing Larry could be proud of in 1979. He was awarded an honorary Oscar, handed to him by Cary Grant in Los Angeles in April, 'for the full body of his work, for the unique achievement of his entire career and his lifetime of contribution to the art of film'.

Laurence Olivier was officially a Hollywood legend.

34

Antony, by Zeus

In 1979 I got to see Larry again after all, when he was playing Zeus in the fantasy adventure *Clash of the Titans*, one of the many successful collaborations between special-effects wizard Ray Harryhausen and producer Charles H Schneer; they had produced films such as *Jason and the Argonauts* and *The Seventh Voyage of Sinbad* and its sequels.

Larry was required for just a few days of filming at Pinewood Studios, with his good friend Maggie Smith as the goddess Thetis as well as Claire Bloom as Hera and Ursula Andress as Aphrodite. All the big action sequences involving Harry Hamlin as Perseus and Judi Bowker as Andromeda, and the assorted monsters such as Medusa and the Kraken, were filmed on more exotic locations. Larry was happy just to play a cameo and to film his few scenes closer to home.

Although I was still intent on becoming a film director, I had decided to try my hand at acting. I'd been an extra in several films and decided to go to the top and ask Lord Larry to give me an acting lesson.

I vaguely knew Charles Schneer, and through him I was able to get a letter to Larry (I never imposed by writing directly to Larry's private address) and one day at work I received a telephone call to come to the studios the next day.

He was in his dressing room waiting for me, in his full loose-fitting costume and Zeus beard, which somehow made him look less frail. He seemed unusually stern with me, and I thought that maybe I was in trouble for daring to ask him to teach me to act.

'And so,' he said, 'you want to be an actor, do you, Eminem?'

'Yes, Lord Larry.'

'What have you done so far?'

I outlined my limited experience in front of a camera.

'What have you done on the stage?'

I explained that my stage work had been limited to a couple of one-act amateur plays.

'Written by whom?' he asked.

'By me.' Well, that's how I got to act – by writing my own material.

He paused for a while, then said, 'Do you know why I agreed to this?'

'No.'

'Because you had the fucking balls to ask.' He laughed, and I knew I wasn't going to be ejected after all.

'Look,' he said, 'I think the best thing is if we choose a play we both know and I'll take you through it. What are you familiar with?'

The obvious choice was *Julius Caesar*: I knew much of it just from listening to the long-playing record of dialogue highlights from the Marlon Brando version over and over. Antony's funeral speech on the forum steps was fixed firmly in my head, as performed by Brando. So I announced, 'I can do Antony's funeral speech.'

'Ah, good! Of course! Then do it, dear boy.'

'What – now?' I suddenly felt ridiculous and ill-equipped now that the moment had come to perform before his Lordship.

'Yes, just do it. It's the only way.'

'Where shall I start?'

'Try starting with "Friends, Romans, countrymen",' he said with great patience and kindness. 'Just do it. Don't stop for anything.'

I was about to begin when he said, 'Wait! Put some cushions down there. Cover them with a sheet.' That was to be the body of Caesar.

Caesar's body in place, I went into the speech, basically playing Marlon Brando as Mark Antony.

Lord Larry sat and watched and listened in silence until I got to the bit where Antony says, 'My heart is in the coffin with Caesar and I must pause till it come back to me.'

Then he suddenly said, 'Methinks there is much reason in his saying.'

'Pardon?' I asked.

'I'm playing the plebeians,' he said, and then carried on delivering the lines of the crowd.

'Now mark him – he begins again to speak.'

That was my cue. 'But yesterday the word of Caesar might have stood against the world . . .' And so it went on, right to the end when I finished on a loud, 'Here was a Caesar. When comes such *anotherrrr*?'

I fell silent, my throat dry from so much ranting. Lord Olivier sat quietly musing. 'You've had no voice training, have you?'

'No,' I admitted.

'And you don't know how to breathe properly, do you?'

'No.'

'But considering all that, you were not *too* awful.' He stood up. 'Right, well, let's do some breathing exercises.' And with that he began showing me how to find my diaphragm and how to use my stomach muscles to get the best from my voice, which has never been a particularly strong one. I was eager for him to tell me the best way to deliver the lines. But there were further technicalities I had to learn about. 'Now,' he said, 'we could have a go at being a tree, but I think that would just be a waste of our time, don't you?'

I agreed with him, not knowing what went into being a tree or why I should be a tree in the first place. He went on to explain that acting requires a mixture of techniques, from summoning up past experiences to developing the ability to simply put yourself into situations or display emotions that may be totally alien by simply *thinking* yourself into the part. That's what being a tree was all about. (I have since been a tree, actually.)

'There are some useful tools for actors,' he told me. 'For me I have to find the right clothing and the right face.' This was something I knew, but I was happy to hear it again.

Then came the bit of the lesson I had been looking forward to. 'Now we will do the whole speech the *right* way.'

And he proceeded to take me through it all, not just telling me how to say the lines but *why* I should say them and what I should be thinking while I said them. His voice was actually quite weak with age, but when he took to delivering the lines himself, the voice grew strong; acting seemed to lift him physically, emotionally and psychologically.

I tried it his way. It was far better than my first attempt.

'Now – *now* come down the steps of the pulpit,' he told me. 'Let the people gather around you. The whole forum opens out before you. Let your voice carry.'

I was getting the best free acting lesson in the world.

There were a few interruptions when he was called to the set. Most of the time on set is spent lighting shots, which actors find boring. He told me he had a stand-in to do that these days, adding, 'I'm much too fucking grand for all that.' And he was, too. I can think of few other actors who could truly say that.

I was able to go on set and watch some of the filming. I was watching Laurence Olivier acting with Maggie Smith, just as I had done back in 1964. I felt a little like I had come full circle, and I felt sure that Larry himself was very close to taking his final bow.

He told me to come back the next day, and I did, getting more tips and advice, and hearing him talk about his life and work. He liked having me there and told me to come back again the next day. I even provided him with an audience while he ran through his lines one morning. He was a master technician. He liked to leave nothing to chance. He wanted to get it right and keep it right. He was rehearsing a scene where he sits upon his throne as Zeus and gives a short monologue.

'I love our director very much,' he told me, 'but I need to know if what I am giving him is right, and I fear he settles for whatever I give. So tell me please, dear boy, what you think.'

And I did. I told him his problem was that he was sounding too austere. Too grand. Too theatrical. I said I felt that Zeus was more of a kindly head teacher.

'That's it,' he said.

And when he did it again, I said, 'I think that's a wrap!'

He thanked me, and told me I would be a very fine director. I don't think he actually took my meagre direction, but he was kind enough to make me think he would.

It was a real honour and a privilege to have spent that time with Laurence Olivier and I was sure that had to be the last time I would see him.

35

The Very Worst

At the end of 1979 Larry began work on the Granada Television series *Brideshead Revisited*, playing the Marquess of Marchmain. He shot only a few scenes, including his death scene, and then took off to America in early 1980 for the remake of *The Jazz Singer*. He would complete his remaining scenes for *Brideshead Revisited* later.

Singer Neil Diamond had been cast in the Al Jolson part, a young Jewish cantor whose desire for success in show business outrages his imperious father, played by Olivier.

Sidney J Furie was originally hired to direct the movie, and during the first several weeks of production, he was constantly rewriting the screenplay. During the first week of filming, actress Catlin Adams had no idea if her character was married to Neil Diamond's character or was just his girlfriend.

Other scenes were reportedly ad-libbed on the spot without anyone having any idea where they would eventually end up in the finished film. Finally, EMI, the production company, fired Furie and Richard Fleischer was contacted to salvage the project.

'When I was asked to do it, I had doubts that you could update that old-hat tale of the cantor and his son,' Fleischer told me in 1994 in London. 'But I was tempted by the prospect of working with Laurence Olivier. So I did it.'

Fleischer had previously met Larry socially, in London in 1978.

I went to dinner with my friends Laurence Evans, who was an agent, and his wife Mary. They had a flat just off Grosvenor Square where I arrived to find Laurence Olivier sitting, or rather stretched out, in an armchair. He was rather rosy-cheeked, his white hair was thinning, and he had the odd appearance of looking fragile and robust at the same time. Laurie hadn't mentioned Olivier would be there, but it was really quite wonderful to meet this man who was probably the greatest actor alive then.

Olivier's sister Sybille was also there. I recall that she looked like one of the short, plump, grey-haired old ladies who you'd expect to find in a production of *Arsenic and Old Lace*. They had come up from their home in Brighton for a day's shopping and had become tired, so they had stopped off to see Laurie and Mary to rest up before they caught their train home.

Olivier struggled to his feet when Laurie introduced us and he very warmly took both my hands in his to greet me and said, 'I am *so* delighted to meet you.' I felt very flattered as he went on, 'I can't tell what a great pleasure it is.'

I said, 'Well, thank you very much, Sir Laurence. I feel very honoured.'

And he said, 'Please, call me Larry.'

I found Sybille to be completely delightful and somewhat unaware of what was happening. She kept insisting that she'd left her shopping in the taxi and everyone was reassuring her over and over that her shopping bag was right there in the flat. Mary brought the bag in to show her, and five minutes later Sybille began telling me again that she had left her shopping in the taxi and was worrying how she would track it down. And through it all, Olivier was so tolerant and kind towards her, and just gently amused by her.

We had dinner, including Olivier and his sister, and by the end of it Olivier was really rather drunk, although it was hard to tell how much because even at his best he found walking difficult, and now he was almost unable to walk at all. So Laurie and I took him under each arm and walked him down the station platform to the train while Mary and Sybille walked ahead of us, talking and with Sybille seemingly unaware that her brother was doing what I thought of as a splendid imitation of Roy Bolger, who did such a wonderful rubber-legged walk and played the Scarecrow in *The Wizard of Oz*.

Olivier wasn't so drunk that he couldn't still talk with great wit and was perfectly charming and even dignified. I thought he was just a wonderful man, a most charming character.

We were almost at his train car when he suddenly stopped, stretched out his arms, and I thought, oh my God, he is going to throw up! And then he said, in a most grieved way, staring at the ladies ahead of us, 'You know, it distresses me to see my sister so unsteady on her feet.' Well, that was priceless, and I was totally captivated by the Olivier charm, which endeared me to him for ever.

Clearly, Fleischer had no idea that Sybille was mentally ill.

Having accepted the somewhat herculean task of trying to rescue *The Jazz Singer*, Fleischer ran as much of the film Furie had shot as he could manage.

There was so much of it, I couldn't get through it all. One of the big problems was that the original director used multiple cameras – often up to seven at a time, and usually no less than five. That's seven cameras that each have to have a crew, and that's a lot of technicians and equipment on one set, which leaves little room for any of the action. The performances were badly affected by all this. Neil Diamond was not a real actor and he was struggling, but to see Laurence Olivier giving a bad performance told the whole story of what had taken place. It wasn't that he didn't try. He tried so hard that he was acting his heart out, and to try to play this very Jewish cantor he was using every cliché you could think of.

Neil Diamond was the opposite. He didn't have the confidence that made Olivier's performance over the top, so Diamond was well under the table, like he didn't want to be noticed. You couldn't understand anything he said.

Two days after I accepted, I met with Larry in his suite [at the l'Ermitage in Beverly Hills] and he greeted me like he was never so pleased to see anyone in his life.

Olivier thought he had good reason to be overwhelmingly delighted to see Fleischer, as he told me: 'Making *The Jazz Singer* was the worst – the *very* worst – experience of my career. Even worse than *Inchon*. Every day we had new scenes. I have a hard enough time these days remembering my lines, but I can manage to fix my lines in my head first thing in the morning for the scenes we are scheduled to do that day, but after I'd learned my lines and was on my way to the set in the car, I'd have three or four new pages shoved through the car window.

'One glorious and ultimately terrible morning, I was walking around the [Goldwyn] studio trying to find the sound stage when a production secretary pushed two pages of new dialogue into my hand. I read through it as I was walking, and as I wandered onto the sound stage I said, "This piss is shit." Everyone who heard it laughed; a most appreciative audience because they all knew I was right.'

That 'piss is shit' comment would later come back to haunt him.

'I was very relieved when they fired the original director,' Larry told me, 'but I was worried about who they could get to salvage the film. I thought it would be best to let it sink, but that's not the spirit, you know. You have to save even a sinking ship.

'Then I heard that Dick Fleischer was being considered and I was asked if I would be happy for him to take over. I believe they asked Neil Diamond also for his approval, but honestly, dear boy, I think they were more concerned about what I thought.

'I called Chuck Heston and asked him about Fleischer because he had worked with him [on *The Omega Man*], and he said that Fleischer was a good craftsman, was somebody very considerate towards actors and I would enjoy working with him. So when the producers offered us Richard Fleischer, I was glad to agree.'

While Fleischer prepared, the production shut down for two weeks. Said Fleischer, 'The biggest pressure on me was to shoot all of Larry's scenes, because he was contracted to be paid $33,333 for every day that went over his schedule.' Larry had been paid a cool million dollars up front.

When production resumed, Fleischer started to reshoot one of Larry's scenes. 'He had overacted so much in the original scene I wanted to get him to do it again, and when he asked me why we were doing the scene again, I felt I couldn't tell Laurence Olivier that he was overacting. So I told him that I didn't like the way the scene had been staged, which was also the truth.

'He'd worked very hard on his Jewish accent. I thought it was terrible. It was a cliché. He told me very proudly that he had worked so hard to perfect it and how different it was from the one he used in *The Boys from Brazil*. I hoped he would allow the accent to slip as we went along, but he was too much of an experienced pro to let that happen. So I said nothing.'

I said to Fleischer that he *should* have told Larry and that I was sure Larry would have preferred to have had his pride hurt for a short while and later realise that Fleischer had been right, rather than come to realise that his performance had been flawed by a terrible Jewish accent.

Fleischer replied, 'How can you tell the world's greatest actor that he's overacting?'

This was a problem many directors faced when directing Laurence Olivier. They were too overawed by him, which is understandable. He knew only too well that this was a problem for some directors.

'They won't tell me what they really want,' he said to me in 1979. 'They think I know it all. Well, maybe I know bloody well too much. I play these parts in films that I do partly because I need the money to leave for my family when I'm gone, but also because acting is what I *do*. And I want to do it well, always, even if I know the script is shit.'

I told Fleischer what Larry had said to me, and he shrugged and said, 'When you have a big-budget movie and a schedule to meet and you have a production company expecting you to save their picture, you have to make decisions on the spot, and sometimes you are right and sometimes you are wrong. I still think I was right in the way I handled Olivier.'

I know how much Larry appreciated constructive direction. But Richard Fleischer had all the pressure of trying to rescue *The Jazz Singer*. He said,

Olivier was quite old and more ill than I realised at the time, and his memory was bad, which angered him more than it ever did me. He would stop in the middle of a take, trying to find the next word and then he'd get angry and yell at himself, 'You damned old fool, don't you realise when it's time to quit this business?'

On the last day Olivier worked, we were shooting the biggest scene in the picture, which was a live concert by Neil Diamond at the Pantages Theatre. Among some fifteen hundred extras we sat Olivier for his reaction shots. I had just the one day to film this.

Olivier was called at 1 p.m. and because he could only work eight hours a day, I had to be finished with him at 9 p.m. Before he arrived, Jerry Leider told me that EMI wanted me to do an extra close-up of Olivier for the 'Kol Nidre' scene in the synagogue. I'd shot it so that when Olivier recognises his son's voice, his eyes lit up, and then a bitter expression comes over his face and he turns away. I wanted to delay the reconciliation between the father and son, otherwise it was just an old cliché. But EMI had wanted a shot of him smiling. Leider said we'd never use it. I said, 'It's always the same; you shoot it, they'll use it.' And then I said, 'Have you talked to Larry about this?' and he said, 'We'll talk to him as soon as he gets here.'

The audience began to arrive – they were mainly young rock fans – and among them sat Laurence Olivier. There was a long delay waiting for Neil Diamond to get on stage. Leider was on stage, and he suddenly said, 'Now, ladies and gentlemen, I am honoured to introduce to you one of the stars of our picture – Lord Laurence Olivier.'

This audience of young rock fans rose to its feet and gave him a standing ovation. It was quite incredible, quite moving. And right after that Leider came over and said to me, 'Olivier has given the OK for the close-up as long as we get it before nine.'

I said, 'If Neil doesn't get out here we won't be ready by then.' Neil didn't know what to sing. Finally he appeared, he did a song, and eventually I knew we were not going to get Olivier's close-up done by nine. So Leider spoke to him and then came to me and said, 'He'll stay past nine but we have to pay him for an extra day's work.'

Now this really floored me. Olivier was insisting he get his $33,333 for one close-up. He saw a chance to make more money, which kind of disgusted me. He knew the close-up wasn't really important, and I felt really let down that he was doing it just for the money. I was suddenly seeing a side to Olivier that I didn't like.

Clearly, Fleischer had not got to know Larry as well as he had thought. Larry made no secret of the fact that he was trying to earn as much money as he could to leave his children and wife as well as pay for his children's schooling. He had never become rich at his peak as a stage actor. He even told me, 'I'm killing myself working to make good money that I never made when I was at my best.'

Fleischer discovered there was still fifteen minutes to go before the clock struck nine. He told me:

Leider told me, 'If you get the shot set up and I see that it can't be done before nine, I'll give you the signal to cancel and send Olivier home because I'm not going to pay him an extra $33,333 for one close-up.'

Well, we just did it, and at one minute to nine, I had the shot in the can, and Larry was dismissed. His work on the picture was over. It is customary after an actor's last shot on a picture that the first assistant announces it, and the crew applauds, and then it's handshakes all round. But there was no time for this. I guess Leider had told the first assistant to stay silent.

Olivier rose from his chair and said, 'I've never been so badly treated on a film in my entire career,' and he stormed off.

I caught up with him and said, 'Larry, I've come to say goodbye and to thank you for all you have done to make the picture work.'

He said, 'My dear Richard, working with you was a blessed redemption and I've been happier in my work with you than I've been allowed to feel in a long time.' Then he put his arms around me, and we hugged and were friends still.

Larry recalled it slightly differently when we met for the very last time in 1981: 'On my last day of filming that dreadful picture, I was not given the traditional farewell applause, which may sound petty. But it's something that happens on *all* films. And when you are greeted with only silence, then it is as good as a slap around the face. It means they are glad to be rid of you.

'The director, Richard Fleischer, caught up with me in my dressing room at the theatre where we filmed on my last day, and said, "I wanted to thank you."

'I felt that at least the director was grateful. I told him how wonderful it had been working with him. But the truth was, I hated every minute of that film and was glad it was all over. I felt I couldn't just leave on a sour note, so I swallowed my pride and humbled myself. Humbling is good for the soul – at times.'

There was more humbling to be done. Olivier stopped off in New York before returning to England, and dined at a restaurant with friends, regaling them with the story of how he came to proclaim, 'This piss is shit.'

Unfortunately, the story found its way into New York's *Daily News*, where the words 'shit' and 'piss' were substituted for less offensive words that the newspaper could publish, and the story went around on the wires that Olivier had called *The Jazz Singer* 'trash'.

The shit really did hit the fan at the EMI offices. There were threats of lawsuits and Larry was forced to issue a statement to the *Daily News*, the United Press International and the Associated Press:

I have nothing but respect for the way in which the film is now being handled. The brilliant ideas instigated by the producer, Jerry Leider, were expertly directed by Richard Fleischer and as for my leading man I am quite sure that the American public, or shall I say the world public, have a great and delightful surprise in store for them.

Two weeks later, in April 1980, Fleischer received a ten-page handwritten letter from Larry, in part explaining and apologising for what had happened as a result of his remarks in the New York restaurant.

He also went on to explain that he was tormented by his behaviour during the 'close-up' incident and of his demand for a full day's pay. He wrote, 'The best possible education for my beloveds is naturally my main concern at this time of life.' That was when Fleischer realised that Larry was working hard to save for his family's benefit.

36

The Last Years

In April 1980 Larry was back on the set of *Brideshead Revisited*, filming many of the scenes in which he is seen as the younger, vigorous marquis. He was now suffering from a bladder infection. From what proved to be an Emmy-winning performance, no one would have known how ill he was.

He had long since abandoned the autobiography he had begun in hospital, but now set about rewriting it, this time typing it himself, even with sore fingers. He finished it in May 1981.

In the April, he had been filming *The Jigsaw Man*, a film that reunited him with Michael Caine, who played a Russian agent defecting to the British. Larry was to spend six weeks on it, and was being paid a million dollars. Many of his scenes were shot in the relative comfort of Shepperton Studios, and I was lucky to be able to get onto the set to interview him. I'm glad I did, because it was the last time I ever saw him.

He was more frail than ever, and unhappy. The film wasn't going well. Financial problems were about to hit it and production would be postponed. But as we talked, he began to reminisce, and then came the revelation that he had been sexually abused.

He told me how Joan was working so much and staying in London while he lived for the most part in Sussex that he hardly saw her, and then he admitted, 'But really, dear boy, I am so jealous of her, and I hate myself for feeling that way.'

He was often in the depths of depression. 'I keep telling Joan, "You're better off if I am dead." How can I say such terrible things to her? But she seems to be doing fine without me, anyway. We're not as close as we once were.'

At the end of my allotted time with him, and after the emotional experience we had shared, he again took my hands in his, very gingerly, shook them very slightly and said through tears, 'Please come and see me again, Eminem.'

'I will, Lord Larry,' I replied. I left, like before, certain that I wouldn't see him again. This time I was right.

I later learned that he collapsed on the set. The money ran out and filming was postponed. It resumed several months later and Larry was able to finish his work on it. The final film was poor and hardly seen anywhere.

Larry still had work to do on television where, in those days, he was getting to do quality drama. This time it was John Mortimer's autobiographical *A Voyage Round My Father*, playing Mortimer's blind father. At the same time Joan was in *Who's Afraid of Virginia Woolf?* at the National, which hurt Larry; he was angry that she would perform at Peter Hall's National Theatre. After his outburst, he was full of remorse that he had been so angry with her and he apologised. Their final years together were not easy.

He was thrilled when he got to work once more, and for the last time, with John Gielgud and Ralph Richardson. The trio played ministers to the court of King Ludwig II in *Wagner*, a ten-hour television miniseries starring Richard Burton in the title role. It was filmed on location in Vienna.

Richard Burton told me (when we were working on *1984*):

There was the greatest rivalry between them. They all gave a great dinner for each other – three dinner celebrations by three great actors for each other, and they did it only to outdo each other. They were all disasters of varying degrees. Larry had given everyone the wrong arrival time and he spent two hours on his own waiting for everyone to arrive. Gielgud had a stand-up argument with his chef, and Richardson hired incompetent waiters who were slow, sloppy and probably more drunk than I was.

I expected so much more of the three of them. Ralph couldn't be bothered to learn his lines so they had to be written on idiot boards for him. Gielgud was easily the best of the trio, doing his scene without a hiccup and then heading for home when he had finished.

But I was disappointed with Larry. He was consumed with technique. There was no room for spontaneity so there was no emotion. He was a caricature of an actor.

It is difficult to take all of what Burton said to heart; I knew him for many years (he was another hero of mine) and never found him to be superficial or egotistical, so no doubt his disappointment about Larry was real enough. Someone had told me that Burton was drunk for much of the time he was making *Wagner*.

'No, not drunk,' Burton protested when I told him what I had heard. 'I drank heavily. I didn't get drunk. I was too *ill* to be drunk.'

Wagner is a film to relish, not because it is good – it was only moderately good – but because together for the one and only time on screen are Laurence Olivier, John Gielgud, Ralph Richardson and Richard Burton; Burton was a great actor who never achieved the legendary status of the other three. 'It was my own fault,' Burton told me. 'When I was making *Cleopatra* Larry wrote to me and said, "Make up your mind. Do you want to be a great actor or rich?" and I replied, "Rich." But, you know, Mick, I wanted so much to be a great actor, really.' (We had a long-standing agreement; he called me Mick and I called him Dick!)

In 1982 Larry was awarded the Order of Merit. That year *Confessions of an Actor* was published to great acclaim and popularity. It was also useful that it earned him around £320,000.

He was back on television again in 1983, playing *King Lear*, giving the part the age it required, but allowing him, through the technique of television recording, the breaks he needed to get through it in his weakened state. In April he and Joan flew to New York, where he received the Film Society of Lincoln Centre Award from Douglas Fairbanks Jr at the Lincoln Centre. Fairbanks described him as 'one hell of an actor'. President Ronald Reagan threw Larry and Joan a party at the White House.

Then the Oliviers flew home and Larry did three days' work playing Admiral Hood for one scene in *The Bounty* and earned £100,000.

During the summer he was ill with pleurisy but recovered in time to travel to France to film a television play, *The Ebony Tower*, based on John Fowles's novel about an old painter and his relationship with two female art students.

He appeared fleetingly in *The Last Days of Pompeii*, another TV miniseries, and for Home Box Office in America, he was in *Mr*

Halpern and Mr Johnson with Jackie Gleason. Back in Britain he made a comedy mystery for the BBC, *A Talent for Murder*, with Angela Lansbury.

On 29 July 1983 David Niven died. Larry attended his memorial and wept. On 10 October Ralph Richardson died; Larry was distraught but nothing could keep him from the memorial service.

He became seriously ill again and underwent surgery to have a kidney removed. Nobody expected him to ever work again. But he amazed everyone when he went to Berlin in July 1984 to play Rudolph Hess in a poor action thriller, *Wild Geese II*. It was supposed to be a sequel to the highly successful 1978 film *The Wild Geese*, which had starred Richard Burton as a mercenary. Burton was to have repeated his role in the sequel, but four days before he was due on the set, Sunday 5 August, he had a cerebral haemorrhage and died. The film went ahead with American actor Scott Glenn in the lead role of a mercenary leading a squad to rescue Rudolph Hess from Spandau Prison.

Burton's death only served to dampen Larry's spirits, but he put all he could into the film; it's a painful picture to watch, seeing Larry, weak and emaciated, in such a second-rate action flick.

But it earned him $300,000 and it gave him work, which he was desperate for. To him, an actor who could no longer act was no longer living. Larry was 77 years old but he looked ten years older, and he was beginning to forget the names of people around him.

He decided to write a second book, *On Acting*, although this time he was too weak to type any of it himself, so he dictated it to Gawn Grainger, who had been in his last play, *The Party*. In March 1985 he flew to Los Angeles to present the Best Film Oscar for *Amadeus*.

He and Grainger finally finished work on the book, and it was published in 1986. That year there was another small cameo in a TV miniseries, as King William III in *Peter the Great*. Then there was one final television play, in September, *Lost Empires*, from J B Priestley's novel, playing the small role of a one-time star of music hall.

He appeared at the Olivier Awards of 1986 at the London Dominion Theatre, where he received tumultuous applause. But he was too frail to stay.

On 1 April he was in hospital again with abdominal pains, the cause of which were never revealed. He needed work, but there was nothing much he could do, although he did appear as a holographic image in a West End musical called *Time* starring pop star Cliff Richard.

At the end of April he was well enough for him and Joan and one of his nurses to stay at a villa near Marbella in Spain for a three-week vacation. In September there was further tension between Larry and Joan. She had received a letter from actor Trader Faulkner complimenting her on her performance in *The House of Bernarda Alba*, but when she showed Larry the letter, he threw it aside and muttered, 'I must get back on the stage.'

Three days before his eightieth birthday, he formally announced that he would do no more film or television work.

To celebrate his birthday, the National Theatre put on a pageant, *Happy Birthday, Sir Larry* in the Olivier auditorium. On stage Albert Finney did a turn as a laid-back comic, Peter Hall portrayed Shakespeare and Peggy Ashcroft walked on as Lilian Baylis. Then, out of a huge birthday cake, jumped Julie-Kate and proclaimed, 'Happy Birthday, Dad.'

'The audience just loved him so much,' Dame Peggy Ashcroft told me in 1989. 'They gave him such applause as he had never known before. He tried to wave at everyone there. The applause just continued on. It was very moving, very beautiful.'

Joan tried to lead him out but he wasn't going to miss a second of this applause. Finally he was led to a balcony overlooking the street, where the huge crowd outside cheered and waved and called for him.

'It was his farewell to them, and their farewell to him,' Peggy Ashcroft said.

In June 1987, Larry's son Richard married a Canadian girl in Los Angeles. Richard and his wife came to live with his parents at the Malthouse, where Larry was being looked after by nurses; Joan always picked the pretty nurses, knowing it would make Larry happy.

There were always friends visiting, such as Derek Jacobi, Anthony Hopkins, Ronald Pickup, John Mills, John Osborne and Ian McKellen. But he was weak and could only manage an hour at most with each visitor. He became more forgetful, unable to remember people's names.

For a man who fought to have control over his life, how ignoble it must have felt to have finally lost control. Joan's brother David went to see him and he told David, 'It's time I was gone, David.'

In March 1989 he fell and had to undergo an operation to replace a hip. The following month his sister Sybille died, aged 87.

Joan continued to work; she had to, as there were medical and nursing bills to be paid. She went that summer to Hollywood to make a film, *I Love You to Death*. In early July, Richard called her to say that his father's remaining kidney was failing. She completed her work on the film in a day and rushed home to find Larry drifting in and out of consciousness.

On the morning of 11 July, Julie-Kate went into his room, and at that moment his breathing stopped – at 11.15 a.m.

Laurence Olivier's life was completed. He was no longer out of control. If there are angels, he was in their hands. He had at last received closure.

He was, according to his wishes, cremated. It was a time only for family and close friends, including Alec Guinness, John Mills, Douglas Fairbanks and Franco Zeffirelli.

John Osborne petitioned for a grand funeral service at Westminster Abbey and for Olivier's ashes to be interred in Poet's Corner. The only other actor to receive this honour was Edmund Kean, one of the great Shakespearean actors whom Olivier always wanted to be numbered with. The ceremony took place on 20 October 1989, and I was lucky enough to find a place inside; it was a sheer privilege being there. Prince Edward represented the Royal Family. As well as the immediate family, Dickie's widow Hester was there, and so was Jill Esmond, sick from cancer and in a wheelchair. Peter O'Toole, Maggie Smith and Richard Attenborough were among the special guests.

Friends carried items that had been of special importance to Larry. I saw Derek Jabobi carrying a crown, which I only later discovered was the crown Larry wore in the film of *Richard III*. Michael Caine carried the special Oscar for lifetime achievement. Frank Finlay had a sword that had been presented to Larry by John Gielgud and which Kean had once worn. Douglas Fairbanks bore the insignia of Olivier's Order of Merit.

Readings were given by John Gielgud, John Mills and Peggy Ashcroft. Alec Guinness spoke, but the most moving moment came when a recording of Olivier delivering the St Crispin's Day speech echoed about the abbey.

It was, I imagine, much like a royal funeral. It was full of pomp and ceremony, and it conveyed the love and awe and respect that people in his profession had for him. I've heard criticism about how grand and theatrical it all was. But that's what Laurence Olivier was – grand and theatrical. I doubt that another actor in my lifetime will ever reach the heights of true greatness that he achieved.

Epilogue

With Richardson and Olivier gone, only John Gielgud was left. I'd written to Sir John in 1988, to ask him about Trevor Howard about whom I was writing a book. He graciously replied, writing his letter entirely by hand.

I wrote again shortly after Larry died, and asked him if he could tell me what his thoughts were about Olivier.

I didn't know Larry as well as I should have, or should have liked to. Now that he is gone, I feel very sad and somewhat disappointed with myself that I didn't make the effort to get to know him much better. There was never the great rivalry between us that the press liked to write about. We did play some of the same great parts, but mostly we played very different parts because we were different actors with different characteristics. So we were never rivals. As for our personal relationship, he enjoyed his privacy and never confided in me as he knew I am a somewhat indiscreet gossip, so we were never that close. As an actor, he was one of the greatest of all time. He followed in the theatrical tradition of Kean and Irving. He respected tradition in the theatre, but he also took great delight in breaking tradition, which is what made him so unique. He was gifted, brilliant, and one of the great controversial figures of our time in theatre, which is a virtue and not a vice at all. He broke new ground when he was at his best. I now realise how very lucky I was to have been his contemporary and colleague.

Gielgud had known Olivier since 1934. I'd known him only since 1972. Richardson had known Olivier most of his life and had admitted, 'I don't really know him at all.'

Everyone seems to have their special memories of him, and their impressions – and indeed many *do* impressions of him. In this book I have shared my memories of him. I can't be sure that the Olivier I saw and got to know was the same others did. He was a chameleon. He could change to suit his surroundings and even to suit the people he was with. He could easily put on an act.

But that last time I saw him, in 1981, was no act. I doubt he shared with anyone else what he shared with me, and he shared it more in spirit than in words. That was a time when we were the closest. And it was no act. There is an old adage; it takes one to know one. I knew more about him from knowing that terrible event in his young life than anything else that he could have ever revealed to me. And if he kept it from all others, even from his family, that is no surprise. I only revealed it to my partner of eighteen years early in 2006, before I had started work on this book. I had only ever told one other person, and that was a friend who had suffered the same thing. So this will come as a surprise to all who know me.

And so it's very likely that Larry kept his secret, and if I am the only one who ever knew, then I feel very blessed. That is what makes this book, for me, such a personal and intimate portrait.

Sources and Acknowledgements

I have been enormously privileged to have mingled with the good and the great over the years and in many ways writing this book is a glimpse into my own past. Here, in alphabetical order, are those I have quoted firsthand, with brief details about where, when and why I talked to them. I like to think of them as my cast– and as Olivier wished to be credited last in *Shoes of the Fisherman*, I have credited him last here too.

Dana Andrews (London, 1974)
Harry Andrews (Shepperton Studios, filming *SOS Titanic*, 1979)
Peggy Ashcroft (BBC Studios, London, recording *BBC2 Playhouse: Caught on a Train*, 1980)
Irving Asher (London, 1975)
John Badham (Shepperton Studios, filming *Dracula*, 1979)
Alan Bates (on location in Devon for *The Shout*, 1977)
Richard Burton (Shepperton Studios, filming *1984*, 1984)
Michael Caine (Dorchester Hotel, London, 1976)
Noël Coward (Claridges, London, 1972)
Tony Curtis (his London home, 1974)
Kirk Douglas (London, promoting *Posse*, 1976; London, promoting his book *The Ragman's Son*, 1988)

Peter Finch (Shepperton Studios, filming *Bequest to the Nation*, 1972)

Frank Finlay (BBC Studios, London, recording *Count Dracula*, 1977)

Richard Fleischer (London, promoting his book *Tell Me When to Cry*, 1994)

John Gielgud (The Apollo, London, 1970; The Old Vic, London, 1975; Norfolk on location for *Tales of the Unexpected*, 1979; by letter, 1989)

Stewart Granger (London, promoting his book *Sparks Fly Upwards*, 1981)

Alec Guinness (London, for a screening of the first episode of *Tinker, Tailor, Soldier, Spy*, 1979)

Guy Hamilton (Twickenham Studios, filming *The Mirror Crack'd*, 1979)

Rex Harrison (on location in Norfolk for *Tales of the Unexpected*, 1982)

Jack Hawkins (London – an event that I remember nothing much more about apart from sitting with Hawkins and being joined by Olivier, probably late in 1972 or early 1973)

Charlton Heston (London, promoting *The Actor's Life*, 1979; Lee Studios, London, filming *The Awakening*, 1999; Haymarket Theatre, London, 1999)

Michael Jayston (in a very nice pub next door to the BBC rehearsal studios at Acton, London, 1979)

Patrick 'Paddy' Jordan (at my home theatre, The Quay, where I was hosting a tribute to Alec Guinness, 2000)

Garson Kanin (in London; he was in England to visit Olivier, 1988)

Jesse Lasky Jr (his London house, 1978)

Joseph L Mankiewicz (Pinewood Studios, filming *Sleuth*, 1972)

James Mason (Shepperton Studios, filming *Murder By Decree*, 1978)

John Mills (on some foggy location for *Quatermass*, 1978)

Kenneth More (Pinewood Studios, filming *A Tale of Two Cities*, 1979)

David Niven (Pinewood Studios, filming *Candleshoe*, 1976; on location in London for *A Nightingale Sang in Berkeley Square*, 1978; Elstree Studios, filming *A Man Called Intrepid*, 1979)

Gregory Peck (London, 1978)

Anthony Quayle (Shepperton Studios, filming *Bequest to the Nation*, 1972; Shepperton Studios when filming *Murder By Decree*, 1978)

Anthony Quinn (Elstree Studios, filming *The Greek Tycoon*, 1977)

Ralph Richardson (The Apollo, London, 1970; The Old Vic, London, 1975; Twickenham Studios, filming *The Man in the Iron Mask*, 1976)

W D Richter (on location in Cornwall for *Dracula*, 1979)

Jean Simmons (Shepperton Studios, filming *Dominique*, 1977)

James Stewart (in Norfolk for an American Air Force reunion, probably in 1985)

Peter Ustinov (Shepperton Studios, filming *The Thief of Baghdad*, 1978)

Robert Wagner (Granada TV Studios, Manchester, recording *Cat on a Hot Tin Roof*, 1976)

Natalie Wood (Granada TV Studios, Manchester, recording *Cat on a Hot Tin Roof*, 1976; London, promoting *The Last Married Couple in America*, 1980)

William Wyler (interview by telephone, 1976)

Terence Young (Shepperton Studios and on location, filming *The Jigsaw Man*, 1981)

Franco Zeffirelli (London, directing *Filumena*, 1977)

and **Laurence Olivier** (Pinewood Studios, filming *Sleuth*, 1972; an event in London where we talked to Jack Hawkins, probably late 1972 or early 1973; The Old Vic Theatre, rehearsing *Saturday, Sunday, Monday*, 1974; The Old Vic, in his office, 1975; The Old Vic rehearsal room, *Eden End*, 1975; Granada TV Studios, Manchester, recording *Cat on a Hot Tin Roof*, 1976; Cornwall, on location filming *Dracula*, 1978; Shepperton Studios, filming interiors for *Dracula*, 1978; Pinewood Studios, filming *Clash of the Titans*, 1979; Shepperton Studios, filming *The Jigsaw Man*, 1981)

I owe a debt of gratitude to a number of people and wish to convey my thanks to Deborah Cote, Cathy Ballard, Melanie Letts, Barbara Phelan of Anova Books, Ian Allen for copy editing this book, and to Jeremy Robson I wish to say, thank you for your faith in me for the past 22 years.

Bibliography

Agee, James, *Agee on Film*, Peter Owen (London), 1967

Barker, Felix, *The Oliviers*, Hamish Hamilton (London), 1953

Coleman, Terry, *Olivier*, Bloomsbury (London), 2005

Coward, Noël, *The Noël Coward Diaries*, Weidenfeld & Nicolson (London), 1982

Douglas, Kirk, *The Ragman's Son*, Simon & Schuster (New York and London), 1988

Faulkner, Trader, *Peter Finch*, Angus & Robertson (UK), 1979

Flamini, Roland, *Scarlett, Rhett and a Cast of Thousands*, Andre Deutsch (New York), 1975, Andre Deutsch (London) 1976

Geist, Kenneth L, *Pictures Will Talk*, Charles Scribner's Sons (New York), 1978

Hawkins, Jack, *Anything for a Quiet Life*, Elm Tree Books (London), 1973

Heston, Charlton, *The Actor's Life*, Penguin Books (Harmondsworth), 1979, E.P. Dutton & Co Inc. (US), 1978

Kanin, Garson, *Hollywood*, Hart-Davis, MacGibbon (London), 1975

Korda, Michael, *Charmed Lives*, Random House (New York), 1979, Allen Lane (London), 1980

Lambert, Gavin, *Natalie Wood*, Alfred A. Knopf (New York), Faber and Faber Ltd (London), 2004

Lasky Jr, Jesse, with Pat Silver, *Love Scene*, Angus & Robertson (UK), 1978

Miles, Sarah, *Serve Me Right*, Macmillan (London), 1994

Morley, Margaret, *Olivier, The Films and Faces of Laurence Olivier*, LSP Books, 1978

Morley, Sheridan, *The Authorised Biography of John Gielgud*, Hodder and Stoughton (London), 2001

Morley, Sheridan, *The Other Side of the Moon*, Weidenfeld & Nicolson (London), 1985

Niven, David, *Bring on the Empty Horses*, Hamish Hamilton (London), 1975

Niven, David, *The Moon's a Balloon*, Hamish Hamilton (London), 1971

Olivier, Laurence, *Confessions of an Actor*, Weidenfeld & Nicolson (London), 1982

Ustinov, Peter, *Dear Me*, William Heinemann (London), 1977

Wood, Lana, *Natalie*, Columbus Books (London), 1984

The Plays, Films and TV Dramas of Laurence Olivier

The Plays

The Merry Wives of Windsor as Servant: The Fellowship of Players, Regent Theatre, London, 1924

Henry IV, Part 2 as Snare and Thomas of Clarence: Regent Theatre, London, 1925

Macbeth as Lennox: St Christopher's School, Letchworth Garden City, 1925

Ghost Train as Policeman, and *Unfailing Instinct* as Armand: A Julian Frank Production, tour of Brighton, Manchester, Birmingham, Eastbourne, Aberdeen, Glasgow and Brixton in London, 1925

The Tempest as Antonio: Lena Ashwell Players, Century Theatre and London tour, 1925

Julius Caesar, as Flavius: Lena Ashwell Players, Century Theatre and London tour, 1925

Henry VIII as Serving Man: Lewis Casson/Bronson Albery Production, Empire Theatre, London, 1925

The Cenci as Servant: Lewis Casson/Bronson Albery Production, Empire Theatre, London, 1926

The Farmer's Wife as Richard Coaker: Birmingham Repertory Theatre, 1926

Birmingham Repertory Theatre performances of 1927
Something to Talk About as Guy Sydney
Well of the Saints as Mat Simon
The Third Finger as Tom Hardcastle
The Mannoch Family as Peter Mannoch
The Comedian as Herald, Guard and Lictor
Uncle Vanya as Vanya
All's Well That Ends Well as Parolles
She Stoops to Conquer as Tony Lumpkin
Quality Street as Ensign Blades
Bird in Hand as Gerald
Advertising April as Mervyn
The Silver Box as Jack Barthwick
The Road to Ruin as Mr Milford

Macbeth as Malcolm: Birmingham Repertory Theatre Company, Royal Court Theatre, London, 1928

Back to Methuselah as Martellus: Birmingham Repertory Theatre Company, Royal Court Theatre, London, 1928

Harold as Harold: Birmingham Repertory Theatre Company, Royal Court Theatre, London, 1928

Bird in Hand as Gerald: Royalty Theatre, London, 1928

Paul Among the Jews as Chanan: Incorporated Stage Society, Prince of Wales Theatre, London, 1928

Journey's End as Captain Stanhope: Incorporated Stage Society, Apollo Theatre, London, 1928

Beau Geste as Beau: a Basil Dean Production, His Majesty's Theatre, London, 1929

The Circle of Chalk as Prince Pao: New Theatre, London, 1929

Paris Bound as Richard Parish: Golders Green Hippodrome, London, tour and Lyric Theatre, London, 1929

The Stranger Within as John Hardy: Garrick Theatre and Golders Green Hippodrome, London, 1929

Murder on the Second Floor as Hugh: Eltinge Theatre, New York, 1929

The Last Enemy as Jerry: Fortune Theatre, London, 1929

After All as Ralph: Arts Theatre, London, 1930

Private Lives, as Victor: Kings' Theatre, Edinburgh; Theatre Royal, Birmingham; Palace Theatre, Manchester; King's Theatre, Southsea; Phoenix Theatre, London, 1930; Times Square Theatre, New York, 1931

The Rats of Norway as Stevan Beringer: Playhouse Theatre, London, 1933

The Green Bay Tree as Julian Dulcimer: Cort Theatre, New York, 1933

Biography as Richard Kurt: Glove Theatre, London, 1934

Queen of Scots as Bothwell: New Theatre, London, 1934

Theatre Royal as Anthony Cavendish: King's Theatre, Glasgow; King's Theatre, Edinburgh; Opera House, Manchester; Lyric Theatre, London, 1934

Ringmaster as Peter Hammond: New Theatre, Oxford; Theatre Royal, Birmingham; Shaftesbury Theatre, London, 1935

Golden Arrow as Richard Harben (also directed): New Theatre, Oxford; Whitehall Theatre, London, 1935

Romeo and Juliet as Romeo and Mercutio: New Theatre, London, 1935

Bess on the Boatdeck as Robert Patch (also co-directed with Ralph Richardson): Lyric Theatre, London, 1936

Hamlet as Hamlet: Old Vic, London, 1937

Twelfth Night as Sir Toby Belch: Old Vic, London, 1937

Henry V as Henry: Old Vic, London, 1937

Hamlet as Hamlet, Kronborg Castle, Elsinore, Denmark, 1937

Macbeth as Macbeth: Old Vic, London, 1937

Othello as Iago: Old Vic, London, 1938

The King of Nowhere as Vivaldi: Old Vic, London, 1938

Coriolanus as Coriolanus: Old Vic, London, 1938

No Time for Comedy as Gaylord Easterbrook: Ethel Barrymore Theatre, New York, 1938

Romeo and Juliet as Romeo: 51st Street Theatre, New York, 1940

Arms and the Man as Sergius: Old Vic Company, Opera House, Manchester; New Theatre, London, 1944

Peer Gynt as Button Moulder: Old Vic Company, New Theatre, London, 1944

Richard III, as Richard: Old Vic Company, New Theatre, London, 1944

Uncle Vanya as Astrov: Old Vic Company, New Theatre, London, 1945; Century Theatre, New York, 1946

Henry IV Part 1 as Hotspur: Old Vic Company, New Theatre, London, 1945; Century Theatre, New York, 1946

Henry IV Part 2 as Justice Shallow: Old Vic Company, New Theatre, London, 1945; Century Theatre, New York, 1946

Oedipus as Oedipus: Old Vic Company, New Theatre, London, 1945; Century Theatre, New York, 1946

The Critic as Mr Puff: Old Vic Company, New Theatre, London, 1945; Century Theatre, New York, 1946

King Lear as Lear: Old Vic Company, New Theatre, London; Theatre des Champes-Elysees, Paris, 1946

The School For Scandal as Sir Peter Teazle (also directed): Old Vic Company, in Australia at the Capitol Theatre, Perth, the Princess Theatre, Melbourne, the Theatre Royal, Hobart, the Tivoli Theatre, Sydney, and His Majesty's Theatre, Brisbane, 1948; and in New Zealand at the St James Theatre, Auckland, the St James Theatre, Christchurch, His Majesty's Theatre, Dunedin, the St James Theatre, Wellington, 1948; New Theatre, London, 1949

Richard III as Richard: Old Vic Company, in Australia at the Theatre Royal, Adelaide, the Princess Theatre, Melbourne, and the Tivoli Theatre, Sydney, 1948; in New Zealand at the St James Theatre, Auckland, the St James Theatre, Christchurch, the St James Theatre, Wellington, 1948; New Theatre, London, 1949

The Skin of Our Teeth as Mr Antrobus: Old Vic Company, in Australia at the Theatre Royal, Adelaide, the Princess Theatre, Melbourne and the Tivoli Theatre, Sydney, 1948; and in New Zealand at the St James Theatre, Christchurch, and the St James Theatre, Wellington, 1948

Venus Observed as Duke of Altair (also directed): St James's Theatre, London, 1950

Caesar and Cleopatra as Caesar: Opera House, Manchester; St James's Theatre, London; Royal Court, Liverpool; Ziegfeld Theatre, New York, 1951

Antony and Cleopatra as Antony: Opera House, Manchester; St James's Theatre, London; Royal Court, Liverpool; Ziegfeld Theatre, New York, 1951

The Sleeping Prince as Grand Duke of Carpathia: Opera House, Manchester; King's Theatre, Glasgow; King's Theatre, Edinburgh; Theatre Royal, Newcastle; Phoenix Theatre, London, 1952

Twelfth Night as Malvolio: Shakespeare Memorial Theatre, Stratford-upon-Avon, 1955

Macbeth as Macbeth: Shakespeare Memorial Theatre, Stratford-upon-Avon, 1955

Titus Andronicus as Titus: Shakespeare Memorial Theatre, Stratford-upon-Avon, 1955; Théâtre des Nations, Paris; La Fenice, Venice; National Theatre, Belgrade; National Theatre, Sagreb; Burgtheatre, Vienna; National Theatre, Warsaw; Stoll Theatre, London, 1957

The Entertainer as Archie Rice: Royal Court Theatre, London, 1956; Palace Theatre, London; King's Theatre, Edinburgh; New Theatre, Oxford; Hippodrome, Brighton, 1957; Royal Theatre, New York, 1958

Coriolanus as Coriolanus: Shakespeare Memorial Theatre, Stratford-upon-Avon, 1959

Rhinoceros as Berenger: Royal Court Theatre; Strand Theatre, London, 1960

Becket as Becket: St James Theatre, New York, 1960

Becket as Henry II: Colonial Theatre, Boston; O'Keefe Centre, Toronto; Shubert Theatre, Philadelphia; Hudson Theatre, New York, 1961

The Broken Heart as Bassanes (also directed): Chichester Festival Theatre, 1962

Uncle Vanya as Astrov (also directed): Chichester Festival Theatre, 1962 and 1963

Semi-Detached as Fred Midway: King's Theatre, Edinburgh; New Theatre, Oxford; Saville Theatre, London, 1962/63

Uncle Vanya as Astrov (also directed): National Theatre Company, Old Vic Theatre, London, 1963; Theatre Royal, Newcastle; King's Theatre, Edinburgh, 1964

The Recruiting Officer as Captain Brazen: National Theatre Company, Old Vic Theatre, London, 1963/64

Othello as Othello: National Theatre Company, Alexandra Theatre, Birmingham; Old Vic, London, 1964; Kremlevsky Theatre, Moscow; Freie Volksbühne, Berlin; King's Theatre, Edinburgh; Theatre Royal, Newcastle, 1965; Queen's Theatre, London, 1966

The Master Builder as Halvard Solness: National Theatre Company, Opera House, Manchester; Grand Theatre, Leeds; New Theatre, Oxford; Old Vic Theatre, London, 1964; King's Theatre Glasgow; Coventry Theatre, 1965

Love for Love as Tattle: National Theatre Company, Kremlevsky Theatre, Moscow; Freie Volksbühne, Berlin; Old Vic Theatre, London; King's Theatre, Edinburgh, 1965; Shakespeare Memorial Theatre, Stratford-upon-Avon, 1966

The Dance of Death as Edgar: National Theatre Company, Old Vic Theatre, London; Theatre Royal, Brighton; Royal Court Theatre,

Liverpool, 1967; Théâtre Maisonneuve, Montreal; O'Keefe Centre, Toronto, 1967; King's Theatre, Edinburgh, 1968
A Flea in Her Ear as Etienne Plucheux: National Theatre Company, Old Vic Theatre, London; Théâtre Maisonneuve, Montreal; O'Keefe Centre, Toronto, 1967
Home and Beauty as A B Raham: National Theatre Company, Theatre Royal, Norwich; Alhambra Theatre, Bradford; Theatre Royal, Nottingham; Old Vic Theatre, London, 1969
The Three Sisters as Chebutikin (also directed): National Theatre Company, Old Vic Theatre, London; Theatre Royal, Brighton, 1970
The Merchant of Venice as Shylock: National Theatre Company, Old Vic Theatre, London; Cambridge Theatre, London, 1970; King's Theatre, Edinburgh, 1971
Long Day's Journey Into Night as James Tyrone: National Theatre Company, New Theatre, London, 1971/72; Old Vic, 1972
Saturday, Sunday, Monday as Antonio: National Theatre Company, Old Vic Theatre, London, 1973
The Party as John Tagg: National Theatre Company, Old Vic Theatre, London, 1973/74

Plays directed by Laurence Olivier in which he did not act

The Skin of Our Teeth, Phoenix Theatre, London; Piccadilly Theatre, London, 1945
Born Yesterday, Garrick Theatre, London, 1947
The Proposal, Old Vic Company, New Theatre, London, 1949
A Streetcar Named Desire, Aldwych Theatre, London, 1949
The Damascus Blade, Theatre Royal Newcastle and tour (Edinburgh, Glasgow, Brighton), 1950
Captain Carvallo, Lyceum Theatre, Edinburgh; Garrick Theatre, London, 1959
Venus Observed, New Century Theatre, New York, 1952
The Tumbler, Shubert Theatre, Boston; Helen Hayes Theatre, New York, 1960
Hamlet, National Theatre Company, Old Vic Theatre, London, 1963
The Crucible, National Theatre Company, Old Vic Theatre, London, 1965

Juno and the Paycock, National Theatre Company, Old Vic Theatre, London, 1966

The Three Sisters, National Theatre Company, Old Vic Theatre, London, 1967

The Advertisement, co-directed with Donald Mackechnie, National Theatre Company, Old Vic Theatre, London, 1968

Loves Labour's Lost, National Theatre Company, Old Vic Theatre, London, 1968

Amphitryon 38, National Theatre Company, New Theatre, London, 1971

Eden End, National Theatre Company, Old Vic Theatre, London, 1974

Filumena, St James Theatre, New York, 1980

The Films

The date of each film denotes the year of release.

Too Many Crooks, 1930

The Temporary Widow, 1930

Friends and Lovers, 1931

Potiphar's Wife (US title *Her Strange Desire*), 1931

The Yellow Passport (US title *The Yellow Ticket*), 1931

Westward Passage, 1932

No Funny Business, 1933

Perfect Understanding, 1933

Moscow Nights (US title *I Stand Condemned*), 1935

As You Like It, 1936

Fire Over England, 1937

The Divorce of Lady X, 1938

Q Planes (US title *Clouds Over Europe*), 1939

Wuthering Heights, 1939

Twenty-One Days (US title *Twenty-One Days Together*), 1939

Rebecca, 1940

Conquest of the Air (This was a documentary tracing the history of flight based on an early draft by H G Wells; Olivier played Lunardi, an early balloonist. It was made in 1935 but held up due to financial and production problems), 1940

Pride and Prejudice, 1940

Lady Hamilton (US title *That Hamilton Woman*), 1941

49th Parallel (US title *The Invaders*), 1941

The Demi-Paradise (US title *Adventure for Two*), 1943
Henry V, 1944
Hamlet, 1948
The Magic Box, 1951
Carrie, 1952
The Beggar's Opera, 1953
Richard III, 1955
The Prince and the Showgirl, 1957
The Devil's Disciple, 1959
The Entertainer, 1960
Spartacus, 1960
Term of Trial, 1962
Othello, 1965
Bunny Lake is Missing, 1965
Khartoum, 1966
The Shoes of the Fisherman, 1968
Oh! What a Lovely War, 1969
The Dance of Death, 1969
Battle of Britain, 1969
The Three Sisters, 1970
Nicholas and Alexandra, 1971
Sleuth, 1972
Lady Caroline Lamb, 1973
Marathon Man, 1976
The Seven Per Cent Solution, 1977
A Bridge Too Far, 1977
The Betsy, 1977
The Boys from Brazil, 1978
A Little Romance, 1979
Dracula, 1979
The Jazz Singer, 1980
Inchon, 1981
Clash of the Titans, 1981
The Bounty, 1984
The Jigsaw Man, 1985
Wild Geese II, 1985

The Television Dramas

John Gabriel Borkman, 1958
The Moon and Sixpence (Olivier won an Emmy), 1959
The Power and the Glory (released theatrically in Europe), 1961
Uncle Vanya, 1963
David Copperfield (released theatrically in Europe), 1969
Long Day's Journey Into Night, 1973
The Merchant of Venice, 1973
Love Among the Ruins (Olivier and co-star Katharine Hepburn both won an Emmy for their performances), 1973
Laurence Olivier Presents The Collection, 1976
Laurence Olivier Presents Cat on a Hot Tin Roof, 1976
(Olivier did not appear in *Laurence Olivier Presents Hindle Wakes* in 1976, but he directed it)
Laurence Olivier Presents Come Back, Little Sheba, 1977
Laurence Olivier Presents Daphne, Laureola, 1977
Laurence Olivier Presents Saturday, Sunday, Monday, 1977
Jesus of Nazareth, 1977
Brideshead Revisited, 1981
Wagner, 1981
A Voyage Round My Father, 1982
King Lear, 1983
Mr Halpern and Mr Johnson, 1983
A Talent for Murder, 1983
The Ebony Tower, 1984
The Last Days of Pompeii, 1984
Peter the Great, 1986
Lost Empires, 1986

Index

INDEX